"Stephen Binz has combined solid scholarship with deep devotion. For those who have never been to the Holy Land, this book will induce you to go. For those pilgrims on their way, it will serve as an excellent guide. And for those who have been blessed in their travels there, this book will keep that memory alive."

—Rev. Michael Patella, OSB, Rector, Saint John's University School of Theology and Seminary

"It is no small task to distill two-thousand years of history on the holy sites into a readable and inspirational format, but Binz has successfully done just that."

—Laurie Brink, OP, Professor of New Testament Studies, Catholic Theological Union

"A marvelous guide for pilgrims to the Holy Land that combines history, personal reflection, and prayers and meditations designed for the holy sites. Stephen Binz's inviting and accessible book will be a great asset to anyone wanting to explore the land often known as the Fifth Gospel."

—James Martin, SJ, author of *Jesus: A Pilgrimage*

"A pilgrimage to the Holy Land is an extraordinary journey of faith, conversion, and joy, which Stephen J. Binz has laid out in brilliant detail. I hope this book inspires the faithful to say 'yes' to this invitation for the most invaluable gift that you can ever give yourself."

—Dr. Peter E. Bahou, President of Peter's Way Tours

"Stephen Binz's *Holy Land Pilgrimage* is a wonderful guide both in preparation for your pilgrimage and a sure help while traveling where Jesus and the apostles walked."

—Jeff Cavins, Creator of The Great Adventure

D1523368

"As a biblical scholar and experienced group leader, Stephen Binz understands how important it is to prepare the pilgrims with knowledge of the biblical sites so they can fully enjoy the richness a Holy Land journey provides. Every pilgrim should read this book before traveling, use it as a reference during the trip, and as a reminder of all the places visited upon return."

—Edita Krunic, President of Select International Tours

"I greatly admire the dedication of Stephen Binz to the Christians of the Holy Land. The support he brings through his work assures us that we will not be forgotten and will be kept in the prayers of our brothers and sisters worldwide, whom we look forward to meeting when they visit the Holy Land."

—Shibly Kando, Holy Land coordinator of Select to Give Foundation, Bethlehem

"In *Holy Land Pilgrimage*, Stephen Binz takes us on a spiritual journey, with intimate reflections and his beautiful photography. Enter the Land of Emmanuel. You'll never be the same!"

—Gus Lloyd, author of *A Minute in the Church*, Host of *Seize the Day* radio program

"*Holy Land Pilgrimage* is a gift to those called to make a journey where the Bible comes alive. Stephen Binz helps us connect the dots between the Scriptures and pilgrimage sites, walking quite literally in Our Lord's footsteps."

—Milanka Lachman, President of 206 Tours

"Stephen Binz's book comes at a most opportune time. Few are better qualified than Stephen to lead us through the Holy Land in a way that brings out both history and spirituality that is applicable to our modern times today."

—John Michael Talbot, musician, author, and founder of The Brothers and Sisters of Charity, Little Portion Hermitage

Holy Land Pilgrimage

Stephen J. Binz

LITURGICAL PRESS
Collegeville, Minnesota

www.litpress.org

1	2	3	4	5	6	7	8	9

Library of Congress Cataloging-in-Publication Data

Names: Binz, Stephen J., 1955– author.
Title: Holy Land pilgrimage / Stephen J. Binz.
Description: Collegeville, Minnesota : Liturgical Press, 2020. | Includes index.
| Summary: "Biblical scholar and seasoned pilgrimage guide Stephen J. Binz offers an up-to-date handbook for experiencing the sites of the Holy Land as a disciple of Jesus"— Provided by publisher.
Identifiers: LCCN 2020010680 (print) | LCCN 2020010681 (ebook) | ISBN 9780814665121 (paperback) | ISBN 9780814665374 (epub) | ISBN 9780814665374 (mobi) | ISBN 9780814665374 (pdf)
Subjects: LCSH: Christian pilgrims and pilgrimages—Palestine—Guidebooks. | Christian pilgrims and pilgrimages—Israel—Guidebooks. | Christian shrines—Israel—Guidebooks. | Christian shrines—Palestine—Guidebooks. | Palestine—Guidebooks. | Israel—Guidebooks. | Israel—Description and travel. | Palestine—Description and travel.
Classification: LCC BX2320.5.P19 B56 2020 (print) | LCC BX2320.5.P19 (ebook) | DDC 263/.0425694—dc23
LC record available at https://lccn.loc.gov/2020010680
LC ebook record available at https://lccn.loc.gov/2020010681

Contents

Preface

The Holy Land is my favorite place on earth. I love it not because God is present there in a way he is not in New York, Paris, or Shanghai, but because I can experience the divine presence more easily there, in the places where God has been revealed in history. I don't believe I'm any better in God's sight because I travel frequently to the Holy Land. In the Christian worldview, every place and every person is holy, irreplaceable in God's creation and unconditionally loved by God. But I love the Holy Land for the place it holds in the history of God's revelation. These are the places where God made his presence and identity known, entering into covenant with our ancestors and revealing himself fully in the life of Jesus Christ.

Ever since my graduate education in Jerusalem, studying with faculty from the Pontifical Biblical Institute and Hebrew University, I have been exploring the Holy Land. For thirty years, I have been leading biblical pilgrimages, enabling many to savor this land and read the Bible with new eyes. It's the fruit of these experiences that I hope to bring to this book. I will explore with you the mountains, seas, deserts, cities, and towns as well as the sanctuaries, altars, peoples, and cultures of the Holy Land. But I will do so not just as a historian, geographer, or archaeologist, but especially as a pilgrim, inviting you to experience these places as sacred, allowing them to deepen your faith and to form you more fully into disciples of Jesus.

My interest in biblical studies and pilgrimage is complemented by my enjoyment of photography. I enjoy making images because it helps me to see more clearly, to take notice of light, color, texture, and detail. The photographs throughout this book are my own, the fruit of several years of shooting in the Holy Land. I hope they help you to imagine and remember your encounter with the Holy Land.

I have chosen the term Holy Land for the land of the Bible in order to avoid the more political designations of the land as Palestine and Israel. Although this land has been designated as Palestine and Israel at alternating periods of its history, it is recognized by all people of faith as the Holy Land. Although using this term to refer to Canaan, ancient Israel, or

Roman Palestine might seem anachronistic, keep in mind that the term "holy land" was used from ancient times, even in the Old Testament and Jewish literature (Zech 2:12; Wis 12:3; 2 Macc 1:7).

I have written this guide for both the adventurous traveler, preparing for a physical journey to the Holy Land, and the imaginative traveler, visualizing the places of the Bible from your armchair. Either way, I hope you will be able to envision these sites and experience them with a biblical understanding and an experience of prayer.

I am grateful to friends at Liturgical Press, with whom I have published this and several other biblical books, especially Peter Dwyer, Hans Christoffersen, Tara Durheim, Stephanie Lancour, Colleen Stiller, Julie Surma, and Monica Bokinskie. I thank, too, my colleagues in offering Holy Land pilgrimages and those who have offered me feedback and direction during the writing. I am especially grateful to the many pilgrims who have traveled with me on pilgrimage to the Holy Land. Each of them has given me new insights and enthusiasm for the art of pilgrimage. Finally, I would like to dedicate this work to the Christians of the Holy Land, whose faithfulness under trial continually inspires me.

Stephen J. Binz, author, biblical scholar, and pilgrimage leader

Old and New Testament Cities in the Promised Land

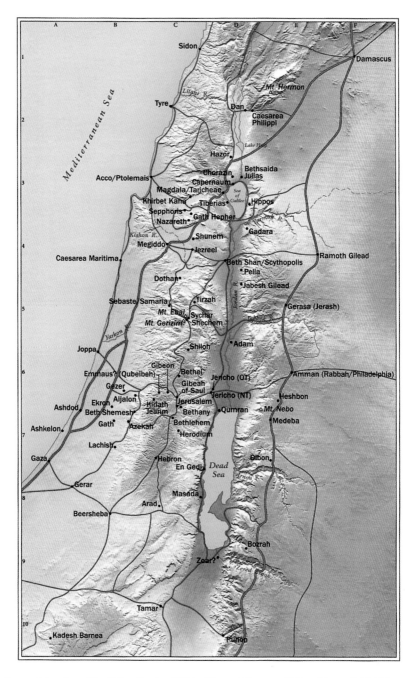

Chapter I

The Way of Pilgrimage

Before going on pilgrimage, would-be travelers must divest themselves of their naive outlooks. Pilgrimage is not an experience of pleasant sightseeing. Rather, pilgrimage immerses travelers in a formative journey, a multifaceted experience that can be described as universal, communal, and liturgical.

By going on pilgrimage, travelers enter an experience that is, first of all, universal. Pilgrimage is an ancient practice that is common to every religious tradition. This journey to a sacred place in search of transcendence could be described as one of the archetypal experiences of humanity. Leaving behind the mundane cares and ordinary responsibilities, pilgrims seek to meet the Holy. There seems to be something deep within our human nature that longs to go on pilgrimage.

Pilgrims enter into an experience that is also communal. They bring along in mind and heart those they love, united in faith and prayer. Pilgrims also unite themselves with residents of the new land, uniting themselves to cultural expressions and customs that may differ significantly from their own. Likewise, pilgrims join with other pilgrims from many different places—people of dissimilar languages, races, and nationalities, but sharing one essential purpose that transcends their many differences.

Finally, pilgrimage is a liturgical experience. At these sacred places, where God is believed to have encountered people in transforming ways, shrines have been constructed to mark and honor the place. At these shrines, pilgrims enact rituals that put them in touch with the event of divine encounter at that location, and they perform rites that continue the accumulated worship of their spiritual ancestors through the ages.

These three aspects of pilgrimage—universal, communal, and liturgical—sometimes lead travelers to the Holy Land to experiences quite different from their expectations. After traveling to the splendors of Catholic

Europe, for example, the shrines of the Holy Land can seem disconcerting: exotic rituals of the East competing with the noble simplicity of the West, Byzantine and modern styles perplexingly juxtaposed, the Way of the Cross running through an Oriental bazaar. When a little girl remarked at the altar of Calvary in the Church of the Holy Sepulcher, "I never knew our Lord was crucified indoors," she was expressing the bewilderment that troubles many who come to the Holy Land with an imagination filled since childhood with conventional biblical pictures.[1] This uneasiness is what prompted the nineteenth-century British Army general Charles Gordon to advocate for "Gordon's Calvary" and "the Garden Tomb," against all historical and archaeological evidence, as the location of Jesus's death and resurrection. The pleasant outdoor scene—a tomb with a rolling stone, surrounded by a flowery garden—is just as the Western imagination would expect. It is undisturbed by the two millennia of building and destruction, conquest and defeat, juxtaposing the Roman, Byzantine, Crusader, and Ottoman periods as well as the Greek, Syrian, Latin, Armenian, Coptic, and other architectural and liturgical expressions.

While there are many sacred places throughout the world frequented by pilgrims seeking to draw closer to God, for the Christian, the Holy Land is unique. There our faith has its deepest roots. Most of the events recounted in the Bible happened within its borders. God was revealed to us not only in specific periods of history, but also in very specific places. As Bargil Pixner wrote, we have inherited not only a history of salvation, but also a "geography of salvation."[2] By traveling to these sites, seeing and touching these places of divine encounter, we can experience how truly incarnational is our Christian faith.

Beginning with the call of Abraham and Sarah, the Bible is filled with people on a journey. Our ancestors in faith left their homelands to travel to a new land that God would show them. They went out not knowing where they were going, traveling by faith at God's direction. God led the Hebrew people out of slavery and set them on a long journey. Under the leadership of Moses, the Israelites encountered God on their way in the wilderness and were formed into God's people through the experience. The New Testament, too, is structured as a journey: the journey of Jesus from Galilee to Jerusalem, traveling from place to place to announce the kingdom

---

1. Evelyn Waugh, "The Plight of the Holy Places," LIFE, December 24, 1951, 61.
2. Bargil Pixner, *With Jesus through Galilee according to the Fifth Gospel* (Rosh Pina, Israel: Corazin Publishing, 1992), 7.

throughout the land, and the journey of the church from Jerusalem to the ends of the earth. As we travel on pilgrimage, we enter into the way of our ancestors with our minds, our hearts, and our feet.

1. Pilgrimage in Ancient Israel and the Life of Jesus

The people and tribes of Israel erected shrines to mark the various places where they experienced God's presence in particular ways. Abraham built an altar at Mamre to commemorate his covenant with God, and there he was told by God that Sarah would bear a son in her old age (Gen 13:18; 18:1). Jacob set up a pillar and anointed it with oil on the spot where he dreamed of the stairway to heaven, naming the place Bethel and describing it as "the house of God" and "the gate of heaven" (Gen 28:16-18). When God spoke to Moses from the flaming bush, God commanded him to remove his sandals because the place where he stood is "holy ground" (Exod 3:5). The people under Moses erected their own traveling shrine that contained the ark of the covenant. Later, the ark was located at various places in the land, including Shechem, Gibeah, Gilgal, and Shiloh, which became places of pilgrimage for God's people.

The Torah of Israel commands God's people to celebrate three annual pilgrim feasts, by which they would remember the travels of their ancestors: Passover (Unleavened Bread), which commemorates Israel's freedom from bondage; Weeks (Pentecost), which remembers God's giving the law on Mount Sinai; and Booths (Tabernacles), which renews Israel's wandering in the wilderness to be formed as God's people. At each of these feasts, the Israelites would travel on pilgrimage to "the place that the LORD will choose as a dwelling for his name" (Deut 16:2, 6, 11, 15, 16). These pilgrimages were opportunities for the Israelites to reassert their identity as God's people and re-center their lives in covenant with God. Eventually these pilgrim feasts were celebrated in Jerusalem, with sacrifices and feasting, praying and singing. The rituals embodied the central narratives and the highest values of God's people.

Throughout the Bible, God's faithful are described through the imagery of pilgrimage. They are people on the journey, always seeking the place that will satisfy them, the place of God's rest. God commanded that the ark of the covenant be constructed with four gold rings attached, through which two poles were placed. In this way, the ark was carried with the people on all their journeys. The text insists that the poles were to always remain in the rings, never separated from the ark, always ready for travel (Exod 25:15). Even when the ark seemed settled in the temple at Jerusalem, the poles could be seen extending from the curtain covering the place where the ark dwelt (1 Kgs 8:8). Even when they seemed established in their own land, the Israelites were always to understand themselves as God's pilgrim people.

In the writings of Israel's prophets, the theme of pilgrimage is increasingly universalized. In the future, says Isaiah, all nations will stream toward Jerusalem, "the mountain of the Lord's house" (Isa 2:2). "The foreigners who join themselves to the Lord" will be brought to God's holy mountain, and God's house will be called "a house of prayer for all peoples" (Isa 56:6-7). "All nations and tongues" will come to Jerusalem to see God's glory (Isa 66:18). Zechariah prophesies that through Judaism, many peoples and strong nations will come to the Lord: "In those days ten men from nations of every language shall take hold of a Jew, grasping his garment and saying, 'Let us go with you, for we have heard that God is with you'" (Zech 8:22-23). God will draw his people from the four corners of the earth for the ultimate, universal pilgrimage.

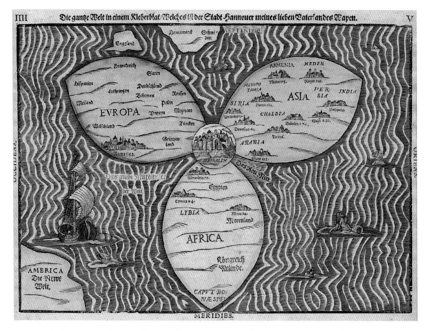

Bünting's depiction of Jerusalem at the intersection of Europe, Asia, or Africa

The life of Jesus was marked by his travels to Jerusalem for the pilgrim feasts of Israel. Luke's gospel describes the journey of the family of Jesus, when he was twelve years old, as they traveled to Jerusalem for the feast of Passover. We know that this was one of many pilgrim feasts that Jesus shared with Joseph and Mary, since the gospel tells us they went every year for the feast (Luke 2:41). During his adult ministry, Jesus continued participating in the pilgrim feasts in Jerusalem. John's gospel describes Jesus's presence in Jerusalem for several of the Jewish feasts, including the festivals of Passover (John 2:13), Booths (7:2), and Dedication (10:22). And all four of the gospels underscore Jesus's final pilgrimage to Jerusalem as the culmination of his sacrificial life. Through his own life, Jesus shows his disciples the way to follow in his footsteps as they journey through life as pilgrims.

Heinrich Bünting's book of woodcut maps, *Itinerarium Sacrae Scripturae*, first published in 1581, provided a comprehensive summary of biblical geography and described the Holy Land by illustrating the travels of notable people from the Scriptures. In addition to conventional maps, the book also contained a figurative map depicting the earth as a three-leaf clover, with each leaf representing either Europe, Asia, or Africa. The three are drawn together by a ring encircling the city of Jerusalem, expressing not only its geographical location at the intersection of the ancient continents but, more importantly, the universal nature of God's saving plan to bring all the nations into unity through the saving life of Jesus Christ.

2. Christian Pilgrimage in the Early Church

Many have called the Holy Land "the fifth gospel." In addition to the four sacred texts, the good news about Jesus is revealed to us by the places that mark the events of his life. By exploring the fifth gospel, the world of the four will open to us. The gospel of the land fills out the written gospels with tangible reality. Here we can imagine Jesus with his disciples along the lake, teaching on the mountainside, praying in the garden, and dying on the cross. These places hold memories that carry an enormous sense of expectation for anyone seeking a fresh encounter with him.

It seems inevitable in a religion founded on historical events and on the conviction that God "became flesh" in human life that the most significant physical places associated with that belief would be remembered and preserved. Oral tradition, sacred texts, and sacred places bridge the gulf between past and present. If there were no places that could be seen and touched, the claim that God had entered history would seem less real. The holy places become witnesses of the truth of biblical history.

St. Justin Martyr, born around AD 100, states that he knew the site of a "certain cave" that the locals venerated as the place of Jesus's birth and that the Christians of the area took care to preserve the historical memory of the nativity. Other writers assure us that Christians in Galilee and especially in Jerusalem preserved the memory of the places of Jesus's life and that believers traveled from near and far to honor these places.

The historian-bishop Eusebius of Caesarea describes the accounts of pilgrims in the Holy Land during the church's early centuries. He tells us that St. Melito of Sardis, a bishop of the second century, made a pilgrimage to the Holy Land to better understand the Bible—to learn "accurate facts about the ancient Scriptures."[3] Eusebius mentions another bishop, St. Alexander of Cappadocia, who went to Jerusalem "to pray there and visit the sites."[4] Eusebius tells us that even though the Romans had landscaped over the holy sites of Jerusalem and converted them to pagan shrines, Christians traveled to Jerusalem to pray at the Mount of Olives overlooking the city.

During the age of persecution, such pilgrimages to the Holy Land were difficult and dangerous. But in AD 306, Constantine became emperor and, convinced of the truth of Christianity, issued the Edict of Milan in 313, by which Christianity became a recognized religion. This new freedom for the church led to a new enthusiasm for the holy places. St. Helena, Constantine's mother, traveled to Jerusalem and there, after the location was pointed out by local Christians, excavated the true cross of the Lord, discovering the place of Calvary and the empty tomb of Christ buried beneath a pagan temple.

For centuries Roman emperors had used their office and the wealth of the empire to build sacred edifices. Now Constantine began his own building program featuring Christian churches, a project that continued relentlessly until his death in 337. After constructing lavish basilicas in

---

3. Eusebius, *Historia Ecclesiastica* IV 26, 14.
4. Eusebius, *Historia Ecclesiastica* VI 11, 2.

Mary depicted as a medieval pilgrim, representing the church on pilgrimage

Rome and Constantinople over the tombs of the martyrs, he turned to the Holy Land and built three major basilicas on the site of "three sacred caves."[5] He constructed the Church of the Resurrection, which included a circular shrine at the empty tomb of Christ as well as a memorial at the site of Calvary. Constantine also erected the Eleona Church on the Mount of Olives, built around the cave honoring the place where Jesus frequently taught his disciples and where he ascended into heaven. The third basilica was the Church of the Nativity in Bethlehem, focused on the cave marking the place of Jesus's birth.

While Constantine's churches were being built, an anonymous pilgrim from Bordeaux in Gaul came to follow in the footsteps of Jesus. From him we have the first writings describing a tour through the Holy Land. Arriving in 333, he carefully noted where he went, what he saw, the routes he took, and the distances between one place and another. His descriptions of places like the house of Caiaphas, the tomb of Lazarus, the place of Elijah's sacrifice on Mount Carmel, and Jacob's well where Jesus met the Samaritan woman confirm the antiquity of many traditions about the holy places.

These early pilgrims were drawn by the desire to see and touch the land of the Bible. St. Jerome, a fourth-century biblical scholar who traveled the land, wrote, "We understand Scripture more clearly when we have seen Judea with our own eyes, and discovered what still remains of ancient towns."[6] Writing to Marcela in the name of the holy women Paula and Eustochium, Jerome urged her to join them in the Holy Land:

> Will the day never come when we shall together enter the Savior's cave, and together weep in the sepulcher of the Lord? Then shall we touch with our lips the wood of the cross, and rise in prayer and resolve upon the Mount of Olives with the ascending Lord. We shall see Lazarus come forth bound with grave clothes, we shall look upon the waters of Jordan purified for the washing of the Lord. . . . If only you will come, we shall go to see Nazareth, as its name denotes, the flower of Galilee. Not far off Cana will be visible, where the water was turned into wine. We shall make our way to Tabor and see the tabernacles there which the Savior shares, not, as Peter once wished, with Moses and Elijah, but with the Father and with the Holy Spirit. Thence we shall come to the Sea of Gennesaret, and when there we shall see the spots where the five thousand were filled

5. Eusebius, *De Laudibus Constantini* 9, 17.
6. *Praef in lib Paralip.*; PL 29, 401.

with five loaves, and the four thousand with seven. The town of Nain will meet our eyes, at the gate of which the widow's son was raised to life. . . . Our eyes will look also on Capernaum, the scene of so many of our Lord's signs—yes, and on all Galilee besides. And when, accompanied by Christ, we shall have made our way back to our cave through Shiloh and Bethel, and those other places where churches are set up like standards to commemorate the Lord's victories, then we shall sing heartily, we shall weep copiously, we shall pray unceasingly. Wounded with the Savior's shaft, we shall say one to another: "I have found Him whom my soul loveth; I will hold him and will not let him go."[7]

A key figure in the promotion of Christian pilgrimage was St. Cyril of Jerusalem, who was bishop from 350 to 386. He developed Jerusalem into the prime "Holy City" of Christianity and center of pilgrimage. His famous *Catechetical Lectures* for the catechumens during Lent and his *Mystagogic Catecheses* for the baptized during Easter Week were delivered in the Church of the Resurrection, a few feet from the places of Christ's death and resurrection. His catechesis is of great importance, as it spotlights the initiation rites and the liturgical practices of the fourth century. In his homilies to pilgrims, Cyril would often refer to the place in which the congregation was standing as bearing witness to the events detailed in Scripture. The many witnesses in Jerusalem include Golgotha, the tomb of Christ, the place of his ascension on the Mount of Olives, and the Upper Church of the Apostles on Mount Zion. As he emphasized when speaking in the holy places, "others merely hear, but we both see and touch."[8]

The most extensive early travelogue was written by a woman from Spain named Egeria in the late fourth century. By this time, Jerusalem was a bustling Christian city, filled with monks, clerics, pilgrims, and adventurers. Its new churches at the holy sites and their elaborate liturgies astonished visitors from throughout the world. Egeria writes to her "revered sisters" back home, leading to the belief that she was a member of a religious community, sharing a common life and interested in both the Scriptures and the church's liturgical life.

The first part of Egeria's written work forms her travel diary, in which she describes her visits to noteworthy sites. Carrying a codex of the Bible

---

7. Jerome, *Epist.* 46.
8. Cyril of Jerusalem, *Catechetical Lectures* 13,22.

with her, she commemorated each sacred site with a ritual consisting of the reading of the appropriate Scripture, psalms, prayer, and at some locations, the offering of Eucharist.[9] The second part details the rituals of Jerusalem during the liturgical year, as developed by Bishop Cyril. Describing Holy Week, she highlights the Palm Sunday procession from the Mount of Olives, the Holy Thursday liturgy, which ended with a walk to Gethsemane by torchlight, and the Good Friday veneration of the cross. She then relates the Paschal Vigil at the Church of the Resurrection with its baptisms and Eucharist.

Although pilgrimage to the Holy Land was increasingly popular in the Byzantine period—from Constantine in the fourth century to the early part of the seventh century—the value of pilgrimage to sacred places was often debated. In some periods and by certain teachers, pilgrimage was discouraged because it was thought that earthly locations and human structures could get in the way of spiritual encounters with God. Had not Jesus said to the Samaritan woman that true worship had nothing to do with Jerusalem or Samaria, but was all about worshiping God in spirit and in truth (John 4:20-24)? We are too easily tempted to believe that going to a particular place or going through a particular ritual earns us God's favor.

Paul articulated the Christian position in his speech at the Areopagus: "The God who made the world and everything in it, he who is Lord of heaven and earth, does not live in shrines made by human hands" (Acts 17:24). Unlike ancient Israel, where God could be experienced as dwelling in the temple, "the place that the LORD will choose as a dwelling for his name" (Deut 16:2), Christians themselves are "the temple of the living God" (2 Cor 6:16). Those who live "in Christ" may worship God at all times and in all places.

Yet, places and rituals can indeed be powerful means to experience God. Although all of creation is sacred and we are capable of seeing God and experiencing his goodness in all things, the particular places where God has been revealed and where Jesus has spent his earthly life can be especially effective signs of divine presence and means of God's grace. But it is not sufficient merely to go on pilgrimage to see these places. External pilgrimage must be accompanied by interior conversion. So that

---

9. *Itinerarium Egeriae* 10,7. Commentary and translation by Anne McGowan and Paul F. Bradshaw, *The Pilgrimage of Egeria* (Collegeville, MN: Liturgical Press, 2018).

pilgrimage is not just another journey, the pilgrim must travel in faith, seeking a new heart, and with a will to interior change. Pilgrimage must be the simultaneous movement of the feet and the soul.

The ambiguity of Christian pilgrimage to holy places can be summed up by the words of the angel at the empty tomb: "He is not here; for he has been raised" is balanced by the invitation, "Come, see the place" (Matt 28:6). Because Jesus is the risen Lord, the sanctity of the empty tomb and all other places of his life are provisional. Yet, there is good reason to come and see the tomb and all the other places associated with his life.

That the church began in Jerusalem is a historical fact that can never be forgotten, but the center of the church is Jesus Christ, present with his people throughout the world by his Spirit. Jesus himself has become the true "place" of worship, so to go on pilgrimage is to come to encounter the risen Christ. The Christian religion neither possesses nor needs a sacred place. What matters is living "in Christ." He is "the place that the Lord will choose as a dwelling for his name," the great I AM. Through the ever-present Holy Spirit, the living Scriptures, and the perpetual sacrament, the Lord is present in any and every local place. He goes before us into all the world, summoning us to follow him.

As we connect the sacred places of our salvation with the sacred texts of Scripture, we become pilgrims. While we look for Christ, we realize that he is really the one looking for us. He is with us walking along our pilgrim way. When we travel humbly, listening for the Lord to speak in the quiet of our hearts, waiting for him to show us his presence, there is no telling in what ways we may be led and changed.

3. The Christian People of the Holy Land

Places are not holy in themselves; places become holy when God is revealed there to his people. From the beginning of the church, an indigenous Christian community has existed in the Holy Land. Many of today's Holy Land Christians descended from those who encountered Jesus in this land and first experienced the Spirit at Pentecost. These indigenous Christians, most of whom are Palestinians, were the first to venerate the holy places where Jesus walked, taught, suffered, died, and rose.

These descendants of the first Christians feel a certain responsibility to remain in the Holy Land and to maintain Christian worship there. Yet,

the Israeli-Palestinian conflict makes life increasingly difficult for them, and many have chosen to emigrate elsewhere for the sake of their families and their future. Because the barrier wall prevents them from entering Jerusalem for work, they experience a severe lack of employment and opportunity. In 1948, the Christian population of the Holy Land was 30 percent; today it is close to 1 percent.

These Christians in the Holy Land are often called "the living stones." The metaphor comes from Peter's first letter in which he refers to Christians as "living stones," built into a spiritual house, a holy priesthood, offering spiritual sacrifices, with Christ as the cornerstone (1 Pet 2:4-6). The living stones join their lives to Christ, the foundation in Zion, to build their lives "upon the foundation of the apostles and prophets," becoming "a dwelling place for God" (Eph 2:20-22).

For those making a pilgrimage to the Holy Land, it is essential not only to see and touch the holy places, but to visit the living stones. For centuries this was a natural process, as pilgrims stayed in monasteries, convents, or the homes of local Christians, participating with them in liturgy and prayer, sharing news, and partaking in the local culture. The mass tourism of today, however, with its international hotels, comfortable coaches, and tightly packed itineraries, has transformed pilgrims into tourists and pilgrimage into vacations. Visitors are isolated from the living stones of the land so visiting the holy places becomes a form of sightseeing.

To experience a genuine pilgrimage today, visitors must try to interact with the local Christians. Worshiping with them in their churches, touring their educational facilities and programs for children in need, sharing meals while discussing their struggles, and shopping in their stores can boost their spirits. Pilgrimages are an important source of aid to the Christian tourism industry. Choosing the services of Christian tour companies, hotels, guides, and restaurants can be a tremendous help to them.

Some of the best souvenirs of the Holy Land are made by Christian artisans, many of whom have perfected their skills for generations. Olive wood carvings, mother of pearl figures, jewelry, antiquities, religious icons, and ceramics make some of the finest memorabilia of your trip and some of the most appreciated gifts. The Christians of Bethlehem take great pride in crafting and selling these handmade souvenirs that typify the pilgrimage experience. By shopping from established merchants, pilgrims can be better assured that the crafts are locally produced rather than imported from abroad.

Pilgrims may also want to experience development projects among the Palestinian Christians. These include educational projects, child development centers, Bethlehem University, and relief services for refugees. Many such projects are coordinated by religious communities and welcome visitors.

Because of the rapid decline of the Christian population of the Holy Land, they need and deserve our support and encouragement. In all of these ways, Christians from abroad can help sustain the living stones, validating their rights in the land and endorsing their courageous sacrifice to stay in the land where Christianity began.

Orthodox man lights a candle in the Church of the Holy Sepulcher

Christian Churches and Their Rites

Pilgrims who seek to encounter the local church will discover a variety of ecclesial traditions and ethnic expressions among the Christians. Churches of all nations and cultures are represented there, and contact with these churches will deepen the pilgrim's understanding of the rich diversity of the Christian faith.

In order to truly encounter Christianity in the Holy Land, the pilgrim must begin to understand Eastern Christianity, a general name for the church traditions that developed in the East, which includes the Holy Land, as opposed to the West, which is mostly Western Europe.

Eastern and Western Christians pray together in the Holy Land

These Eastern churches are many, with diverse origins, each of which developed distinctly over centuries. They have their own traditions and ways of worship, all of which are externally characterized by splendid liturgies: chanted by priests and choirs, focused on icons that glow in the warmth of oil lamps and candles, and elevated with wafting incense uniting heaven and earth. The major bodies include the Eastern Orthodox Church, the Oriental Orthodox Churches, and the Eastern Catholic Churches that are in communion with Rome but still maintain Eastern liturgies.

Among the Eastern Orthodox, the Greek Orthodox form the largest Christian community in the Holy Land, encompassing a large majority of the Christian Arabs. Their patriarch claims direct descent from St. James, the first bishop of Jerusalem. In the New Testament, the Greek language and way of life was predominant in the eastern regions of the Roman Empire and many of the first converts belonged to this Greek culture. The Greek Orthodox hold major rights to the Church of the Holy Sepulcher in Jerusalem and the Church of the Nativity in Bethlehem.

The Russian Orthodox are also numbered among the Eastern Orthodox. Russians began coming on pilgrimage in great numbers in the nineteenth century. For many it was a preparation for death and resurrection, so they brought back dirt to be sprinkled on their coffin and a shroud placed on the stone of unction in the Holy Sepulcher. Many Russian pilgrims have stayed, and they have several churches, monasteries, and convents. The Romanian Orthodox also began immigrating in recent centuries and now are well-established in the Holy Land.

Within Eastern Christianity, theological disagreements arose in the fourth century over the nature of Christ, leading to divisions that formed the Assyrian Church of the East and the Oriental Orthodox Churches. These Oriental Churches developed in reaction to the Council of Chalcedon in 451, which defined the human and divine nature of Christ. These non-Calcedonian Churches, including those of the Armenians, Syrians, Ethiopians, and Copts, have been present in the Holy Land since the earliest centuries.

The Armenian Orthodox began to travel to Jerusalem after Armenia became the first nation to adopt Christianity as a state religion in 301. They settled mostly in the southeastern part of the city, which is today called the Armenian quarter. St. James' Cathedral, dedicated to both James, son of Zebedee, and James, the brother of the Lord, forms the center of the quarter. The relics of this second James, the first bishop of the city, are buried under the main altar. The Armenian presence has grown since many survivors of the Armenian genocide in 1915 fled to the Holy Land.

The Syriac Orthodox trace their church to first-century Antioch, where Peter was the first patriarch for seven years before he traveled to Rome. Their liturgical language is Aramaic, the language that Jesus spoke. Their Church of St. Mark is said to be built over the house of Mark, the place of gathering for the early Christians and the place where Peter went when an angel released him from prison (Acts 12:12).

The Ethiopian Orthodox trace their Christianity to the Ethiopian eunuch of Queen Candace, who was baptized by Philip while returning from Jerusalem (Acts 8:26-40). Yet, the Ethiopians trace their link to Jerusalem back to the Ethiopian Queen of Sheba who visited King Solomon 3,000 years ago (1 Kgs 10:1-10). Proud of their Hebrew roots, the Ethiopians follow many Jewish customs, such as male circumcision and dietary laws. The Ethiopian chapel in the Holy Sepulcher leads out to the roof of the church, where monks live in small cells. The festive liturgies are colorful and animated, often with singing and drumming.

The Copts are the Christians of Egypt. Their Christian roots go back to Pentecost when pilgrims from Egypt received the Holy Spirit. The Coptic Church was founded in Alexandria by the evangelist St. Mark. The Coptic Patriarchate of Jerusalem and St. Anthony's Monastery is located on the roof of the Church of the Holy Sepulcher. The Copts also have a tiny chapel at the back of Christ's tomb within the church. Their liturgy is in Coptic, the ancient language of Egypt, with readings in Arabic.

In the eleventh century, long-standing disputes between the Eastern (Greek) and Western (Latin) branches of Christianity incited the East-West Schism, resulting in Eastern Orthodoxy and Roman Catholicism. From that time on, only the Maronites within Eastern Christianity remained in communion with Rome. However, beginning in the sixteenth century, some within the Eastern churches returned to communion with Rome. These Catholic Churches have retained their Eastern liturgies and theology for the most part, while in union with the bishop of Rome. The largest such group in the Holy Land is the Greek Catholics, also known as Melkites. Others include the Chaldeans, who separated from the Assyrian Church of the East, the Armenian Catholics, and the Syriac Catholics.

The Latin Patriarchate is the Catholic episcopal see of Jerusalem. It was established in 1099 with the conquest of the Holy Land by the First Crusade. In 1342, Pope Clement VI gave the custodianship of the holy places to the Franciscan Order. St. Francis himself had visited the Holy Land and encouraged his followers to travel there. The brown-robed Franciscans administer many of the holy places and have active parishes and schools throughout the land. In addition to the Franciscans, dozens of other Roman Catholic religious orders, both women and men, serve in the Holy Land. Since the mid-1950s there has also been a Hebrew-speaking Catholic community—including converted Jews, Catholic spouses of Jews, and immigrants who have assimilated into the Hebrew-speaking society—which now has its own patriarchal vicar.

Protestant Christian communities began to be established in the Holy Land in the nineteenth century. The Lutheran Church of the Redeemer is close to the Holy Sepulcher, and its tall bell tower offers an overview of the city. The Anglicans have St. George's Cathedral and Christ Church in Jerusalem. Several other Reformed, Pentecostal, and Evangelical communities are established throughout the land. Also, diverse groups of Messianic Judaism are growing in number. These groups profess Jesus as the Messiah while maintaining Jewish practices. Many of them express a Zionist ideology, seeing the modern state of Israel as a fulfilment of biblical prophecies.

In the Holy Land we see the diversity within Christianity to its greatest degree, yet it is also the land in which Jesus prayed that his followers would be one, as he and his Father are one (John 17:11). Cultural diversity and differences in languages, history, and rites are not expressions of division among Christ's followers; rather they express the richness of his church. Division is the result of animosity, the scars of history, entrenched separation, and the lack of ecclesial communion within the body of Christ. How marvelous it would be if the church in the Holy Land, with its beautiful diversity, could become the place where the unity of the church was regained.

4. The Sacred Practice of Pilgrimage

The gospel account of the journey along the road to Emmaus (Luke 24:13-35) describes some of the most important aspects of Christian pilgrimage. The travelers encounter Jesus, who accompanies them on their journey. They discuss their life experiences along the way and they read from Scripture. The travelers offer hospitality and they break bread together. Their travel is more than a journey; it is a pilgrimage because they experience the risen Lord. He is present with them on the road—in the words they exchange, in the Scriptures, in the signs of hospitality, in the Eucharist, and in the community formed through the experience. The encounter with the risen Lord on the journey offers new possibilities and new hope for their Christian lives. These, then, are the elements of genuine pilgrimage: journey, community, Scripture, sacrifice, hospitality, ritual, sacrament, and spiritual encounter.

Unlike traditional pilgrimage, contemporary tourism—with its high-rise hotels, to-do lists, and isolating comforts—has many disadvantages. While pilgrimage is a metaphor of the Christian life, tourism may be seen as a metaphor for modern secular life. Tourists don't belong to the places they visit, and they keep their distance from the locals. While they may observe other cultures and customs, they return to their own whenever they like. Tourists are concerned with amusement, novelty, and pleasure. Reconstructing a world to their own liking, they have experiences made up of disconnected episodes that do not last beyond their own duration.

Pilgrims, on the other hand, travel in search of encounter and transformation. The tourist becomes a pilgrim when the observer becomes a participant. Cynthia Ozick describes the difference: "I would distinguish between a visitor and a pilgrim: both will come to a place and go away again, but a visitor arrives, a pilgrim is restored. A visitor passes through a place; the place passes through the pilgrim. A visitor comes either to

Pilgrims from Brazil gather for prayer

teach or to learn, or perhaps simply and neutrally to observe; but a pilgrim comes on purpose to be taught renewal."[10]

Pilgrimage to the Holy Land is an especially cherished spiritual practice for followers of Jesus because Christianity is a historical, incarnational, sacramental religion. God's decisive work in Jesus Christ occurred in a particular historical and spatial setting. Yet, through his resurrection, Jesus Christ is unbounded from these particularities.

God uses the visible, material, and particular to mediate the invisible, immaterial, and universal divine presence. For this reason, pilgrimage functions in a way analogous to the sacraments. Through the sacred words, symbolic elements, and ritual gestures of sacraments, God offers us grace, which forms us more deeply into the image of Christ. Likewise, pilgrimage is concrete, relational, and embodied, leading to a divine encounter. Through the sacred places, biblical readings, ritual gestures, communal prayer, and song, pilgrims are formed more fully into disciples of the Lord.

Paulinus of Nola, a fifth-century bishop, expressed this reality well when he said, "No other sentiment draws people to Jerusalem but the desire to see and touch the places where Christ was physically present, and to be able to say, from their very own experience: We have gone into his tabernacle and have adored in the places where his feet have stood."[11]

Make sure your travel becomes a pilgrimage by following a few simple pieces of advice:

- Travel lightly by keeping your clothing and your baggage simple, so you don't get weighed down by too much stuff.

- Travel expectantly by looking forward to the learning and change you will experience through your encounters.

- Travel humbly by visiting the people of this land with respect and reverence for their traditions and way of life.

- Travel gratefully by realizing you are guests in this land and by displaying appreciation for the people who are providing for you.

- Travel softly by seeking an attitude of inner quietness and attentive listening, making time for silence when you stand on holy ground.

10. Cynthia Ozick, *Art and Ardor* (New York: Knopf, 1983), 154.
11. Paulinus of Nola, *Letters*, 49, 14.

- Travel courteously by showing consideration for your hosts and fellow travelers and by helping to smooth the way through difficulties.

- Travel patiently by staying flexible and adaptable, realizing that unexpected changes, delays, and glitches are part of the whole experience.

- Travel relaxed by letting go of tensions and by deciding to have a good time.

Pilgrims rest and converse in the Holy Land

5. Novena in Preparation for Travel

Preparing the heart to encounter God in sacred places is one of the most important elements of pilgrimage. This novena, a nine-day period of spiritual preparation, invites us to get ready, to focus on the experience ahead, and to invoke the assistance of those who have traveled ahead of us. Just as Mary and the disciples waited after Jesus's ascension for nine days of prayerful anticipation of the Holy Spirit at Pentecost, so we prepare with an expectant spirit for the graces of pilgrimage that God wants to bestow upon us.

Each day of the novena will be dedicated to a character from the Bible or a saint of the church. We pray for the intercession of these holy pilgrims who have prepared the way before us. Each day also has a focal symbol, which is a reminder of our upcoming journey. Place this focal symbol in front of you and create a prayer space with a candle, crucifix, or icon. These symbols will direct you to prepare each day for a different aspect of your pilgrimage.

In ancient times, pilgrims were blessed in their parish church, using their walking stick and pilgrim cloak as symbols of the journey. Like our ancestors, we pray each day of this novena that God will bless us as we prepare for all that God has in store for us on pilgrimage.

The ancient pilgrim cry, "Onward," with walking sticks

DAY 1

Holy patron: The Archangels Michael, Gabriel, and Raphael

Focal symbol: travel packet with airline reservation

Reflection: How can I better trust in God for my protection and guidance?

Reading: Genesis 28:10-17
He dreamed that there was a ladder . . . and the angels of God were ascending and descending on it. . . .

Response: In you my God, I place my trust.

You who live in the shelter of the Most High,
   who abide in the shadow of the Almighty,
will say to the LORD, "My refuge and my fortress;
   my God, in whom I trust." R.

For he will deliver you from the snare of the fowler
   and from the deadly pestilence;
he will cover you with his pinions,
   and under his wings you will find refuge. R.

Those who love me, I will deliver;
   I will protect those who know my name.
When they call to me, I will answer them;
   I will be with them in trouble (Ps 91). R.

Prayer: All powerful and merciful God, who is always close to those who trust in you, send your angels to guard us and guide us along our pilgrim way. As you showed Jacob the ladder with angels ascending and descending between heaven and earth, giving him comfort and hope, help us to know that we do not travel alone. As we prepare to travel to the land you made holy, give us heavenly companions to escort us and protect us. Amen.

DAY 2

Holy patron: Abraham and Sarah

Focal symbol: walking shoes

Reflection: What can I do to prepare my mind and body for the challenges of pilgrimage?

Reading: Hebrews 11:8-10
By faith Abraham obeyed when he was called to set out. . . .

Response: Lord, let your mercy be on us, as we place our trust in you.

The word of the LORD is upright,
    and all his work is done in faithfulness.
He loves righteousness and justice;
    the earth is full of the steadfast love of the LORD. R.

Truly the eye of the LORD is on those who fear him,
    on those who hope in his steadfast love,
to deliver their soul from death,
    and to keep them alive in famine. R.

Our soul waits for the LORD;
    he is our help and shield. . . .
Let your steadfast love, O LORD, be upon us,
    even as we hope in you (Ps 33). R.

Prayer: God of salvation, who called Abraham and Sarah to leave their homeland not knowing where they were going, give us the faith of our ancestors to set out at your directive. Strengthen us in mind and body for the challenges of the journey ahead. Give us firm purpose and expectation of new experiences. Show us how to walk in the way that many have walked for generations, so that we, too, may be numbered among your pilgrim people. Amen.

DAY 3

Holy patron: Moses the liberator

Focal symbol: name tag/luggage tag

Reflection: In what ways has God cleared the way and prepared me for this pilgrimage?

Reading: Exodus 3:1-15
God called to him out of the bush, "Moses, Moses. . . ."

Response: Holy is the Lord our God.

Extol the LORD our God;
>   worship at his footstool.
>   Holy is he! R.

Moses and Aaron were among his priests,
>   Samuel also was among those who called on his name.
>   They cried to the LORD, and he answered them. R.

He spoke to them in the pillar of cloud;
>   they kept his decrees,
>   and the statutes that he gave them. R.

Extol the LORD our God,
>   and worship at his holy mountain;
>   for the LORD our God is holy (Ps 99). R.

Prayer: Lord our God, who called Moses by name from the flaming bush, you have summoned each of us to be your instrument for the salvation of others. By taking off his sandals, Moses prepared himself to encounter your holy presence and to be commissioned as liberator of your people. Open our ears to hear you call us by name, and make us ready to listen to your word on holy ground. Amen.

DAY 4

Holy patron: Elijah the prophet

Focal symbol: smartphone/camera

Reflection: How does God desire to work in my life and change me during this pilgrimage?

Reading: 1 Kings 19:4-13a

The word of the LORD came to him, saying, "What are you doing here, Elijah? . . ."

Response: "The LORD is near to all who call on him."

The LORD is faithful in all his words,
    and gracious in all his deeds.
The LORD upholds all who are falling,
    and raises up all who are bowed down. R.

The LORD is just in all his ways,
    and kind in all his doings.
The LORD is near to all who call on him,
    to all who call on him in truth. R.

He fulfills the desire of all who fear him;
    he also hears their cry, and saves them. . . .
My mouth will speak the praise of the LORD,
    and all flesh will bless his holy name forever and ever (Ps 145). R.

Prayer: Just and merciful Lord, who manifests your presence through fiery mountains, thundering skies, and gentle whispers, help us to encounter you in the holy people and places of our journey. Give us an inner quiet, a contemplative spirit, so that you can work gently within us. As we photograph and remember the experiences of our pilgrimage, mold our hearts and form our minds with the character of your prophets and saints. Amen.

DAY 5

Holy patron: St. Mary Magdalene

Focal symbol: cross, icon, or rosary to bring on pilgrimage

Reflection: How can I become a witness to the risen Lord to those around me?

Reading: John 20:1, 11-18
Mary Magdalene went and announced to the disciples, "I have seen the Lord. . . ."

Response: Proclaim God's marvelous deeds to all the nations.

O sing to the LORD a new song;
    sing to the LORD, all the earth.
Sing to the LORD, bless his name;
    tell of his salvation from day to day. R.

Declare his glory among the nations,
    his marvelous works among all the peoples. . . .
Honor and majesty are before him;
    strength and beauty are in his sanctuary. R.

Ascribe to the LORD, O families of the peoples,
    ascribe to the LORD glory and strength.
Ascribe to the LORD the glory due his name;
    bring an offering, and come into his courts (Ps 96). R.

Prayer: Holy and risen Lord, who first showed your glorified body to Mary Magdalene, make us witnesses to the good news of eternal life. As we follow in your footsteps on this pilgrimage, teach us how to be missionary disciples, so that our words and actions may reveal your life to those around us. In our discussions, prayers, and good deeds for others, may we be seen as living icons, made in the divine image. Amen.

DAY 6

Holy patron: St. Helena

Focal symbol: luggage with empty space to return with memorabilia

Reflection: What will I bring to the people of the Holy Land and what will I bring home with me?

Reading: 1 Corinthians 1:18-25
For Jews demand signs and Greeks desire wisdom, but we proclaim Christ crucified. . . .

Response: Do not forget the works of the Lord!

Give ear, O my people, to my teaching;
    incline your ears to the words of my mouth. . . .
    We will tell to the coming generation
the glorious deeds of the LORD. . . . R.

He divided the sea and let them pass through it,
    and made the waters stand like a heap.
In the daytime he led them with a cloud,
    and all night long with a fiery light. . . . R.

He chose the tribe of Judah,
    Mount Zion, which he loves.
He built his sanctuary like the high heavens,
    like the earth, which he has founded forever (Ps 78). R.

Prayer: Compassionate God, you led St. Helena, mother of Emperor Constantine, to travel to the Holy Land and discover the true cross of your Son in Jerusalem. May she, as the patron saint of archaeologists, inspire our journey to every excavation and discovery in the land of God's promise. Through the power of the glorious cross of Jesus Christ, may we share in his triumph over sin and his victory over death. Amen.

DAY 7

Holy patron: St. Cyril of Jerusalem

Focal symbol: passport

Reflection: What will I do to lead others to Christ and to his church?

Reading: Acts 2:42-47
Day by day the Lord added to their number those who were being saved. . . .

Response: Listen to me, my children, I will teach you to honor the Lord.

I will bless the LORD at all times;
    his praise shall continually be in my mouth.
My soul makes its boast in the LORD;
    let the humble hear and be glad. R.

O magnify the LORD with me,
    and let us exalt his name together.
I sought the LORD, and he answered me,
    and delivered me from all my fears. R.

Look to him, and be radiant;
    so your faces shall never be ashamed.
This poor soul cried, and was heard by the LORD,
    and was saved from every trouble (Ps 34). R.

Prayer: Risen Lord, who appointed St. Cyril as bishop of your church in Jerusalem and led him to bring many catechumens to baptism at the Easter Vigil, show us how to lead others to you. As Bishop Cyril welcomed pilgrims from many lands to the city of Jerusalem, help us to transcend the nationality of our passports and, through the graces received in Jerusalem, become the multicultural church of all the nations. Amen.

DAY 8

Holy patron: Sts. Jerome and Paula

Focal symbol: portable Bible or pocket New Testament

Reflection: What obstacles must I remove so that God's word can take root and grow within me?

Reading: 2 Tim 3:14-17

All Scripture is inspired by God and is useful for teaching. . . .

Response: Lord, gather your scattered people.

Hear the word of the LORD, O nations,
    and declare it in the coastlands far away;
say, "He who scattered Israel will gather him,
    and will keep him as a shepherd a flock." R.

For the LORD has ransomed Jacob,
    and has redeemed him from hands too strong for him.
They shall come and sing aloud on the height of Zion,
    and they shall be radiant over the goodness of the LORD. R.

Then shall the young women rejoice in the dance,
    and the young men and the old shall be merry.
I will turn their mourning into joy,
    I will comfort them, and give them gladness for sorrow (Jer 31). R.

Prayer: O God, who led St. Jerome and St. Paula on pilgrimage to the Holy Land to study the places of Sacred Scripture, give us the ability to imagine the events of our salvation through contact with these holy sites. May the scholarship of your saints inspire us to devoted reading of your Word and to delight in it as the fountain of life. Amen.

DAY 9

Holy patron: St. Francis of Assisi

Focal symbol: this pilgrimage guidebook

Reflection: What do I expect to receive from God as a result of this pilgrimage?

Reading: Isaiah 2:2-4
All the nations shall stream toward [Jerusalem.] . . .

Response: I rejoiced when I heard them say: let us go to the house of the Lord.

I was glad when they said to me,
   "Let us go to the house of the LORD!"
Our feet are standing
   within your gates, O Jerusalem. R.

Pray for the peace of Jerusalem:
   "May they prosper who love you.
Peace be within your walls,
   and security within your towers." R.

For the sake of my relatives and friends
   I will say, "Peace be within you."
   For the sake of the house of the LORD our God, I will seek
     your good (Ps 122). R.

Prayer: God of our ancestors, who established Jerusalem at the center of the nations, you now call us to go up to the mountain of the Lord's house. May we travel in the spirit of St. Francis, pursuing peace among the nations streaming to Jerusalem and seeking healing among the many peoples who live within its walls. By walking in the footsteps of St. Francis, may we follow your Son, and may we be united in expectant faith and joyful charity.

Galilee and Surrounding Regions in the Time of Jesus

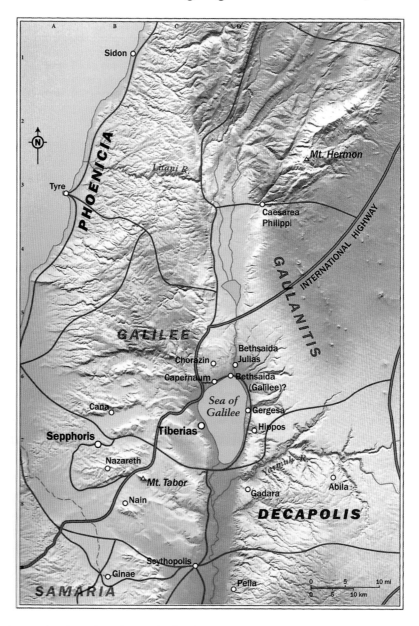

Chapter II

Galilee

Galilee is the Holy Land's northern region, an area richer in vegetation than other regions because of its lower temperatures and higher amount of rainfall. The mountainous upper Galilee contains many streams and waterfalls, while lower Galilee is dominated by the Sea of Galilee and the fertile Jezreel Valley. Colorful wildflowers carpet the hillsides in springtime, and many species of birds annually migrate through the region. In addition to its flora and fauna, Galilee is dotted with small towns and villages of biblical importance.

Isaiah described the region as "Galilee of the nations" and prophesied that God would make it glorious "in the latter time" (Isa 9:1). Because the ancient trade routes passed through Galilee, connecting Egypt with Damascus and beyond, the people of this region found themselves in contact with the peoples of the world, whether they be traveling merchants or the marching warriors of the Midianites, Philistines, Assyrians, Babylonians, Greeks, and Romans.

After the death of Herod the Great, his son Herod Antipas was appointed by Emperor Augustus as tetrarch of Galilee. The region remained a Roman client state as Antipas paid tribute to the emperor in exchange for Roman protection and the ability to govern as he wished. During Jesus's lifetime, Herod Antipas rebuilt Sepphoris and founded Tiberias, two cities that became Galilee's largest cultural centers.

Matthew shows that the launch of Jesus's ministry in "Galilee of the Gentiles" fulfilled God's plan to reach the nations with the gospel of salvation (Matt 4:14-15). "Jesus went throughout Galilee, teaching in their synagogues and proclaiming the good news" (Matt 4:23). After his resurrection, Jesus delivered his great missionary commission to his disciples on a mountain of Galilee. From there, God's saving grace was brought to all the peoples of the world.

Galilee was a great storehouse of imagery for the teachings of Jesus, and its landscapes were the setting of many of his parables. Since the bulk of Jesus's life and ministry took place in Galilee, today's pilgrims can learn from the birds of the air and the flowers of the field, the climate and the terrain, and the towns and villages crisscrossed by Jesus, how to embody his teachings and let the kingdom of God come to birth and mature within us.

1. Nazareth, Basilica of the Annunciation

Nestled in a hollow among the hills of Galilee, Nazareth is the place where the life of Jesus began. The town is dominated by the towering cupola of the Basilica of the Annunciation, built directly above the house of Mary. The facade features images of the angel Gabriel and Mary, and declares in Latin, "The angel of the Lord declared unto Mary," and beneath images of the four evangelists, "The Word became flesh and lived among us" (John 1:14). The bells of churches throughout the world echo the bells of Nazareth as Christians pray the Angelus, professing faith in the incarnation of God's word in the womb of the Virgin Mary as she conceived by the Holy Spirit.

Past the monumental bronze doors depicting the life of Christ, the entrance leads to the lower level of the basilica. The structure is focused on the remains of a natural cave, which ancient tradition describes as the house of Mary, where the angel revealed Mary's essential role in God's saving plan. Many houses of Nazareth, even today, are built up against a rock slope with a cave hewn into the rock.

*Grotto of
the Annunciation
in Nazareth*

A Jewish-Christian shrine was built on this site in the third century and at least four churches have enclosed this site through the centuries: Byzantine, Crusader, eighteenth-century Franciscan, and the present basilica. The present mid-twentieth-century structure incorporates remains of each of these periods. On the front of the altar, at the spot where the angel spoke to Mary, these words are inscribed: *Verbum Caro Hic Factum Est* (Here the Word was made flesh). Every March 25, nine months before the celebration of Jesus's birth, the church throughout the world focuses on this event as it celebrates the feast of the Annunciation.

Early pilgrims left their markings—called "graffiti" by archaeologists—on the early church-synagogue at the site. Among the graffiti scratched into the columns and ornamentation for the shrine were found many titles for Christ and brief invocations to Jesus and Mary. Most remarkably, the Greek letters XE MAPIA, "Hail Mary," the oldest known inscription honoring Mary, was found, an indication of early Marian veneration.

In the gospel scene of the Annunciation, the angel Gabriel is sent to announce the culmination of God's saving plan for the world. Gabriel had already appeared in the Old Testament as the interpreter of Daniel's prophetic dreams. Now he appears to Mary, revealing that the time has arrived when God is going to give the world what the prophets awaited.

"The Most High," "the Son of God," and "the Holy Spirit" are all named by Luke in the gospel scene—the Trinity present to Mary at this climactic moment of grace.

To this day, the people of the Middle East make a bow with one of their hands placed against their chest to indicate that they are willing to obey another's wish. Mary, the humble virgin, bowed before God: "Let it be with me according to your word." She has consented to God's will and she knows this will determine everything that happens in her life from now on.

Upper Church of the Basilica of the Annunciation

The spiral stairway near the entrance leads to the vast upper church. If the simple cave presented Mary as the humble mother of Jesus of Nazareth, the upper church presents her as mother of the universal church. On the walls, as well as in the courtyard surrounding the church, are mosaic, bas-relief, and tile images of Mary, donated from dozens of countries, showing ways she is visualized in the many cultures and ethnicities of the world. The mosaic apse expresses the triumph of the one, holy, catholic and apostolic church. The dome represents a lily, blooming downward into the church as it draws its light from the incarnation.

Meditation

- In what ways is Mary a model of trust for me?

- What do I desire to ask of Mary, my mother, at this holy place?

Reading: Luke 1:26-38

The angel Gabriel was sent by God to a town in Galilee called Nazareth. . . .

Response: Blessed are you among women, and blessed is the fruit of your womb.

Hail Mary, full of grace, the Lord is with you. R.

Chosen by God before all other creatures, the singular ray of hope illumining humanity's darkness. R.

Beloved daughter of the Father, gentle mother of the Son, and faithful spouse of the Holy Spirit. R.

Mother of the Child Jesus, sanctifier of the vocation of motherhood, protector of families. R.

Humble mother of Jesus of Nazareth, Mother of the universal church, glorious Queen of Heaven. R.

Prayer: Virgin Mary, Mother of the Word incarnate, who bore in your womb him whom the heavens cannot contain, pour out your heavenly mercy on all mothers and help them to be holy. Teach us how to form our hearts to be receptive to the word of God. Show us how to respond to God's call to us with simple trust and to say "yes" to his will with the obedience of love.

2. Nazareth, Church of St. Joseph

The Basilica of the Annunciation exits into a great elevated plaza, containing a small eight-sided baptistery. Excavated remains of Nazareth are found in a museum beneath the plaza. Past the large Franciscan Terra Sancta Convent stands the Church of St. Joseph. A lovely white statue of the Holy Family is built into the wall of the church. Pilgrims from the seventh century identified this site as the "carpentry shop of Joseph." In later centuries it was described as the "house of Joseph." Inside the church, the apse contains paintings of the Holy Family, the dream of Joseph, and the death of Joseph in the arms of Jesus and Mary.

As Luke's gospel describes the annunciation to Mary, Matthew's gospel recounts the annunciation to Joseph. The obedient responses of both Mary and Joseph were necessary for the Savior's coming. Through Joseph's compliant response to God's will, Jesus is called Son of David; and through the conception by the Holy Spirit in Mary, Jesus is Son of God.

Church of St. Joseph windows, betrothal of Mary and Joseph and death of St. Joseph

In the gospels, Jesus is called the son of the *tekton* (Matt 13:55) and the *tekton*, the son of Mary (Mark 6:3). The Greek word is usually translated "carpenter," but a *tekton* was an experienced worker in the local build-ing materials of all kinds, be they wood, stone, or metal. Every town or group of villages had a tekton to service its specialized building needs.[1] So, Joseph was not a carpenter in our limited sense of the word, but a skilled craftsman who built houses, made agricultural tools, and repaired almost anything. Joseph taught his son both the faith of Judaism and the skills of his trade.

Stairs lead down under the church to caves and rock-cut installations used by the Nazareth dwellers of the Roman period to store grain. In the Byzantine period, the space was used for Christian worship. One of the rock-cut cavities was converted to a baptismal pool with a mosaic floor. A chapel has been built inside the caves, which includes stained glass images of Joseph's life, including a scene of his betrothal to Mary. A Crusader church was built over the entire site in the twelfth century, and the present Franciscan church dates to 1914.

In the days of the Holy Family, Nazareth was literally "off the map." After the birth of Jesus in Bethlehem and their time as refugees in Egypt, Joseph brought his young family back to this village, and Jesus would henceforth be known as "a Nazorean" (Matt 2:23). In the opening scenes of John's gospel, Nathaniel was skeptical when Philip said to him, "We have found him about whom Moses in the law and also the prophets wrote, Jesus son of Joseph from Nazareth." Since Nazareth is not even mentioned in the Old Testament, it is not surprising that Nathaniel re-torted, "Can anything good come out of Nazareth?" (John 1:45-46). The answer to Nathaniel's question, of course, is obvious in retrospect.

Meditation

- Why would God come among us in such humble and human ways?

- What does Joseph teach me about the value of my work and family life?

Reading: Matthew 1:18-25

"Joseph, son of David, do not be afraid to take Mary as your wife, for the child conceived in her is from the Holy Spirit. . . ."

1. Yizhar Hirschfeld, *The Palestinian Dwelling in the Roman-Byzantine Period* (Jeru-salem: Franciscan Press, 1995), 112–43.

Response: St. Joseph, pray for us.

Spouse of the Virgin Mary and protector of the Holy Family. R.

Adoptive father of Jesus, who gave to Jesus his lineage from King David. R.

Bearing in your arms the Son of God and teaching him the faith of Judaism. R.

Witnessing the hidden life of Jesus and dying in the arms of Jesus and Mary. R.

Patron and inspiration for husbands and fathers. R.

Model for workers, consecrating the labor of our hands to God. R.

In all our homes, in all our afflictions, in the hour of death, and in the day of judgment. R.

Prayer: God of our ancestors, who gave to the just man from Nazareth, St. Joseph, the privilege of serving as earthly Father to Jesus your Son, through his intercession watch over our families and guide us in your ways. May this son of David, in whom the shoot from the stump of Jesse has blossomed, guide your people with care and protect your church from harm. United with Mary his spouse and Jesus our Lord, may we be joined forever in the joys of your heavenly kingdom.

3. Nazareth, Mary of Nazareth International Center

Located across the street from the Basilica of the Annunciation, the Mary of Nazareth International Center is one of the newest attractions of this ancient town. The four-story complex welcomes visitors of all faiths and uses modern technologies to celebrate Mary's role in salvation history. The center has received the support of all the Christian churches of the Holy Land—Catholic, Orthodox, and Protestant. The impetus for establishing the center came from the Association Marie de Nazareth, a Catholic group based in France, and has been run by the Chemin Neuf community since its opening in 2012. In addition to its focus on Mary in Christianity, the programs at the center emphasize Mary as a Jewish woman and Mary in the Qur'an.

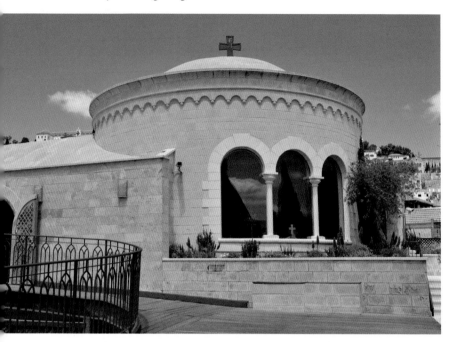

Unity Chapel of the Mary of Nazareth International Center

When workers were preparing the foundations of the center, they uncovered the walls of an ancient house from the Roman period. Archaeologists then excavated the simple house with walls of slightly hewn limestone. Its storage and living areas form an L-shape around a small courtyard where rainwater was collected from the roof into a rock-hewn cistern. The Israel Antiquities Authority declared that the remains were of the first residential building ever discovered in Nazareth that dated back to the time of Jesus. Since the house is only fifty meters from the cave of the annunciation, it seems almost certain that Mary knew the family and visited there.

Visitors may follow a multimedia presentation, giving them a sweeping perspective of Mary's place in Scripture. The content is divided into four parts, each viewed in a separate room, presented with surround sound, wide-screen cinema, and 3D effects, available in multiple languages. It is firmly grounded in Scripture, ranging from ancient Israel and the prophets to the death and resurrection of Jesus and the beginnings of the church. The rooftop garden offers visitors a place to reflect and enjoy spectacular views of Nazareth.

View of Nazareth from the Unity Chapel

The Unity Chapel in the midst of the gardens provides a place for prayer and liturgy. Twenty icons are featured within the walls of the domed church, each representing one of the mysteries of the rosary. The joyful, luminous, sorrowful, and glorious mysteries are enhanced through these ancient-styled icons from the Eastern tradition of the Christian faith.[2]

2. These twenty icons are reproduced with gospel texts and reflections by Stephen J. Binz, *Transformed by God's Word: Discovering the Power of Lectio and Visio Divina* (Notre Dame, IN: Ave Maria Press, 2016).

Meditation

- In what ways do icons, paintings, music, and devotional practices enhance my experience of the Bible?

- What new perspectives do I receive when imagining the joys and sufferings of Jesus through the mind and heart of Mary?

Reading: Luke 2:33-40

Simeon . . . said to his mother Mary, "This child is destined for the falling and rising of many in Israel. . . ."

Response: "Holy Mary, Mother of God, pray for us sinners, now and at the hour of our death."

Mary, Mother of Sorrows, Simeon's prophecy foretold that a sword of suffering would pierce your heart. We lift up all parents who suffer over their children, that they be given comfort and hope. R.

Mary, Comforter of the Afflicted, you followed your son as he displayed divine compassion for humanity. We lift up the poor, the displaced, the marginalized, and vulnerable members of society, that Christ's disciples may help them in their needs. R.

Mary, Intercessor and Advocate, you come to the aid of all who flee to your protection and implore your help. We lift up one another, that you will hear our petitions and plead for us before your son in heaven. R.

Mary, Queen of Heaven and earth, you desire to lead the world to the salvation offered by your son. We lift up all those called to God's kingdom, that they may know the freedom of being God's children and come to the fullness of life. R.

Mary, Our Lady of the Rosary, you present to the world the blessed fruit of your womb. We lift up those who meditate on these holy mysteries, that we may imitate what they contain and obtain what they promise. R.

Prayer: Son of God and Son of Mary, we pray for the coming of your kingdom on earth as it is in heaven. Help us to continue the work you have begun in us. Inspire us to works of justice, compassion, and forgiveness until you come in glory to crown all our efforts with your eternal blessings.

The Synagogue Church of Nazareth

4. Nazareth, Synagogue Church

Beneath the cars and buses, houses and hotels of today, lies the Jewish peasant village. In modern Nazareth, we can still observe many characteristics of an ancient oriental town. The *souk*, or marketplace, displays fruits and vegetables, live chickens and fresh meat, woven cloths and jewelry. In the shop owners of the town we can still see people like Mary and Joseph, with their olive skin and deep-set eyes. We can see Jesus in the children as they run through the streets and out into the hills overlooking the great valley below. We see Jesus in the youth who help the elders of the town in their shops and learn new skills from their parents. Jesus is in the young men who go to the churches for the feasts, just as Jesus went into the synagogue on Saturdays and learned the Scriptures.

The Synagogue Church is located in the middle of Nazareth's old market, adjacent to the Greek Catholic Church of the Annunciation. The Jewish synagogue from the Roman period was located on this site, according to the Byzantine tradition. Here is where Jesus was brought by his parents on the Sabbath to study the Torah and the prophets. In the twelfth century, the Crusaders built the present church as a simple, single-hall structure. The Franciscans controlled the church until the eighteenth century when it was passed to the Greek Catholics.

When Jesus returned to Nazareth during his adult ministry, Luke's gospel tells us, "he went to the synagogue on the sabbath day, as was his custom" (Luke 4:16). As a learned visitor, Jesus would have been invited to read a section of Scripture and offer a comment on the text. As Jesus unrolled the scroll, he read a passage from Isaiah (61:1-2), which told of one anointed by God's Spirit. The description of this anointed Messiah's work previews the ministry of Jesus himself: bringing good news, proclaiming liberty, giving sight, freeing the oppressed—in sum, announcing a time of favor from God. After rolling up the scroll and sitting in the chair of the teacher, Jesus began his commentary on the text by saying, "Today this scripture has been fulfilled in your hearing" (Luke 4:21). He identified himself as this anointed one of Isaiah's prophecy and signaled that the longed-for time of God's favor would be given through him.

The initial reaction to Jesus's words was encouraging; all were amazed at his teachings. Yet, soon doubts began to arise, prompted by a question about Jesus's simple origins in their own town. Why should Jesus claim any distinctions for himself or any unique relationship with God? As the mood of the people changed, Jesus began to show them how God's people had always rejected their prophets. And with these words, the people expelled Jesus from their synagogue and drove him from Nazareth.

Meditation

- In what ways do I see Jesus in the streets of Nazareth today?

- In what ways am I in need of the healing, forgiveness, and liberation that Jesus, God's anointed Servant, offers?

Reading: Luke 4:14-24

"The Spirit of the Lord is upon me, / because he has anointed me / to bring good news to the poor. . . ."

Response: Come Lord Jesus with your saving power.

In the latter time he will make glorious the way of the sea, the land beyond the Jordan, Galilee of the nations.

The people who walked in darkness
    have seen a great light;
those who lived in a land of deep darkness—
    on them light has shined (Isa 9:1-2). R.

Then the eyes of the blind shall be opened,
    and the ears of the deaf unstopped;
then the lame shall leap like a deer,
    and the tongue of the speechless sing for joy (Isa 35:5-6). R.

Here is my servant, whom I uphold,
    my chosen, in whom my soul delights;
I have put my spirit upon him;
    he will bring forth justice to the nations.
He will not cry or lift up his voice,
    or make it heard in the street (Isa 42:1-2). R.

Who has believed what we have heard?
    And to whom has the arm of the LORD been revealed?
For he grew up before him like a young plant,
    and like a root out of dry ground;
he had no form or majesty that we should look at him,
    nothing in his appearance that we should desire him (Isa 53:1-2). R.

Prayer: Come Lord Jesus with your saving power. As God's anointed Servant, you fulfill the words of God's prophet and bring light, healing, forgiveness, and liberation to those who receive you. Let the poor, captive, blind, and oppressed hear the good news you proclaim, so that all may experience the time of God's favor you have brought to the world.

5. Nazareth, Mount Precipice

The Nazareth Ridge rises sharply from the Jezreel Valley on the south side of Nazareth. We can imagine Joseph bringing the young Jesus here at sunset and teaching him about the history of Israel by pointing out the sites of countless biblical events in the Valley of Jezreel and the mountains beyond. Moving from left to right, we first see the dome-shaped Mount Tabor, which is associated with the battles of Deborah and Barak (Judg 4-5). Next, the Hill of Moreh is the site of Gideon's battle with the Midianites

(Judg 6-7), and Mount Gilboa is the place of the Philistine victory, where King Saul and his sons met their deaths (1 Sam 31). Megiddo witnessed the death of King Josiah (2 Kgs 23:29), and Mount Carmel, on the right, was the stage for Elijah with the prophets of Baal (1 Kgs 18:17-46).

This high precipice, while providing the town of Nazareth with a dramatic view, would have offered a sense of seclusion and protection from the vast arena that had served as a highway and a battleground through the ages. Yet, the adolescent Jesus would come to this view and imagine the great world beyond his hometown. It provided an ideal setting for the years of preparation Jesus needed as he "increased in wisdom and in years, and in divine and human favor" (Luke 2:52).

After the adult Jesus had enraged the people in the synagogue of Nazareth, they brought him to this ridge, intending to throw him to his death. By reminding them of the stories of the prophets Elijah and Elisha, Jesus reiterated how Israel had drifted away from God to idolatry and corruption. The accounts of the prophets revealed how God bestows mercy upon the humble and how God would rather give blessings to foreign Gentiles, such as the widow in Sidon and Naaman the Syrian, than to ungrateful Israelites (Luke 4:25-27).

A small chapel, Our Lady of the Fright, can be seen on the hillside southeast of Nazareth. It commemorates the place where Mary was standing as she watched Jesus being led to the edge of the cliff to be thrown down. With great fear, she prayed here for her son as she continued to experience the maternal suffering that the life of Jesus would bring. But Jesus passed through the midst of those seeking his life and went on his way to Capernaum by the Sea of Galilee.

Meditation

- What might Jesus have thought when he visited this ridge in his adolescence?

- Why did Jesus's recalling stories of God's mercy to foreigners so enrage his hearers in Nazareth?

Reading: Luke 4:22-30

They got up, drove him out of the town, and led him to the brow of the hill. . . .

Response: "I will give you as a light to the nations, / that my salvation may reach to the end of the earth."

Listen to me, O coastlands,
    pay attention, you peoples from far away!
The LORD called me before I was born,
    while I was in my mother's womb he named me. R.

And now the LORD says,
    who formed me in the womb to be his servant,
to bring Jacob back to him,
    and that Israel might be gathered to him,
for I am honored in the sight of the LORD,
    and my God has become my strength. R.

"It is too light a thing that you should be my servant
    to raise up the tribes of Jacob
    and to restore the survivors of Israel;
I will give you as a light to the nations,
    that my salvation may reach to the end of the earth." R.

Sing for joy, O heavens, and exult, O earth;
    break forth, O mountains, into singing!
For the LORD has comforted his people,
    and will have compassion on his suffering ones (Isa 49). R.

Pilgrims on the windy Mount Precipice

Prayer: Divine Prophet of Israel, formed and named in the womb of Mary but disdained and rejected in your own hometown, you are a light to the nations that God's salvation might reach to the ends of the earth. Like Elijah and Elisha, you bestow divine mercy on the humble and give blessings to foreigners who trust in God. Make us zealous in our love for the Father and generous in our care for neighbor, so that we may not reject you but follow you as our Savior and Lord.

6. Cana, Church of the Wedding Feast

Cana is remembered as the place where, according to John's gospel, Jesus performed "the first of his signs," the miraculous transformation of a large quantity of water into wine at a wedding feast (John 2:1-11). Although historians and archaeologists do not agree on the historical location of the town, the Franciscans chose Kafr Kanna in 1641 as the place to commemorate the miracle. The town is about five miles northeast of Nazareth on the road toward Capernaum on the Sea of Galilee. Weddings are frequently performed here and married pilgrims often renew their wedding vows at this place where Jesus honored marriage with his presence.

The gospel account shows no concern for the details of who was getting married, who invited Jesus and his mother, or why the wine gave out. Mary is the first to notice the lack of wine, and she takes the matter to Jesus. Despite Jesus's dismissive remarks, Mary tells the servants, "Do whatever he tells you." On the first level of meaning, Mary wants to save the couple's family from the embarrassment of not providing sufficient wine for the guests. But the quantity and quality of the wine that Jesus produces indicates a deeper level of meaning. Indications of the size of the six stone water jars—"each holding twenty to thirty gallons"—filled "to the brim" designates an enormous amount of wine. On tasting the wine, the steward remarked to the bridegroom that he had waited to serve the best wine last. The prophets had described God's future blessings as an abundance of wine: "The mountains shall drip sweet wine, / and all the hills shall flow with it" (Amos 9:13). Mary is asking Jesus to bring about the plentiful banquet and abundant wine expected for God's kingdom in the age to come.

Church of the Wedding Feast in Cana

The wedding banquet shows us that Jesus was not a desert ascetic like John the Baptist. He celebrated with people, and abundant life and joy seems to have characterized much of his life. His first miracle must have delighted the wedding guests with an extravagance of the finest quality wine. The joy of God's kingdom is a new creation. Never again would life be as predictable, bland, and colorless as water; life in Jesus becomes vibrant, luscious, and crimson. Jesus comes to show people what they have been missing, what they thought had run out. Christian marriage and the whole of life in Christ anticipate the joys of God's kingdom.

The miracle at the wedding was the first of the seven "signs" of Jesus in John's gospel. A sign is not merely a miraculous wonder, but a revelation of who Jesus is and an invitation to have faith in him. The "second sign" of John's gospel also occurred at "Cana in Galilee": the healing from a distance of the son of a royal official (John 4:46-54). Although the official implored Jesus to come to his ill son in Capernaum, about a day's journey away, Jesus healed the boy at a distance in Cana and assured the official that his son would live.

The Franciscan church, often simply called The Wedding Church, holds a painting of the wedding feast above the altar along with decorative jars recalling the miracle. Beneath the church remains were found of a first-century dwelling, a Jewish synagogue, and a Byzantine basilica with three apses in the form of a cross. A small stone cistern was also discovered. Near the Franciscan church is the Greek Orthodox church, filled with frescoes in icon style. Around the churches, the local shops offer sweet "wedding wine" for tasting and purchasing.

Meditation

- Do I trust Jesus enough to follow the advice of Mary: "Do whatever he tells you"?

- In what ways does the wine of Cana express the life that Jesus offers me?

Reading: John 2:1-12

The mother of Jesus said to him, "They have no wine." . . .

Response: Lord, hear our prayer.

We pray for all married couples here, that God will continue to bless their lives and enrich their love for one another. We pray to the Lord. R.

We pray for all preparing for marriage and for those discerning God's call for their lives, that God will give them wisdom and guidance. We pray to the Lord. R.

We pray for all couples experiencing difficulties in their marriage, that God give them courage and help in their struggles. We pray to the Lord. R.

We pray for all single adults and for all committed to consecrated service in your church, that God will bless their lives and enrich their call. We pray to the Lord. R.

We pray for those whose spouses have died, that God will comfort them in their loss and give eternal life to the deceased. We pray to the Lord. R.

We pray for those who have experienced divorce or separation, that God will transform their pains and bring healing to their families. We pray to the Lord. R.

We pray for extended families, blended families, and single-parent families, that all family members be enriched through dedication to one another and the love that comes from life in Christ. We pray to the Lord. R.

We pray for all married couples, that they may see their marriages as true vocations in Christ and that they may see their relationships as a call to holiness. We pray to the Lord. R.

Couples with their marriage renewal certificates

Renewal of Marriage:

Turn toward one another, join your hands together, and renew your marriage vows before God and his church.

Husband, repeat after me, inserting your name and the name of your spouse.

I, _____, renew to you, _____,
the promise I made to you on our wedding day.

We have grown up and grown older together / We have seen good times and bad / sickness and health.

We have seen our love threatened / and we have felt our love deepen.

I will stand by you / and I will love you / all the days of my life.

Wives, repeat after me, inserting your name and the name of your spouse.

I, _____, renew to you, _____,
The promise I made to you on our wedding day.

We have grown up and grown older together / We have seen good times and bad / sickness and health.

We have seen our love threatened / and we have felt our love deepen.

I will stand by you / and I will love you / all the days of my life.

Blessing of Rings:

I invite you to hold out the hand with your wedding ring.

Let us now ask for God's blessings upon them:

Loving God, bless + these wedding rings and the Christian marriages which they symbolize. Grant that those who wear them may always have a deep faith in one another. May they do your will and always live together in loving commitment and peace. We ask this through Jesus Christ, the spouse of your church, and our Lord forever. Amen.

On behalf of the entire church, we accept the renewal of your vows. May your marriages be less predictable, bland, and colorless like water, and more vibrant, luscious, and crimson like wine.

Prayer: Father, we rejoice in your gift of love that fills our hearts. You have so exalted the bond of marriage that it has become the sacramental sign on your Son's union with the church as his spouse. We ask you to bless all married couples, especially those here today. May they both praise you when they are happy and turn to you in their sorrows. May they be glad that you help them in their work and know that you are with them in their need. May they pray to you in the community of the church and be your witnesses in the world. May they reach old age in the company of their family and friends, and come at last to the kingdom of heaven. We ask this through Christ our Lord. Amen.

7. *Mount Carmel, Stella Maris*

Although Mount Carmel sometimes refers to only the high, steep ridge overlooking the Mediterranean Sea, it is more accurately a mountain range stretching from the crest at today's city of Haifa toward the southeast. The mountain formation is an admixture of limestone and flint, containing many caves and covered in volcanic rock. In the writing of the prophets, Carmel is a symbol of strength, beauty, and fertility, but it is most associated with the prophet Elijah, who often lived in Carmel's caves. In ancient Canaanite culture, Carmel was a sacred high place where the gods were honored, and thanks to the prophet Elijah, it became a sanctuary for the God of Israel.

Ahab, the king of the Israelites in the ninth century BC, abandoned the worship of Israel's God and embraced the religion of Baal, under the influence of his foreign wife, Jezebel. Then God's prophet Elijah proclaimed a great drought upon the land, and in the third year of the drought, the prophet challenged Ahab to a contest at Mount Carmel. He told the king to gather all the Israelites as witnesses and to bring all the prophets of Baal. The challenge was to see which deity would send down fire upon the altar to consume a sacrifice. While the prophets of Baal sought a response for many hours, Elijah mocked them with sarcastic humor: "Cry aloud! Surely he is a god; either he is meditating, or he has wandered away, or he is on a journey, or perhaps he is asleep and must be awakened" (1 Kgs 18:27). As evening came, Elijah built an altar to the Lord, placed the sacrifice upon it, drenched the wood with water, and called upon the God of Abraham, Isaac, and Jacob. Immediately fire fell from the sky

Stella Maris,
Our Lady of Mount Carmel

Cave of Elijah in the Stella Maris Church

and consumed the sacrifice, wood, stones, dust, and water, at which the Israelites bowed and cried, "The Lord indeed is God."

Mount Carmel is the place of origin of the Carmelite spiritual tradition. In the twelfth century, during the Crusader rule, groups of hermits, who had come either as pilgrims or crusaders, began to inhabit the caves of this area in imitation of Elijah. Eventually they asked St. Albert, the patriarch of Jerusalem, to provide them with a written rule of life. This was the originating act of the Carmelites, who took the name Order of the Brothers of Our Lady of Mount Carmel. They focus their lives on prayer, community, and service, taking particular inspiration from Elijah and the Virgin Mary, the two patrons of the order. The motto on their crest is the words of Elijah in Latin, "I have been very zealous for the LORD, the God of hosts" (1 Kgs 19:10), and their unique charism is contemplation, based on the message God gave to Elijah at Mount Sinai, not being manifested in the wind, earthquake, or fire, but in the still voice heard in silence (1 Kgs 19:11-12).

The Carmelite Monastery and Church of Stella Maris is built over the cave of Elijah at the highest point of the Carmel range. It is dedicated to Mary under her title our Lady, Star of the Sea, guide and protector of seafarers. It is the foundation house of the order and, after being destroyed several times, was rebuilt in the 1830s. The cave now forms the crypt of the church, while a statue of Our Lady of Mount Carmel dominates the upper altar. The colorful paintings on the ceiling depict Elijah rising to heaven on a chariot, David playing the harp, the prophets Daniel, Ezekiel, and Isaiah, the Holy Family, and the Carmelite founders. Images on the side altars include St. Simon Stock receiving the scapular from our Lady and Sts. Teresa of Avila and John of the Cross, the sixteenth-century reformers and founders of the Order of Discalced Carmelites. The spiritual writings highlighted on the church walls include *Interior Castle* by St. Teresa of Avila, *Ascent of Mount Carmel* by St. John of the Cross, *Story of a Soul* by St. Therese of Lisieux, and works of St. Teresa Benedicta of the Cross (Edith Stein).

Outside the church, a pyramid-shaped memorial stone, with an iron cross on top of it, forms a memorial to the French soldiers who died here after Napoleon's retreat. An earlier monastery complex on this site served as a hospital for Napoleon's soldiers in 1799. The bones of the fallen soldiers were later collected and buried in the garden under the stone. The text of the memorial reads in Latin: "How the mighty have fallen, / and the weapons of war perished!" (2 Sam 1:27), from King David's lamentation over Saul and Jonathan.

Meditation

- What events have brought me back to the worship of the one true God?

- How can I prepare to discern the voice of God in the still voice heard in silence?

Reading: 1 Kings 18:20-39

Ahab sent to all the Israelites and assembled the prophets at Mount Carmel. . . .

Response: Make us zealous for you, O Lord, like Elijah your prophet.

The LORD roars from Zion,
 and utters his voice from Jerusalem;
the pastures of the shepherds wither,
 and the top of Carmel dries up (Amos 1:2). R.

The land mourns and languishes;
 Lebanon is confounded and withers away;
Sharon is like a desert;
 and Bashan and Carmel shake off their leaves (Isa 33:9). R.

Elijah said to Ahab, "Go up, eat and drink for there is a sound of rushing rain." So Ahab went up to eat and drink. Elijah went up to the top of Carmel; there he bowed himself down upon the earth and put his face between his knees (1 Kgs 18:41-42). R.

"Look, a little cloud no bigger than a person's hand is rising out of the sea." Then [Elijah] said, "Go and say to Ahab, 'Harness your chariot and go down before the rain stops you.'" In a little while the heavens grew black with clouds and wind; there was heavy rain (1 Kgs 18:44-45). R.

The wilderness and the dry land shall be glad, / the desert shall rejoice and blossom. . . . The glory of Lebanon shall be given to it, / the majesty of Carmel and Sharon (Isa 35:1-2). R.

A chariot of fire and horses of fire separated the two of them, and Elijah ascended in a whirlwind into heaven (2 Kgs 2:11). R.

Rock cliff and cave at Banias

Prayer: God of our ancestors, who gave Elijah the grace of living in your presence, may we listen for you in the rain and storms, as well as in the still quiet voice. We ask you today to help us be rid of any other gods, any idols, any false ideas, or any unhealthy attitudes that may prevent us from worshiping you with all our hearts. May we consume our lives with zeal for your glory and be witnesses to your love.

8. Caesarea Philippi

The ruins of Caesarea Philippi are found in Upper Galilee at Banias, in the foothills of Mount Hermon, the Holy Land's highest mountain. Although the site has no Christian church, pilgrims will immediately notice three natural formations here: a large rock cliff against which the city was built, a large cave at the base of the cliff, and fresh water flowing from within the earth. These help explain why Jesus brought Peter and the disciples here at a climactic moment of his ministry.

The cave of Pan, the part-goat part-man Greek god of fertility and springtime, became a center of pagan activity starting in the third century BC. This gave the city its name, Panias, which is pronounced in Arabic as Banias. Animal sacrifices were cast into the seemingly bottomless cave in which the water flowed. The sacred sanctuary received a higher

status after Herod constructed a temple in honor of Augustus in 16 BC. After Herod's son Philip made the city his capital, it became known as the Caesarea of Philip to distinguish it from another Caesarea by the sea. Additional temples and rock-hewn niches and inscriptions were added as pagan worship continued until the middle of the Byzantine period, around the fifth century, when it was abandoned.

For the Greeks, the mouths of deep caves, especially those with flowing water within, were believed to be entrances to the murky darkness of *Hades*, the realm of the dead. In a famous line of Homer, Achilles says: "For hateful to me, even as the gates of Hades, is the man who hides one thing in his mind and says another."[3] In Hebrew, the fearsome aspects of the grave and the realm of death is *Sheol*. King Hezekiah expressed his fear of being "consigned to the gates of Sheol" (Isa 38:10).

For the Jews of Jesus's day, Caesarea Philippi seemed to be the most pagan place in all of Galilee. Most Jews would avoid it altogether because of its connection to bestiality and the fertility rituals of Pan. And nothing could be further from worship of the one God than offering sacrifice to the emperor and calling on him as lord of the world and savior of all. It seems that Jesus brought his disciples to this distant pagan setting in order to push the boundaries of their understanding of God's saving love. In contrast to the Greco-Roman religions, whose foremost concern was appeasing the gods by doing whatever ritual action would gain their favor, the kingdom preached by Jesus involved bringing God's saving presence to those who are most lost. Realizing that many people misunderstood his identity, mistaking him for one of the prophets, Jesus asked his disciples the question to which the gospel had been leading: "Who do you say that I am?" Peter's response declared that Jesus is not only the Messiah, the fulfillment of all who precede him in Israel's tradition, but also "the Son of the *living* God," in contrast to all the stone dead images of divinity that surrounded them in the temples and niches of the rock.

Since Simon Peter announced who Jesus is, Jesus declared who Peter is. Standing in front of the massive cliff, Jesus used the vivid metaphor "rock." "You are Peter [*Petros*, in Greek] and on this rock [*petra*] I will build my church" (Matt 16:18). Jesus had already urged people to build their own lives upon rock (*petra*) (Matt 7:24); now Jesus was building

---

3. Homer, *Illiad* 9.312–13.

Author points out the ruins of Caesarea Philippi

the foundations of his church. In Aramaic, the language Jesus spoke, the metaphor is even more exact: "You are *Kepha*, and on this *kepha* I will build my church." Truly Christ's church would be indestructible, despite the coming storms of persecution from the Roman empire. Even "the gates of Hades," which represent all the dark and terrifying powers of the underworld, would not prevail against Christ's church. Jesus gave Peter the keys not to this gate, but the "keys of the kingdom of heaven." These keys would open the way to God's kingdom through his preaching and leadership. Like Eliakim, who was made master of the household and given "the key of the house of David" with the authority to open and shut the gates for those seeking entry into the realm (Isa 22:22), Peter is the keeper of the keys, the prime minister or vicar of the King. While Jesus the King never relinquishes his authority over the church, he delegates his authority to his highest official to regulate the affairs of the realm.

The gates of Hades were the way for the fertility gods to go to the underworld in the dry season, only to be coaxed out again with fertility rituals when the rains were due. But Jesus began teaching his disciples about a radically different death and resurrection, unlike the recycled myths of the gods (Matt 16:21). When the impulsive Peter began to reject the way of the cross, Jesus took him aside and issued some of the harshest words of the gospel, calling him "Satan," a tempter. Yet, Jesus did not say, "Away with you, Satan," as he told the devil when he tempted him in the wilderness. Rather, Jesus told Peter, "Get behind me, Satan," commanding him to resume his position as a follower; walking behind Jesus, he would gradually discover through his mistakes and failures what it meant to be a disciple of the Lord and the leader of his church.

Meditation

- Why did Jesus bring Peter and the disciples to the far northern city of Caesarea Philippi?

- Why do the gospels highlight both Peter's misunderstanding and his leading role among the disciples?

Reading: Matthew 16:13-23

When Jesus came into the district of Caesarea Philippi, he asked his disciples, "Who do people say that the Son of Man is?" . . .

Response: You are Peter and on this rock I will build my church.

Jesus saw two brothers, Simon, who is called Peter, and Andrew his brother, casting a net into the lake—for they were fishermen. And he said to them, "Follow me, and I will make you fish for people" (Matt 4:18). R.

"Everyone who hears these words of mine and acts on them will be like a wise man who built his house on rock" (Matt 7:24). R.

"The rain fell, the floods came, and the winds blew and beat on that house, but it did not fall because it had been founded on rock" (Matt 7:25). R.

Prayer: Jesus, we believe that you are the Messiah, the Son of the living God. We thank you for the gift of this faith, and we ask that you reveal to us a deeper understanding and practical implications of this faith each day. Through the intercession of your apostle St. Peter, let nothing shake our faith or the solid foundations of your church.

9. *Mount Tabor, Basilica of the Transfiguration*

Although the gospels do not name the "high mountain" on which the transfiguration of Jesus took place, an early tradition named Mount Tabor as the site. The mountain rises majestically from the Jezreel Valley south of the hills of Galilee. It is hemispherical and almost perfect in its symmetry. From its top, where it flattens out, a panorama of the whole of central Galilee can be viewed.

In the fourth century a basilica was built on the top of the mountain, and St. Cyril of Jerusalem is the first to note that the transfiguration occurred "at Mount Tabor."[4] A sixth-century pilgrim reported three churches there, honoring Moses, Elijah, and Jesus. The present site is surrounded by ruins of a church and monastery from the Crusader period. After the Crusaders were defeated, all the religious buildings were destroyed in the thirteenth century. Tabor remained deserted for nearly 400 years until the Franciscans negotiated permission to settle there. The grounds of the mountaintop are now divided between the Greek Orthodox Church of St. Elijah and the Franciscan Basilica of the Transfiguration and its friary.

Early pilgrims used to climb 4,300 steps cut into the rocky slope to reach the pinnacle. These days taxi vans negotiate a succession of hairpin bends before arriving at the summit. The basilica was the first of many Franciscan churches designed by the Italian architect Antonio Barluzzi. A bas-relief of the designer is set into a wall on the right of the entrance. Completed in 1924, the two bell towers rise over the ancient oratories of Moses and Elijah. The roofline

4. Cyril of Jerusalem, *Catechetical Lectures* 12.16.

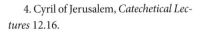
The sacred summit of Mount Tabor

forms three triangles, reminders of the three tents Peter desired to erect for Jesus, Moses, and Elijah.

The upper level of the interior church is dominated by a glowing mosaic of the transfiguration in the apse. The gospel account speaks of a wondrous change in Jesus's appearance on the high mountain. The dazzling garments of Jesus and his glowing face are expressions of his divinity, the glory of God's Son. Moses and Elijah, representing the Torah and prophets, appear with him. They had each previously experienced a theophany of God on a mountaintop, which was for them Mount Sinai. Peter, James, and John are standing below, amazed at the scene. The voice of God identifies Jesus as his Son and asks that his disciples "listen to him."

Steps lead down to a lower level, which is also the level of the Byzantine church. In the center is a stained glass of a pair of peacocks, a symbol of immortality. On both sides of the convex ceiling are beautiful mosaics that show different phases of Christ's transformation for us—his birth, gift of the Eucharist, sacrificial death, and resurrection. In Eastern Christian spirituality, the transfiguration expresses the belief that God wants to transform us all into his own divine likeness. In the transfiguration, we experience a person totally possessed by God, completely on fire with God, perfectly reflecting the divine image. This divinization is what our transforming God would do with us if he were given free rein in our lives. We have all had glimpses of this experience: when we touch God personally in deep prayer, when our hearts are lifted listening to glorious music, when awesome worship fills our spirits with holiness.

The account of the transfiguration occurs in the gospels immediately after Jesus first prophesies his death and begins his journey toward Jerusalem. This context reminds us that transforming experiences of God's presence are never given to us simply to be enjoyed for their own sake. The gift is given within the context of our vocation, to strengthen us for God's calling—a calling that, for the Christian, always includes the call to come down the mountain, take up the cross, and follow Jesus toward Jerusalem.

The upper and lower levels of the Church of the Transfiguration

Meditation

- What gives me hope when my faith is weak and challenged by discouragement?

- When have I had a glimpse of the transformation God desires in my life?

Reading: Matthew 17:1-9

Jesus took with him Peter, James, and his brother John and led them up a high mountain, by themselves. . . .

Response: Lord, make us attentive to your voice!

Moses and Elijah appeared and revealed Jesus Christ as the accomplishment of the Torah and the prophets. May we be attentive to these holy texts so that we may be transformed by the inspired word of God. R.

He received honor and glory from God the Father when that voice was conveyed to him by the Majestic Glory, saying, "This is my Son, my Beloved, with whom I am well pleased." We ourselves heard this voice come from heaven, while we were with him on the holy mountain (2 Pet 1:17-18). R.

You will do well to be attentive to this as to a lamp shining in a dark place, until the day dawns and the morning star rises in your hearts (2 Pet 1:19). R.

May we be transformed into the likeness of our Lord whose radiant splendor we have experienced on this holy mountain in his glorious transfiguration. R.

Prayer: Lord, Jesus, you gave your disciples the vision of your transfiguration as a sign of hope as you made your way toward Jerusalem. When we get discouraged along the way and stop trusting you, give us glimpses of divine glory in the midst of our ordinary lives. With the intercession of Moses and Elijah, give us confidence in your saving plan for us. May all glory be yours forever and ever.

Chapter III

Around the Sea of Galilee

Life in Galilee is centered on its large lake, the Sea of Galilee. Fed by the Jordan River, which flows into the lake at its north side and out of the lake on its south side, as well as by springs and runoff from the mountains to its north and east, the sea provides freshwater fishing to local residents. The sea was known as the Sea of Chinnereth in the Old Testament, and the gospels also refer to it as the Lake of Gennesaret and the Sea of Tiberias. It is about twelve miles long from north to south and about eight miles across at its widest point, between Magdala on the west and Kursi on the east. Although pilgrims today often comment on how the area around the sea is undeveloped, supposing it to be similar to the way it looked in the days of Jesus, in reality, the shores of the sea were much more developed in the first century than today. The slopes and heights around the sea today are dotted with ruins, the remnants of booming activity during the Roman era. Their mute testimony gives evidence of a prosperous population in the towns and villages to which Jesus came to proclaim the coming of God's kingdom.

After leaving Nazareth, Jesus went down to the Sea of Galilee and began his public ministry. Around these usually serene waters, Jesus taught in the synagogues and healed the sick, using the lake, its boats, and its shores to spread the gospel of God's kingdom. Jesus focused his ministry on the northwest side of the lake, the area controlled by Herod Antipas, which contained the largest concentration of Jews. The northeast corner of the Sea of Galilee belonged to the region of Gaulanitis and was governed by Herod Antipas's half-brother Philip. This area held a dramatic mix of Jewish and Greek culture. The southeast side of the sea belonged to the Decapolis, a region of ten cities loosely associated with each other. The cities were bastions of Greek culture and places that religious Jews generally avoided. Jesus traveled to this area on occasion, healing the sick and possessed, and gaining crowds of followers. Three political regions, each controlled by different rulers and representing a variety of lifestyles and worldviews, shared the same small shoreline. The fact that each region included sizable cities around the shoreline demonstrates that the entire area was flourishing with fishing, agriculture, and access to international roads and trade.

As Jesus walked along the shore, the Sea of Galilee was thick with fishing boats. The fishermen cast nets into the water from their boats to catch fish. The nets were weighted with lead around their edges, and as they sank, they surrounded the fish, which were then hauled into the boats. Jesus called the first four of his disciples—Peter, Andrew, James, and John—while they were about their work as fishermen (Matt 4:18-22). Jesus's words emphasized that they would both follow Jesus and share in his mission: "Follow me, and I will make you fish for people." The metaphor of fishing for people is found nowhere else in ancient writings. Jesus must have created it for this occasion, perhaps with some playful humor. It reflects the seaside location of the calling and the way Jesus tailored his message to his audience, using images of their career to declare their new vocation.

Because so much of Jesus's ministry concerned fishing, the fish became a symbol of Jesus in the early church. The Greek word for fish, ΙΧΘΥΣ (*ichthys*), consists of five letters, each of which is the initial of a Christian profession of faith in Greek that translates as "Jesus Christ, Son of God, Savior." For second-century Christians undergoing persecution, the *ichthys* served as a covert sign of identity and soon was used as ornamentation on sarcophagi, frescoes, catacombs, seals, and rings. A pilgrimage around the Sea of Galilee highlights many fishing expeditions, wondrous catches, and fish miracles in Jesus's ministry. And to make the experience even more real, the pilgrim should enjoy a meal of the so-called St. Peter's fish (*musht*, in Arabic), a tasty white fish that can be enjoyed at local restaurants.

1. In a Boat on the Sea

The best way to experience the lake itself is to take advantage of the many boats available for pilgrims to charter. Whether the sea is tranquil or restless, an expedition across the lake can be an inspiring and contemplative experience. By day, the lake affords the ideal view of the surrounding mountains and hills; by night, the sea is uniquely lovely as the boats set out with their lamps alight.

Traveling the Sea of Galilee

Jesus conducted much of his ministry on the sea: crossing from one town to another by boat, teaching from a boat to the crowds on the shore, and displaying his power over the wind and the waves. The fishing boats of Jesus's disciples were made of wood and propelled by a single sail. Because the sea is relatively small and surrounded on most sides by steep hillsides, inhabitants of the surrounding towns could often view the entire surface area of the lake. The crowds following Jesus could follow the progress of his boat as it sailed from one harbor to another. Keeping track of Jesus's movements, the crowds were sometimes able to arrive at a destination before Jesus (Mark 6:33).

The entire lake is located within a great topographical depression. At about 685 feet below sea level, the Sea of Galilee is the lowest freshwater lake in the world. Because it lies low and is surrounded by hills, it is prone to sudden turbulence. Treacherous storms are often generated in mid-afternoon, as the heat on the lake sucks down the cool air of the heights. When winds funnel through the Galilee hills or come off the Golan Heights to the east, the peaceful calm of the lake can quickly become transformed by strong gusts and violent waves.

In the gospels, the storms on the sea represent the challenges of discipleship and the need to trust in the power of Jesus (Matt 8:23-27). The

A meal of the fresh and tasty St. Peter's fish

boat tossing on the violent sea has become an image of the church in the treacherous world. It can also be an apt image of our individual lives. When we seem to be on the verge of going under, we cry out to Jesus to save us. Even when he seems to be asleep, we know that he is with us and we are safe in his care.

Because the shoreline was often crowded when Jesus was present, he would often get in a boat, put out a short distance from the shore, and then speak to the people while sitting in the boat. Since sound carries well over water, the boat served as a pulpit from which he taught the crowds. At the foot of the Mount of Beatitudes, there is a semicircular bay with exceptional acoustic qualities, which is sometimes called Sower's Cove or the Bay of the Parables. It is believed that Jesus taught the parable of the sower from a boat moored in this bay (Mark 4:1-9). The slope of the hill forms a natural amphitheater, and as with a Roman theater, a speaker can be heard when speaking to thousands.

Meditation

- What are my greatest fears? How can I entrust my life more fully to Jesus?

- What qualities of fishermen do I need for the work of "catching people" for God's kingdom?

Reading: Luke 5:1-11

[Jesus] asked him to put out a little way from the shore. Then he sat down and taught the crowds from the boat. . . .

Response: "Put out into the deep water and let down your nets for a catch."

Who is as mighty as you, O Lᴏʀᴅ?
   Your faithfulness surrounds you.
You rule the raging of the sea;
   when its waves rise, you still them (Ps 89:8-9). R.

They cried to the Lᴏʀᴅ in their trouble,
   and he brought them out from their distress;
he made the storm be still,
   and the waves of the sea were hushed (Ps 107:28-29). R.

Jesus said to them, "Why are you afraid, you of little faith?" Then he got up and rebuked the winds and the sea; and there was a dead calm (Matt 8:26). R.

They were amazed, saying, "What sort of man is this, that even the winds and the sea obey him?" (Matt 8:27). R.

Prayer: Lord, grant us a trusting faith in you, even when the circumstances seem unbelievable. As Mary's acceptance—"Let it be with me according to your word"—marked the beginning of the age of salvation, Peter's acceptance—"If you say so, I will let down the nets"—marked the beginning of Christian discipleship. Help us overcome our doubts and fears, so that we can hear your word and accept your will. May we put out into the deep and be your missionary disciples, proclaiming the kingdom in word and deed.

2. Magdala

At the time of Jesus, Magdala was a major trade center on the northwest shore of the Sea of Galilee. Here fishermen sold their catch to be salted and thus preserved for export to Rome and other places throughout the empire. The city, called by its Greek name Taricheae (the place of salted fish), became an important city in the Hellenistic period and the early Roman period. Its location on the ancient trade routes, fertile land, and the fishing industry made it one of the most important cities of Galilee. During the Jewish revolt, the city became a fortified base for rebels who defied the Romans, but it suffered a disastrous end in AD 67 by the Roman forces. It continued on a smaller scale as a Byzantine village, with a fourth-century church built on the reputed site of Mary Magdalene's house.

Beginning in the 1960s, Franciscan archaeologists discovered Magdala's ancient port and a city grid, with a marketplace, paved streets, water canals, villas, and mosaics—one notably depicting a sailing boat. The discovery of the massive foundations of a tower may account for the city's name: *magdala* in Aramaic and *migdal* in Hebrew mean "tower." More archaeological remains were uncovered in 2009 on an adjacent property acquired by a religious congregation, the Legion of Christ, planning to build a guesthouse and retreat center. The archaeologists discovered more of the Jewish city, including a first-century synagogue, the oldest synagogue found to date in Galilee. Since the gospels state that Jesus preached in synagogues "throughout Galilee," and Magdala was in the midst of Jesus's primary region of ministry, he would have undoubtedly taught in

Mary Magdalene first encounters Jesus along the shore

The Duc in Altum Church at Magdala

the Magdala synagogue. The building was adorned with ornate mosaics and brightly colored frescoes. Archaeologists also uncovered the Magdala stone, which has a seven-branched menorah carved on it and other symbols artistically depicting the temple in Jerusalem. This stone block was likely used to place the scrolls of Scripture during ritual readings.

Magdala's fame down the centuries rests on its relationship to Mary Magdalene. Rather than being identified as the daughter of her father or wife of a husband, she is identified by the city in which she lived. This probably indicates that she was an unmarried, independent, and perhaps wealthy woman. She is first identified in the gospels as the woman from whom Jesus had cast out seven demons (Luke 8:2; Mark 16:9). Luke lists her first among the women who accompanied Jesus and supported his ministry from their own resources. Mary Magdalene continued to follow Jesus to Jerusalem where she witnessed his crucifixion and was the first recorded witness of his resurrection. Because she was the first to proclaim the good news of the resurrection to Jesus's apostles, by the third century she was given the exalted title "apostle of the apostles."

Little is known with certainty about Mary Magdalene, especially about her life before meeting Jesus. One of the women in her company was Joanna, the wife of Chuza, who managed the household of Herod Antipas, the ruler of Galilee. Was Mary Magdalene also involved in the

court life of Herod Antipas in Tiberius? The church in the West has steadfastly identified Mary Magdalene with the sinful woman of Galilee, who anointed the feet of Jesus and dried them with her hair, and Mary the sister of Martha, who performed a very similar action in Bethany. This understanding of Mary Magdalene as the repentant woman at the feet of Jesus has been fixed in the theological, liturgical, and artistic tradition of the church through the centuries. Whatever her earlier life involved, we know for sure that the unconditional love and acceptance of Jesus penetrated her heart, restored her dignity and peace of mind, and radically changed her life.

In 2014 the Legion of Christ opened a new church on the site and named it Duc in Altum (Latin for "Put out into the deep"). The altar is in the shape of the first-century boat from which Jesus taught, placed in front of an infinity pool leading the eye to the lake beyond. The Women's Atrium features eight pillars, seven of which represent women in the Bible who followed Jesus, while the eighth honors women of faith across all time. This is surrounded by four Mosaic Chapels, illustrating events from the ministry of Jesus around the Sea of Galilee: Jesus calling his first disciples, Jesus inviting Peter to walk on the water, Jesus encountering Mary Magdalene and casting out the seven demons, and Jesus raising the daughter of Jairus with the words *"Talitha koum!"* (which means "Little girl, I say to you, get up!"). Each features the hand of God, which creates, saves, heals, and frees, expressed through the divine hand of Jesus. Viewers are invited to meditate and dialogue with the scene in view of its original site. In the crypt is the ecumenical Encounter Chapel. We can imagine encountering Jesus in this place, paved with authentic stones from Magdala's first-century marketplace. The mural depicts the hemorrhaging woman who trusts that she will experience the healing power of Jesus if only she can touch the fringe of his garment.

Meditation

- Imagine the first encounter of Jesus and Mary Magdalene. What does she see in him? What does he see in her?

- What does Mary Magdalene teach me about encountering Jesus and trusting in him?

Reading: Luke 8:1-3

Mary, called Magdalene, from whom seven demons had gone out. . . .

Response: Mary Magdalene, teach us to long for Jesus.

I waited patiently for the LORD;
    he inclined to me and heard my cry.
He drew me up from the desolate pit,
    out of the miry bog,
and set my feet upon a rock,
    making my steps secure (Ps 40:1-2). R.

He put a new song in my mouth,
    a song of praise to our God.
Many will see and fear,
    and put their trust in the LORD.
Happy are those who make
    the LORD their trust,
who do not turn to the proud,
    to those who go astray after false gods (Ps 40:3-4). R.

Blessed be the God and Father of our Lord Jesus Christ, the Father of mercies and the God of all consolation, who consoles us in all our affliction, so that we may be able to console those who are in any affliction with the consolation with which we ourselves are consoled by God (2 Cor 1:3-4). R.

If anyone is in Christ, there is a new creation: everything old has passed away; see, everything has become new! All this is from God, who reconciled us to himself through Christ, and has given us the ministry of reconciliation (2 Cor 5:17-18). R.

Jesus said to her, "Do not hold on to me, because I have not yet ascended to the Father. But go to my brothers and say to them, 'I am ascending to my Father and your Father, to my God and your God'" (John 20:17). R.

Prayer: Risen Lord, who is the way, the truth, and the life, may we follow you wherever you may lead. May we seek you and long for you, whom our heart most desires. As you dramatically converted the life of Mary Magdalene, transform us into a new creation so that we may honor you as our healer and Lord.

3. Mount of Beatitudes

Matthew's gospel tells us that "great crowds followed [Jesus] from Galilee, the Decapolis, Jerusalem, Judea, and from beyond the Jordan" (Matt 4:25). When Jesus saw the crowds flocking to him, he climbed up the hill overlooking the Sea of Galilee and sat down there to teach. The Sermon on the Mount (Matt 5–7) is a commanding discourse, a gathering of Jesus's teachings on the Christian way of life.

Here, on the mountain, Jesus is the new Moses, teaching a law of holiness that magnifies but does not replace the ancient law of Israel. The gentle beauty of this mountain contrasts with the fiery and thunderous Mount Sinai. Moses had warned the people not to come near the mountain, but Jesus invites his disciples to come up the mountain to listen. The eight Beatitudes proclaim the inner attitudes or ways of living that characterize the follower of Jesus: humble, single-minded, seeking justice, and willing to undergo persecution for the sake of Jesus. On this mount, Jesus taught a message that is not easy, yet one that makes us truly blessed and deeply happy.

A few remains from a fourth-century church farther down the slope remind us that the Byzantine Christians also came to this hillside to reflect

on the manifesto Jesus gave to the crowds. Today, Christians gather at the top of the hill in a church built in 1938. In this octagonal chapel, the architect Barluzzi honors the eight Beatitudes, each presented with a stained-glass window in Latin and a panoramic window below that looks outward. The floor of the chapel around the altar features mosaic symbols on the seven virtues championed throughout the Sermon on the Mount: justice, prudence, fortitude, temperance, faith, hope, and charity.

Many pilgrims enjoy the landscaped lawns, gardens, and benches

The octagonal Church of the Beatitudes

Site of Jesus's Sermon on the Mount

around the church to read the chapters of Jesus's sermon in the hope of hearing and heeding its message afresh. The view of the lush Galilee region from this mount shows us the world that surrounded Jesus. He observed the sower, the harvester, and the vine grower. He learned the secrets of the fig tree, the briar, the sycamore, and the tiny mustard seed. He saw the ways of the birds building their nests, the foxes hiding in their shelters, and flowers of the field arrayed in vibrant color. Jesus looked over at Magdala and saw the fish being salted, and he knew that his followers must be like that salt that adds flavor to people's lives and preserves creation from decay. As the sun went down, Jesus looked over on the eastern shore of the lake at the great Decapolis city of Hippos. This "city built on a hill" was brightly visible because of the light produced by its torches. All these images came to life in the teachings and parables of Jesus.

Meditation

- Which of the Beatitudes do I most want to focus on living today?

- What does the natural world teach me about God and God's will for my life?

Reading: Matthew 5:1-16

When Jesus saw the crowds, he went up the mountain; and after he sat down, his disciples came to him. . . .

Response: May our light shine so that others may see our good works and give glory to God.

Blessed are the poor in spirit. Lord, help us acknowledge our total dependence on you so that we may begin experiencing your kingdom. R.

Blessed are those who mourn. Lord, help us lament our sins and those of the world so that we may begin experiencing your comfort. R.

Blessed are the meek. Lord, help us possess an unassuming humility like your own so that we may inherit the earth rather than those who are stocked with wealth, status, and arms. R.

Blessed are those who hunger and thirst for righteousness. Lord, give us a deep desire that justice permeate our society so that your will may be done on earth as it is in heaven. R.

Blessed are the merciful. Lord, help us to demonstrate compassion based on your life and teachings so that we may experience the promises of your faithful love. R.

Blessed are the pure in heart. Lord, help us become single-hearted so that we may see you with clear vision. R.

Blessed are the peacemakers. Lord, help us strive for the end of hostilities and active reconciliation between people so that genuine peace may come upon the world. R.

Blessed are those who are persecuted for righteousness' sake. Lord, help us know that maltreatment will indeed come our way if we are genuine disciples so that we may begin experiencing your kingdom. R.

Prayer: Divine Teacher, who guides your disciples to understand the ways of the kingdom, we believe that you desire to bring blessings into our lives as we follow your way. Let us listen to your word in the quiet of this mountaintop. Continue to call us to that peace and joy that the world cannot give and cannot take away.

The Byzantine-style church at Tabgha

4. Tabgha, Church of the Multiplication of the Loaves and Fishes

The place where Jesus multiplied the loaves and the fish for the hungry crowd is traditionally located at Tabgha, a name derived from the Greek *Hepta-pegon*, meaning "seven springs." The water from these springs, some of which are warm sulfuric springs, flows through the area and into the Sea of Galilee. The warmth caused the fish to gather here, especially in the cooler winter months, and so were an easy catch for the fishermen.

The Church of the Multiplication of the Loaves and Fishes stands on the site of two earlier churches. A small fourth-century church first commemorated the miracle; then a significantly larger fifth-century church was built over the floor of the more ancient church. This church contained the Byzantine mosaic floors seen today that are among the most elegantly executed in the Holy Land. The Persian invasion of 614 destroyed and covered the site, which was in ruins until its excavation in the 1930s.

The new church was built in 1982 around the ancient churches, following the Byzantine architectural style. Visitors first enter a peaceful atrium, which serves as a transition zone from the outside world, before entering the sanctuary for prayer. The austere interior is marked by stone columns and soaring arches. Built to the same floor plan as the fifth-century church,

the new church includes some of the ancient black basalt walls that have survived and remain visible.

The mosaic artistry on the floor has been preserved and restored. It depicts water plants and water birds, scenes that are typical of the marshes on the north side of the Sea of Galilee. The best-known mosaic is the loaves and fish image in front of the altar. Between the two fish sits a basket with only four loaves visible. Perhaps the artist intended to suggest that the fifth loaf will be placed on the altar as the bread of the Eucharist. The ancient rock beneath the altar, according to an ancient tradition, is the stone on which Jesus placed the loaves and fish for the blessing. To the right of the altar, under the glass protective cover, lie the foundations of the older fourth-century church. To the left of the altar is an inscription of Patriarch Martyrios of Jerusalem (479–486), founder of the Byzantine church. Today the church is administered by Benedictine monks.

The miracle of the multiplication is the only miracle that is recorded in all four gospels. Mark tells us that Jesus was moved with compassion for the crowd that was "like sheep without a shepherd." His initial response was not to feed them with food but to "teach them many things." The gospels emphasize that the teachings of Jesus are as important for life as was bread in the wilderness for their ancestors in the exodus. Although

the disciples could not understand it, the meager loaves and fish fed the hungry crowd of five thousand. As Jesus teaches the people and satisfies their hungers, he shows himself to be the Shepherd that the Scriptures anticipated. The dry wilderness of the exodus has become fertile with green grass as the Good Shepherd leads his sheep to green pastures and seats them for a banquet.

The similarities between the words of Jesus's feeding miracle and the words of the Last Supper are obvious: "He looked up to heaven, and blessed and broke the loaves, and gave them to his disciples to set before the people." The words and gestures recounted here would certainly have reminded gospel readers of the Eucharist as it was celebrated in groups of hundreds and fifties within their Christian communities, and Jesus's first teaching and then feeding the crowd anticipates the sequence of the eucharistic liturgy as it has been celebrated in word and sacrament through the ages. The rock preserved in the church beneath the altar and the mosaic basket with the missing loaf emphasize the continuity of the miraculous feeding with every Eucharist celebrated at the altar. In every era, Jesus feeds the deepest hungers of his pilgrim people with the living word and with the bread of life.

Meditation

- How does this place remind me of my own deepest hungers?

- When have I seen Jesus multiply the human efforts of his church into superabundant gifts?

Reading: Mark 6:30-44

[Jesus] said to them, "How many loaves have you? Go and see." . . .

Response: You open your hand to feed us, Lord, you answer all our needs.

The LORD is my shepherd, I shall not want.
    He makes me lie down in green pastures;
he leads me beside still waters;
    he restores my soul (Ps 23:1-3). R.

The stone and mosaic of the loaves and fishes beneath the altar

You prepare a table before me
   in the presence of my enemies;
you anoint my head with oil;
   my cup overflows.
Surely goodness and mercy shall follow me
   all the days of my life (Ps 23:5-6). R.

I myself will search for my sheep, and will seek them out. As shepherds seek out their flocks when they are among their scattered sheep, so I will seek out my sheep (Ezek 34:11-12). R.

I will bring them out from the peoples and gather them from the countries, and will bring them into their own land; and I will feed them on the mountains of Israel, by the watercourses, and in all the inhabited parts of the land (Ezek 34:13). R.

I will feed them with good pasture, and the mountain heights of Israel shall be their pasture; there they shall lie down in good grazing land, and they shall feed on rich pasture on the mountains of Israel. I myself will be the shepherd of my sheep, and I will make them lie down, says the Lord God (Ezek 34:14-15). R.

Prayer: Good Shepherd, who has compassion on your people and satisfies our hungry hearts, may we not neglect our spiritual health with food that does not nourish us. Continue to feed your flock with the living word of Scripture and the bread of life in the Eucharist. May we find in this food the strength to follow you as your disciple and to live in your Spirit.

5. Eremos Grotto

Early in his gospel, Mark demonstrates how Jesus sought a balance of active ministry and contemplative prayer. The text first narrates Jesus's eventful activity: "That evening, at sunset, they brought to him all who were sick or possessed with demons. And the whole city was gathered around the door" (Mark 1:32-33). Then we are told that Jesus sought prayerful solitude: "In the morning, while it was still very dark, he got up and went out to a deserted place, and there he prayed" (Mark 1:35). Luke's gospel tells us that Jesus often went off to pray alone and shows us Jesus at prayer especially before important transitions in his ministry. For example, before appointing the Twelve who would be his apostles, Luke writes, "Now during those days he went out to the mountain to pray; and he spent the night in prayer to God" (Luke 6:12).

Early pilgrims tell of a cave in the hillside near Tabgha where Jesus would often go to pray alone. Egeria relates that the cave is in the hillside that Jesus ascended when he taught the Beatitudes. The cragginess of the hillside meant it was left uncultivated by farmers and off the beaten path. Today, this cave is often overlooked by pilgrims because it is still in its natural state, without a shrine built around it or a parking lot beside it. This cave called *eremos,* a Greek word meaning "solitary" or "uninhabited," can be reached by walking downhill toward the lake from the Mount of Beatitudes, or it can be reached by walking uphill from the road that passes the area of Tabgha.

Sitting at the mouth of the Eremos Grotto and looking outward offers a beautiful view over the lake and surrounding towns. Toward the lake, Jesus would have seen the small waterfalls of the seven springs where the fishermen cleaned their nets and where he probably met James and John. He also could view the shoreline where he so often taught his disciples and encountered the crowds. And because fishermen often worked from dusk to dawn, when the fish were less likely to see the nets around them, Jesus was able to watch the boats throughout the night, which were often illumined with torches.

Author in the Eremos Grotto looking toward the Sea of Galilee

Here we can imagine Jesus saying to us, "Come away to a deserted place all by yourselves and rest a while" (Mark 6:31). Here in solitude, we can hear the disciples' request, "Lord, teach us to pray" (Luke 11:1). In the Sermon on the Mount, Matthew relates the words of Jesus as he urged his followers to establish their own dedicated place for prayer: "Whenever you pray, go into your *[tameion]* and shut the door and pray to your Father who is in secret" (Matt 6:6). The Greek word *tameion* is most often translated simply as "room," but it is more accurately translated as "inner chamber," "secret place," or "storeroom." It sometimes refers to a treasure room where people could hide their most valuable possessions. Jesus invites us to set aside an inner chamber where we can pray intimately to God. Christians, especially in the Eastern church, create a prayer space in their homes, adorned with crosses, icons, candles, and other "valuables." The space is consecrated for communion with God in prayer. Jews often use a prayer shawl (*tallit*) to cover their head in prayer, forming a personal tent or portable chamber where one can be alone with God.

We ought to create an Eremos Grotto in our home, where we can withdraw to pray in solitude. But we must know that we can take our cave with us wherever we go. While taking the metro, waiting in line, or sheltering from the rain, we can slip into our inner chamber to commune with our God. Within our secret hollow, we become sensitive to the ways that God is directing our lives. The teaching and example of Jesus show us that we can't hope to live the gospel with joy, bring healing to the lives of others, or find victory over sin in our own lives if we don't practice contemplative prayer in the midst of our busy lives.

Meditation

- What does Jesus want to teach me about solitary prayer?
- Where might Jesus be inviting me to carve out a cave of prayer?

Reading: Matthew 14:22-33

[Jesus] went up the mountain by himself to pray. When evening came, he was there alone. . . .

Response: "Lord, teach us to pray."

"Whenever you pray, go into your room and shut the door and pray to your Father who is in secret; and your Father who sees in secret will reward you" (Matt 6:6). R.

"Come to me, all you that are weary and are carrying heavy burdens, and I will give you rest. Take my yoke upon you, and learn from me; for I am gentle and humble in heart, and you will find rest for your souls" (Matt 11:28-29). R.

"Ask, and it will be given you; search, and you will find; knock, and the door will be opened for you. For everyone who asks receives, and everyone who searches finds, and for everyone who knocks, the door will be opened" (Luke 11:9-10). R.

Prayer: Lord, teach us to pray and to create a solitary cavern where we can be alone with you. Forgive us for making time for everything except for you. Help us to carve out time each day for contemplative intimacy with you, when we can listen to your voice and pour out our heart to you. Then, faithful to this sacred time, may we be energized and revitalized with the strength we need to be your disciples and to face any situation that might come our way.

6. Tabgha, Church of the Primacy of St. Peter

The shoreline of Tabgha was a favorite spot for fishermen from nearby Capernaum, and its shoreline was familiar to Jesus and his disciples. Here seven disciples had returned after the death of Jesus, and at Peter's initiative, they decided to go fishing. After they tried all night and caught nothing, the risen Jesus stood on the shore at daybreak and told them where to find a wondrously abundant catch of fish. Recognizing the Lord, Peter jumped into the water and swam ashore, while the others brought the boat to land. The great catch represents the

"Peter, do you love me? Then feed my sheep."

mission Jesus has given to his disciples. The number of fish—153—in some way emphasizes the all-embracing character of the church's mission. St. Jerome speculates there were 153 varieties of fish known at the time. The great catch seems to be a symbolic enactment of the apostolic commission Jesus gave to his followers at the end of Matthew's gospel: "Go . . . and make disciples of all the nations" (Matt 28:19). These fishers of men and women must now evangelize the world.

The Church of the Primacy of St. Peter is a small edifice of black basalt commemorating this event. First constructed in the fourth century, the structure that stands today, built in 1934, incorporates the remains of the first church, which can still be seen around the foundation. The projection of limestone rock enclosed by the church is called *Mensa Christi*, meaning "the table of Christ." It has been revered since at least the Byzantine period as the place where the risen Christ prepared a breakfast of bread and fish for his disciples. The charcoal fire on which Jesus cooked the meal would have reminded Peter of the charcoal fire in the high priest's courtyard the night Peter had denied Jesus. How different these burning coals must have looked to Peter in the light of dawn, as Jesus invited his disciples to come and eat a sacred meal.

Beside the church, in a garden setting, is an area designed for group worship. Between this and the lake stands a modern bronze statue of Jesus symbolically commissioning Peter with his shepherd's crook. After the breakfast, Jesus challenged Peter three times with the question, "Do you love me?" enabling Peter to face up to the memories of his threefold denial on that shameful night. The three responses of Peter expressed the essence of true discipleship and reconciled Peter with his Lord. Jesus's threefold command to Peter—feed my lambs, tend my sheep, feed my sheep—established him as the shepherd of God's flock with the task of teaching and nourishing the flock in imitation of Jesus the Shepherd.

Sitting just outside the church near the shoreline are six heart-shaped rocks that once made up the bases of second-century columns. These stones represent the three questions of Jesus, "Do you love me?" and the three answers of Peter, "You know that I love you." The stones form the path of love that Jesus marked out and then urged Peter to follow. Peter is the rock of Christ's church, the fisherman of God's people, and the shepherd of the flock. Like the love of Peter, our love for Jesus must be translated into service as we follow the path of discipleship.

The Mensa Christi *within the Church of the Primacy of St. Peter*

Meditation

- Placing myself in the gospel scene at the lakeshore, what do I see, hear, smell, taste, and feel?

- How do I answer the question of Jesus, "Do you love me?"

Reading: John 21:1-19

Simon Peter said to them, "I am going fishing." They said to him, "We will go with you." . . .

Response: Lord, you know that I love you.

Blessed be the God and Father of our Lord Jesus Christ! By his great mercy he has given us a new birth into a living hope through the resurrection of Jesus Christ from the dead, and into an inheritance that is imperishable, undefiled, and unfading (1 Pet 1:3-4). R.

Although you have not seen him, you love him; and even though you do not see him now, you believe in him and rejoice with an indescribable and glorious joy, for you are receiving the outcome of your faith, the salvation of your souls (1 Pet 1:8-9). R.

He was destined before the foundation of the world, but was revealed at the end of the ages for your sake. Through him you have come to trust in God, who raised him from the dead and gave him glory, so that your faith and hope are set on God (1 Pet 1:20-21). R.

He himself bore our sins in his body on the cross, so that, free from sins, we might live for righteousness; by his wounds you have been healed. For you were going astray like sheep, but now you have returned to the shepherd and guardian of your souls (1 Pet 2:24-25). R.

Above all, maintain constant love for one another, for love covers a multitude of sins. Be hospitable to one another without complaining. Like good stewards of the manifold grace of God, serve one another with whatever gift each of you has received (1 Pet 4:8-10). R.

Prayer: Good Shepherd, who calls your church to bring in a great catch for your kingdom, give us worthy shepherds for your people. Help us to teach, feed, and evangelize the people you have entrusted to us. In the service we render to your flock—our children, students, clients, patients, and others given to our care—give us the love we need to accomplish the mission you give us.

7. Capernaum, Synagogue

Walking through the gate into the Franciscan property, the visitor is welcomed with the words "Capernaum—the Town of Jesus." Built along the northern shore of the Sea of Galilee, Capernaum was an important center for the fishing industry and a post for tax collection. Nearby Jesus called at least five of his disciples to follow him: Peter, Andrew, James, John, and Matthew (also called Levi). After leaving Nazareth, Jesus came to Capernaum, what Matthew calls "his own town" (Matt 9:1), the hub of his ministry in Galilee.

The grounds have been extensively excavated, revealing fascinating ruins. The most obvious is the white synagogue, a fifth-century limestone structure built over the first-century synagogue where Jesus taught and healed. Jewish images are seen on the ornately carved ruins; among them are the shofar (ram's horn), an incense shovel, a menorah (seven-branched candelabrum), and a representation of the ark of the covenant. The first-century synagogue, which Jesus and his disciples frequented, was made of black basalt stones. The foundations can be seen

The limestone synagogue in Capernaum

beneath the white limestone of the present ruins. This synagogue was built by a Roman centurion. When this centurion's servant was on the verge of death, he sent for Jesus. As a man of great humility and trust, he said to Jesus, "Lord . . . I am not worthy to have you come under my roof. . . . But only speak the word, and let my servant be healed" (Luke 7:5-7). Jesus was amazed at such faith, praised the centurion to his followers, and healed his servant.

The white synagogue built upon the remains of the synagogue of Jesus

Jesus taught in this synagogue with an authority that his listeners knew was from God. Here he healed a man with an unclean spirit, which caused his fame to spread throughout Galilee (Mark 1:21-28). The gospel of John tells us that, after Jesus performed the miracle of the multiplication of the loaves and fish, he delivered his Bread of Life discourse "while he was teaching in the synagogue at Capernaum" (John 6:59). The words that Jesus spoke here were not written on the Torah scrolls of the synagogue; they were a new word of God. Although Capernaum with its synagogue has fallen into ruins, this word endures forever.

Meditation

- How can I trust more deeply in Jesus like the centurion (Luke 7:6-7)?

- How can I let God feed the deepest hungers of my heart?

Reading: John 6:48-59

"I am the living bread that came down from heaven. Whoever eats of this bread will live forever." . . .

Response: The Lord gave them bread from heaven.

He commanded the skies above,
    and opened the doors of heaven;
he rained down on them manna to eat,
    and gave them the grain of heaven.
Mortals ate of the bread of angels;
    he sent them food in abundance (Ps 78:23-25). R.

Jesus said to them, "Very truly, I tell you, it was not Moses who gave you the bread from heaven, but it is my Father who gives you the true bread from heaven. For the bread of God is that which comes down from heaven and gives life to the world" (John 6:32-33). R.

"Very truly, I tell you, unless you eat the flesh of the Son of Man and drink his blood, you have no life in you. Those who eat my flesh and drink my blood have eternal life, and I will raise them up on the last day; for my flesh is true food and my blood is true drink" (John 6:53-55). R.

Because of this many of his disciples turned back and no longer went about with him. So Jesus asked the twelve, "Do you also wish to go away?" Simon Peter answered him, "Lord, to whom can we go? You have the words of eternal life" (John 6:66-68). R.

Prayer: Bread of Life, sent from heaven by the Father to feed the hearts of hungry people, you invite us to union with you by eating your flesh as true food and drinking your blood as true drink. Thank you for the grace of your Eucharist and for your gift of eternal life. Help us to remain in you as you remain in us.

8. Capernaum, House of Peter

A short distance from the synagogue, past the foundations of a first-century neighborhood made of black basalt stone, are the remains of Peter's house, which is today covered with a modern church built upon pillars over the ruins. Similar to the other simple houses in Capernaum at the time of Jesus, the house consisted of a few rooms, with coarse walls and a roof of earth and straw, clustered around a courtyard. This house of Peter and his family was the place Jesus called "home" during his ministry

St. Peter's house near Capernaum's synagogue

in Galilee. Here Jesus returned at the end of each day, relaxed with his disciples, and planned for the next day, talking with his friends into the night. Here, too, people came seeking Jesus—the sick, the possessed, and all who were in need (Mark 1:32-34). They knew they could find in Jesus a refreshing word, a healing touch, a saving presence. Here the four friends of the paralyzed man dug out panels from the mud-thatched roof and lowered him on a mat to the feet of Jesus because of the crowd. Jesus must have smiled at this beautiful gesture of trusting friendship. Sometimes people are unable to come to Jesus on their own, not because of paralysis as in the gospel account, but because of fear, insecurity, or shame, so they need to be brought by others.

Peter's house looked like all the other houses of Capernaum; it is what happed to the house by the middle of the first century that marked it as exceptional. The largest room of the house was plastered—a rarity for houses of the day. At the same time, the house's pottery, which had previously been household cooking pots and bowls, now consisted entirely of large storage jars and oil lamps, indicating that the space had been repurposed as a place of assembly. Over the ensuing centuries, the plastered room was converted into the central hall of a house church. The old stone walls were strengthened by a two-story arch that supported a new stone roof. The plastered room was then painted with floral and geometric designs, and more than a hundred graffiti were etched into the walls, saying such things as "Christ have mercy" and "Lord Jesus help your servant" in Greek, Syriac, and Hebrew. These are accompanied by etchings of small crosses and, in one case, a boat.

By the fifth century, this house church was replaced by a well-built octagonal church. The inner sanctum of this Byzantine church was built directly above the remains of the first-century room that had formed the central hall of the earlier church. The modern church is suspended over this entire complex of ruins. In the center of the church, a glass floor allows visitors to look into the excavations below and stand directly above the place that Jesus called home. Because the glass floor is at about the same level as the original mud-thatched roof, pilgrims can read the gospel while imagining they are watching the paralyzed man being lowered to the feet of Jesus.

The new church covers the ruins of Peter's house

Meditation

- What is sacred about the place I call home?

- In what ways am I able to bring others to Jesus?

Reading: Mark 2:1-12

When [Jesus] returned to Capernaum after some days, it was reported that he was at home. . . .

Response: Lord Jesus, bless our homes with your abiding presence.

Jesus, you were nurtured at your home in Nazareth with Joseph and Mary, and you made your new home in Capernaum with your disciples. Teach us the irreplaceable value of life in our homes with family and friends. R.

Jesus, transform our homes into sacred dwellings, filled with your presence. Protect our homes from evil, bitterness, sickness, storm, or destruction, and fill our homes with joyful peace. R.

Jesus, bless the doorways of our homes. May all our comings and goings, our hellos and good-byes, be done in a spirit of love. Give us a spirit of hospitality to welcome visitors with kindness and not turn away the person in need. R.

Jesus, bless all the activities of our homes: our conversations and entertainment, our work and our prayer. May the gifts of family and friendship grow and flourish in our homes, giving joy to all who share them. R.

Prayer: Lord of life and love, as we reflect upon your ministry in your home at Capernaum, we ask you to help us see our homes as places of genuine encounter as we go about our daily lives. As you have blessed us with the hospitality, compassion, and healing you brought to Peter's house, give us the grace to transform our homes into places where we can share with others the joy of the gospel.

9. *Kursi*

When Jesus sailed with his disciples "to the other side of the lake, to the country of the Gerasenes" (Mark 5:1), they were not just changing locations; they were traveling to a completely different cultural setting.

This eastern side of the Sea of Galilee was a non-Jewish area. Everything about this locality suggests it is unclean and non-kosher—the tombs on the hillside and the herders raising swine—meaning it was likely a Gentile setting where observant Jews would not be found. In this region of the Decapolis, Jesus performed two striking miracles: an exorcism that resulted in evil spirits being cast into pigs (Mark 5:1-20) and the feeding of four thousand with "seven loaves" and "a few small fish" (Mark 8:1-10). These two miracles of compassion demonstrate that the authority and healing power of Jesus is just as great here as in Jewish Galilee, making it clear that there is no human disorder or need anywhere that Jesus cannot remedy.

When Jesus stepped out of the boat, he was confronted by a dangerous and violent man who lived in the nearby caves used as tombs. All human attempts to subdue him, including binding his hands and feet with shackles and chains, had repeatedly failed. This wretched man was continually crying out with howling agony and injuring his body with self-mutilation. Yet, despite his miserable condition, the man saw hope in Jesus as he ran to him and bowed before him.

The demons, with their supernatural knowledge, knew the full identity of Jesus and cried out in the man's voice, "What have you to do with me, Jesus, Son of the Most High God?" When Jesus asked their name, the demons replied, "My name is Legion," a Roman military unit of several thousand soldiers, indicating their numbers and strength. The legion of demons inhabited the pitiable man, just as the Roman troops occupied the people of the land. The demons begged Jesus not to torment them or send them out of the territory, showing their subservience to the Son of God. Then Jesus, ordering them out of the man, permitted them to enter a nearby herd of swine, numbering about two thousand. As a result, the entire herd rushed down the steep bank and drowned in the sea.

Like the stormy sea that had become calm at the word of Jesus, the former demoniac sat in the presence of Jesus, clothed, calm, and sane. As Jesus got into the boat to leave, the healed man expressed his desire to go with Jesus. But instead, Jesus commissioned him to be a missionary to his own people. His new task was to be the first witness to the saving power and mercy of Jesus among the Gentiles.

On a different occasion Jesus came to this same region of the Decapolis with his disciples and encountered a hungry crowd. The feeding of the four thousand offers a complementary miracle to the feeding of the five thousand in the Jewish territory. Jesus performed these near-identical miracles in two different locations for two different ethnic groups, indicating that he does not make a distinction between Jews and Gentiles. Jesus is the Savior of all.

The size of the monastery complex built here in the fifth century indicates how highly the Byzantine Christians regarded this location. Around it stood a defensive stone wall with a watchtower. At its heart was a large church, divided by two rows of stone columns into a nave and two side aisles, with a spacious courtyard in front of it. The partially restored church and its sur- viving floor mosaics may be entered. In addition to living quarters for the monks, a guesthouse and bath complex for pilgrims have been uncovered. A paved road led from the monastery to the harbor where pilgrims arrived.

The remains of an earlier chapel, built into a cave, are located on the side of the hill behind the monastery. It overlooks a huge boulder enclosed in a retaining wall of stones—apparently identifying the site as the place of the miracle. From here, one can see the Sea of Galilee and, to the south, the ruins of Hippos, a major city of the Decapolis at the time of Jesus. This rounded hilltop city may have been the place toward which Jesus pointed when he said, "A city built on a hill cannot be hid" (Matt 5:14). The remains of a Byzantine cathedral and several other churches have been found at Hippos, and a bishop from Hippos is recorded as attending the church

councils of Nicea and Constantinople in the fourth century. The city was devastated by a massive earthquake in 749, which left it in ruins.

Meditation

- In what way is the divine image distorted within me by the powers of evil?
- What convinces me that Jesus cares for all people, no matter their ethnic origins?

Reading: Mark 5:1-20

When [Jesus] had stepped out of the boat, immediately a man out of the tombs with an unclean spirit met him. . . .

Response: "Go home to your friends, and tell them how much the Lord has done for you, and what mercy he has shown you" (Mark 5:19).

Put on the whole armor of God, so that you may be able to stand against the wiles of the devil. For our struggle is not against enemies of blood and flesh, but against the rulers, against the authorities, against the cosmic powers of this present darkness, against the spiritual forces of evil in the heavenly places (Eph 6:11-12). R.

Like a roaring lion your adversary the devil prowls around, looking for someone to devour. Resist him, steadfast in your faith, for you know that your brothers and sisters in all the world are undergoing the same kinds of suffering (1 Pet 5:8-9). R.

And after you have suffered for a little while, the God of all grace, who has called you to his eternal glory in Christ, will himself restore, support, strengthen, and establish you. To him be the power forever and ever (1 Pet 5:10-11). R.

Prayer: Jesus, Son of the Most High God, your power over evil is without limit and your compassion for people is without boundaries. Cast out from our lives all that distorts the divine image within us and free us to love and experience your peace. Enable us to be ministers of your healing presence to those imprisoned in darkness and fear.

Remains of the Byzantine monastic church at Kursi

Chapter IV

Samaria

In the days of Jesus, Samaria was the central region of the land, bordered by Galilee to the north and Judea to the south. Because of a history of animosity between Jews and Samaritans, Galileans traveling to Jerusalem would usually bypass Samaria on their journey southward, going instead down the Jordan Valley and then making the steep climb to Jerusalem from the east. John summed up the situation in his gospel: "Jews do not share things in common with Samaritans" (John 4:9).

The animosity between the Jewish people and the Samaritans went back a long way. After the unifying era of King David and King Solomon in the tenth century BC, the northern tribes of "Israel" split off from the tribes of "Judah." The northern kingdom of Israel was later conquered by the Assyrians in 722 BC. Many of its inhabitants were deported and Samaria was largely repopulated by foreigners. When Judah suffered a similar fate 150 years later under the Babylonians and then returned to rebuild Jerusalem, they experienced significant opposition from the Samaritans. From then on, the Jews viewed the Samaritans as outsiders and their religion as compromised. At the same time, the Samaritans claimed to practice a purer form of faith than the Jews, focusing exclusively on the first five books of Moses. The Samaritans built their temple on Mount Gerizim in the middle of the fifth century BC, but it was destroyed under the Hasmonean king John Hyrcanus of Judea in 110 BC. The Samaritans of today still worship among its ruins.

It's important to understand the antagonism between Samaritans and Jews when considering the encounter of Jesus with the Samaritan woman at the well. Likewise, in the parable of the Good Samaritan, the hero of the story, the one who cared for the injured stranger, was the despised Samaritan (Luke 10:25-37). When Jesus healed ten lepers on the border of Samaria and Galilee, only the Samaritan returned to give thanks to

Jesus (Luke 17:16). Jesus anticipated a time when tensions between Jews and Samaritans would become irrelevant because of the new era he was bringing into the world, a day when fighting over ethnic differences and geographical locations would be unnecessary because God's salvation would be available to all people everywhere.

In the Acts of the Apostles, Luke describes how the gospel, impelled by the Holy Spirit, went out from Jerusalem through Judea and Samaria. Philip first brought the good news to Samaria with his teaching and healings (Acts 8:12). When the apostles in Jerusalem heard that Samaria had accepted the word of God, they sent Peter and John to pray for and lay hands on the baptized believers, who then received the Holy Spirit (Acts 8:17). They then returned to Jerusalem, "proclaiming the good news to many villages of the Samaritans" (Acts 8:25).

1. Burqin, Church of the Ten Lepers

Off the beaten path and just west of the Palestinian city of Jenin, the village of Burqin is home to the Orthodox Church of St. George, otherwise known as the Church of the Ten Lepers. The church is located on the northern slope of the historic center of the village, overlooking Wadi Burqin.

According to Luke's gospel, Jesus was traveling "through the region between Samaria and Galilee" on his way to Jerusalem. When he entered a village, Jesus encountered ten lepers who were calling out to him, "Jesus, Master, have mercy on us!" (Luke 17:11-13). According to early Christian tradition, the village was Burqin, and the lepers were quarantined in an underground cave, a common practice at the time for people afflicted with contagious skin diseases. Leprosy is manifested as white patches on the skin, running sores, and the loss of parts of the body that have become necrotic. Jesus responded to the lepers' cries for mercy, telling them to go and show themselves to the priests, the only ones able to make the diagnosis that a person has been made clean.

The gospel narrates that all were healed of their leprosy while on their way, not only cured of their disease but also restored to the community. Yet, only one of the cleansed lepers turned back to give thanks. Jesus makes the point to his disciples that this single individual, who prostrated himself at the feet of Jesus in thanksgiving, was a Samaritan. Where were the other nine? Did none of them return to praise God except this "foreigner"? Samaritans were considered outsiders, shunned by Jews as much as lepers were. Although all ten were healed, only one responded in a personal way and entered a relationship with Jesus. As in other places in the gospels, a Samaritan is the model of faithful response to God's grace.

Archaeology indicates that the cave where the lepers were quarantined and then healed was a Roman-era cistern. The place was remembered and honored during the early centuries of Christian persecution, but in the fourth century a church was built there by St. Helena. Destroyed and rebuilt several times throughout history, the church was renovated during the Crusader period and enclosed by a stone wall.

The stonework within the church today probably dates to the Crusader era. This includes the icon wall separating the nave from the sanctuary, the chair of the patriarch with its lion-headed arms, and the baptismal font. Visitors can walk into the ancient cave of the lepers that includes a small opening in the top through which food and drink was provided for the lepers. The cave contains an altar and an icon of Jesus healing the ten lepers.

Meditation

- What is Jesus teaching me by pointing out that the one healed leper who returned to give thanks was a Samaritan?

- How do I give thanks for the blessings and healing I have been given?

Reading: Luke 17:11-19

On the way to Jerusalem Jesus was going through the region between Samaria and Galilee. . . .

Response: Give thanks to the Lord for he is good; his love endures forever.

They cried to the Lord in their trouble,
    and he saved them from their distress;
he brought them out of darkness and gloom,
    and broke their bonds asunder.
Let them thank the Lord for his steadfast love,
    for his wonderful works to humankind (Ps 107:13-15). R.

Then they cried to the Lord in their trouble,
and he saved them from their distress;
he sent out his word and healed them,
and delivered them from destruction.
Let them thank the Lord for his steadfast love,
for his wonderful works to humankind.
And let them offer thanksgiving sacrifices,
and tell of his deeds with songs of joy (Ps 107:19-22). R.

Enter his gates with thanksgiving,
and his courts with praise.
Give thanks to him, bless his name.
For the Lord is good;
his steadfast love endures forever,
and his faithfulness to all generations (Ps 100:4-5). R.

Prayer: Gracious God, we are filled with awe at your immeasurable mercies and love. Receive the sincere praise and thanksgiving of our unworthy hearts for all that you have provided for us in this world and the next. Enable us to walk before you in holiness all the days of our life with fitting gratitude for your healing and saving love.

2. Shechem, Mount Gerizim and Mount Ebal

No place was more sacred than Shechem in the early period of biblical history. Originally a Canaanite settlement, the town is located in the narrow sheltered valley between Mount Ebal on the north and Mount Gerizim on the south. Israel's national story began at Schechem, where the Lord appeared to Abraham and promised, "To your offspring I will give this land." Abraham then built an altar here and offered sacrifice so his descendants would never lose sight of this founding moment (Gen 12:6-7). Jacob later bought a parcel of land and settled here with his household, digging a well which bears his name to this day (Gen 33:18-20; John 4:5-6).

After the exodus, Moses instructed the Israelites, "When the Lord your God has brought you into the land that you are entering to occupy, you shall set the blessing on Mount Gerizim and the curse on Mount Ebal"

*Drawing of covenant renewal
at Mount Gerizim
and Mount Ebal
at Samaritan Museum*

(Deut 11:29). Moses told them to hold a covenant renewal ceremony here, using the natural amphitheater formed by the two mountains, to rededicate themselves to the Torah (Deut 27:1-8). Doubtless, this location was chosen because it stands in the center of the land both from north to south and from east to west.

When Joshua led the people into the Promised Land, he brought the new nation to this sacred spot where he built an altar and offered sacrifices. With the Levitical priests carrying the ark of the covenant in the valley between the mountains, and with half of the people in front of Mount Gerizim and half in front of Mount Ebal, Joshua read the words of the law along with its accompanying blessings and curses (Josh 8:30-35). Later, when Joshua was old and dying, he gathered all the tribes of Israel and addressed them, summarizing their saving history under God's guidance and calling forth the commitment of all the people (Josh 24:1-28). Joshua asked them to choose between serving the God of Abraham who had delivered them from Egypt and the false gods whom their ancestors had served. Joshua's final impassioned speech echoed off these mountainsides: "As for me and my household, we will serve the LORD."

Archaeological excavations on Mount Gerizim

After the Israelites declared their will to serve the Lord, they buried Joseph's bones in Shechem on the land Jacob purchased to fulfill the request Joseph had made before he died in Egypt (Gen 50:25; Josh 24:32). Because of its central location and because of the presence of places sacred to Abraham, Jacob, Joseph, and Joshua, Shechem became a place of hope and expectation of all that God would do for his people.

After the forty-year reign of King Solomon, his son Rehoboam succeeded him. Rehoboam traveled to Shechem, "for all Israel had come to Shechem to make him king" (1 Kgs 12:1). But the northern tribes rebelled against the house of David and chose Jeroboam as their king and Shechem as the capital of the northern kingdom (1 Kgs 12:19-20, 25).

In Samaritan tradition, Mount Gerizim is the sacred location chosen by God for a holy temple, rather than Jerusalem's Temple Mount. The Samaritan temple stood from the fifth to the second century BC, before being destroyed by the Hasmonean king John Hyrcanus. The mountain continues to be the center of Samaritan religion to this day, and most of the Samaritans live nearby. The largest festival is Passover, which is still celebrated on the mountain around the temple's ruins.

The summit of Mount Gerizim offers a great view over central Samaria. A tour of the ruins includes the foundations of the temple as well as the base of an octagonal church and monastery built over the Samaritan ruins in the Byzantine period. Also discovered is a holy place known as the

Twelve Stones. According to the Samaritan tradition, this was the altar that Joshua and the Israelites built after crossing the Jordan into the land (Deut 27:1-8). Although the biblical texts prescribe that this altar be built on Mount Ebal, the Samaritan Torah text states that Mount Gerizim is the location of the altar.

Meditation

- In what way is this pilgrimage helping me dedicate myself more fully to the Lord?

- What foreign gods must I expel from my life in order to serve the Lord?

Reading: Joshua 24:14-28

Joshua gathered all the tribes of Israel to Shechem, and summoned the elders, the heads, the judges, and the officers of Israel; and they presented themselves before God (24:1). . . .

Response: "As for me and my household, we will serve the LORD."

All Israel, alien as well as citizen, with their elders and officers and their judges, stood on opposite sides of the ark in front of the levitical priests who carried the ark of the covenant of the Lord, half of them in front of Mount Gerizim and half of them in front of Mount Ebal, as Moses the servant of the Lord had commanded at the first, that they should bless the people of Israel (Josh 8:33). R.

[Joshua] read all the words of the law, blessings and curses, according to all that is written in the book of the law. There was not a word of all that Moses commanded that Joshua did not read before all the assembly of Israel, and the women, and the little ones, and the aliens who resided among them (Josh 8:34-35). R.

"Thus says the LORD, the God of Israel: . . . When you went over the Jordan and came to Jericho, the citizens of Jericho fought against you, and also the Amorites, the Perizzites, the Canaanites, the Hittites, the Girgashites, the Hivites, and the Jebusites; and I handed them over to you. . . . It was not by your sword or by your bow. I gave you a land on which you had not labored, and towns that you had not built, and you live in them; you eat the fruit of vineyards and oliveyards that you did not plant" (Josh 24:2, 11-13). R.

[Joshua said to all the people,] "Then put away the foreign gods that are among you, and incline your hearts to the LORD, the God of Israel." The people said to Joshua, "The LORD our God we will serve, and him we will obey" (Josh 24:23-24). R.

Prayer: God of our ancestors, who brought your people out of bondage and into a land where they could experience freedom and life, listen to the committed response of your people today. We are witnesses to your saving deeds and we reaffirm the covenant you made with our ancestors. This day we choose to forsake all other gods and we choose to serve you alone, our God and our Lord.

3. Jacob's Well, Church of St. Photina

By the days of Jesus, ancient Shechem had been abandoned, but a village called Sychar grew up nearby, not far from "the plot of ground that Jacob had given to his son Joseph. Jacob's well was there" (John 4:5-6). Although most Jews would travel between Galilee and Judea by way of the Jordan Valley in order to avoid passing through Samaria, John's gospel says Jesus "had to go through Samaria." Because this route was not a geographical necessity, the impulse that drove Jesus to travel through Samaria was the divine necessity to extend the gospel beyond the Jewish people. Here, Jesus encountered the Samaritan woman at the well.

Today Jacob's well lies in the crypt of a modern Greek Orthodox church in the city of Nablus. The Samaritan woman reminded Jesus that Jacob "gave us the well, and with his sons and his flocks drank from it" (John 4:12). Jewish, Samaritan, Christian, and Muslim traditions all associate the well with Jacob. The church is named for St. Photina, the name the Orthodox tradition has given to the Samaritan woman.

Pilgrims' writings refer to Christian veneration of Jacob's well from the third century. A cruciform church built around 380 was the first of a succession of churches erected over the well. In the nineteenth century, the Orthodox Church acquired the property and began restoring the crypt. The present church, completed in 2007, is spacious and airy, modeled on a church from the Crusader era. Brightly colored icons and frescoes adorn the walls and ceilings.

The well was the center of communal life for the ancient people of the Bible. It tapped into groundwater and in dry summers was their source

of life-sustaining water and their salvation from slow famine. It was also a gathering place, a site where people met for conversation and laughter. The water of Jacob's well today is still fresh and good for drinking. It may be drawn up in a bucket while reading from the gospel scene.

The woman was shocked that Jesus, a Jew, was speaking to her, a Samaritan. Jesus was fully aware of the social rules and the Jewish intolerance of Samaritans. Yet, he frequently crossed social and religious boundaries for a higher good. Jesus used his physical thirst as the occasion to address the deeper thirst of the Samaritan woman. Jesus responded that if the woman knew who he was, she would have asked *him* for a drink—and he would have given her not well water but "living water." On the natural level, living water is flowing water, the water of a spring that is always fresh and sparkling. The real contrast is between the well water of ordinary existence and the living water of abundant life in God's Spirit, the "spring of water gushing up to eternal life." Jesus wants to bestow upon her a new kind of life, a life that begins with forgiveness and baptism and then extends into eternal life.

Jesus's prophetic insight about the woman's marriages—"You are right in saying, 'I have no husband'; for you have had five husbands, and the one you have now is not your husband" (John 4:17-18)—quite possibly recounted a tragic marital history. But a different interpretation, in which the woman represents all the people of Samaria, might express a fuller meaning of the text. During the resettlement of Samaria after the Assyrian conquest, five foreign nations settled there, mixing and intermarrying with the remaining Israelites. Each of these peoples brought their own gods and religious practices, compromising the covenant faith of Israel (2 Kgs 17:24, 29-34). If the five husbands of the Samaritan woman symbolize Samaria's relationships with these five idolatrous peoples, then the sixth, or present liaison, would be Samaria's infidelity to God by their worship and practices on Mount Gerizim.

This interpretation seems more probable in light of the Samaritan woman's response to Jesus, which has nothing to do with marriage, but is concerned with the correct place for worshiping God. The Samaritans considered Mount Gerizim the proper place for sacrifice, while the Jews viewed Jerusalem as the only suitable place (John 4:20). Jesus replied

Jacob's well in the crypt of the Church of St. Photina

Jesus meets the woman of Samaria between Mount Gerizim and Mount Ebal

that the place of worship will be relatively unimportant in the new relationship with God that he offers. The new temple for all people will be his own risen body, in which people will worship in spirit and truth (John 4:24).

In his earthly ministry, Jesus continually broke down the barriers that divided people. Jesus's visit to Samaria sowed the seeds of evangelization that would bring early Christian missionaries into Samaria and then outward to the whole world (Acts 1:8). Jesus demonstrates, in his encounter with the woman of Samaria, that God's grace is available to all people and that the gospel is destined for everyone.

Meditation

- What are the barriers that I erect between myself and other people?
- How does Jesus's encounter with the Samaritan woman challenge me?

Reading: John 4:3-26

Jacob's well was there, and Jesus, tired out from his journey, was sitting by the well. . . .

Response: Savior of the world, give us living water that we may never thirst again.

As a deer longs for flowing streams,
    so my soul longs for you, O God.
My soul thirsts for God,
    for the living God.
When shall I come and behold
    the face of God? (Ps 42:1-2). R.

He split rocks open in the wilderness,
    and gave them drink abundantly as from the deep.
He made streams come out of the rock,
    and caused waters to flow down like rivers (Ps 78:15-16). R.

Surely God is my salvation;
    I will trust, and will not be afraid,
for the LORD GOD is my strength and my might;
    he has become my salvation.
With joy you will draw water from the wells of salvation (Isa 12:2-3). R.

[Jesus] cried out, "Let anyone who is thirsty come to me, and let the one who believes in me drink. As the scripture has said, 'Out of the believer's heart shall flow rivers of living water'" (John 7:37-38). R.

The Spirit and the bride say, "Come." / And let everyone who hears say, "Come." / And let everyone who is thirsty come. / Let anyone who wishes take the water of life as a gift (Rev 22:17). R.

Prayer: Source of living water, help us to thirst deeply for you and for the new life you offer us. Quench our thirst with the gift of your Spirit, and renew the grace of baptism within us. Take away all that diverts our hearts from genuine devotion to you, so that we may worship in spirit and truth.

4. Samaria/Sebaste

The ruins of the ancient city of Samaria cover the hillside overlooking today's village of Sebastia. From here, beginning in the ninth century BC, the kings of Israel's northern kingdom ruled their extensive domain. From the highest point of the ruins, where the royal citadel stood, we can imagine the infamous royal couple Ahab and Jezebel looking over their wealthy city and realm. Because Samaria was built of stone instead of mud brick, many of the ancient buildings were reused in later construction, leaving little of the ancient Israelite city intact. Over the Israelite ruins, remains have been found from the Hellenistic, Herodian, Roman, and Byzantine eras.

The history of Samaria began with Omri, the Israelite king who wanted to build a new capital for his kingdom. He purchased the mount from its owner, Shemer, for two talents of silver, fortified the hill, and called the city Samaria. Rather than focus on Israel's God-given mission, Omri sought to make his realm as wealthy as that of his neighbors, the Phoenicians. To facilitate his financial relationships, he arranged for his son Ahab to marry a Phoenician princess named Jezebel. For his efforts, Omri is described as being more sinful than any of the kings who preceded him (1 Kgs 16:24-25). Ruins of the royal citadel, constructed of fine ashlar masonry, have been uncovered on the hill.

Ahab and Jezebel extended trade with Phoenicia, added to the kingdom's wealth, and became notorious for their decadent arrogance. They expanded the palace and decorated it with ivory. Excavations revealed many of these ivory items in a building dubbed "the ivory house." The royal couple built a temple to Baal in Samaria, presuming that the financial success of the Phoenicians was associated with their worship of this pagan deity. Their reign aroused the ire of Elijah the prophet and the condemnation of Amos for their idolatry and social injustice. Ahab succeeded his father in earning the title of worst of the worst kings (1 Kgs 16:29-33). During excavations, two tombs were discovered under the palace at Samaria, possibly those of Omri and Ahab, although First and Second Kings claim that six kings were buried in Samaria: Omri, Ahab, Jehu, Jehoaz, Joash, and Jeroboam II. The royal city remained the kingdom's political hub until the fall of Israel to Assyria in 721 BC, when the entire surrounding area became known as Samaria.

In 30 BC, during the New Testament period, Emperor Augustus gave the city of Samaria to Herod the Great, who renamed it Sebaste to honor the emperor (*Sebaste* is the Greek form of the Latin *Augustus*). At the highest point in the city, Herod built a temple to Augustus over the palace of Omri, the steps and ruins of which may still be seen. Other visible remains include a stadium, a theater, a forum, an aqueduct, and a colonnaded street running east-west. At Sebaste, Herod celebrated one of his many marriages and executed two of his sons.

Byzantine-period basilica
dedicated to John the Baptist

Ruins of the acropolis of Samaria and the Herodian temple

Despite the infamy of the city, the Acts of the Apostles narrates the travels of Philip the deacon to "the city of Samaria" to announce the good news of Jesus Christ (Acts 8:5). The notorious city witnessed healing miracles, the grace of many baptisms, and the joy of forgiveness. When the news of these conversions reached Jerusalem, the community sent Peter and John to the converts. The apostles laid their hands on the newly baptized and prayed that the Holy Spirit might come upon them. The long history of Samaria/Sebaste has made it a place of hope, a witness to the power of the gospel to redeem and transform people, places, and history.

In the Byzantine period, Christian tradition associated the city with the infamous birthday banquet at which Herod Antipas had John the Baptist beheaded. A sixth-century church was built on the southern slopes, beneath Herod's temple to Augustus, to commemorate the finding of John the Baptist's head. The church was rebuilt in the eleventh century to support a central dome. Another church, a large cathedral enshrining the reputed tomb of John the Baptist, was constructed east of the ruins of the city in the twelfth century. Although the church is in ruins, the tomb is beneath a small domed structure within the nave, which is today a mosque.

Meditation

- What does the conversion of the people of Samaria teach me about the power of the gospel?

- How does the example of Philip inspire me to be a missionary disciple?

Reading: Acts 8:5-25

Philip went down to the city of Samaria and proclaimed the Messiah to them. . . .

Response: Send the power of the Holy Spirit upon us.

As you go, proclaim the good news, "The kingdom of heaven has come near." Cure the sick, raise the dead, cleanse the lepers, cast out demons (Matt 10:7-8). R.

You will receive power when the Holy Spirit has come upon you; and you will be my witnesses in Jerusalem, in all Judea and Samaria, and to the ends of the earth (Acts 1:8). R.

Repent, and be baptized every one of you in the name of Jesus Christ so that your sins may be forgiven; and you will receive the gift of the Holy Spirit (Acts 2:38). R.

How are they to believe in one of whom they have never heard? And how are they to hear without someone to proclaim him? And how are they to proclaim him unless they are sent? As it is written, "How beautiful are the feet of those who bring good news!" (Rom 10:14-15). R.

The gifts he gave were that some would be apostles, some prophets, some evangelists, some pastors and teachers, to equip the saints for the work of ministry, for building up the body of Christ (Eph 4:11-12). R.

Prayer: Risen Lord, who desires the salvation of all people, you send your disciples to continue your mission in ways they don't expect. Help us not to set limits on where you might ask us to go, what you might ask us to do, or how you might ask us to serve you.

5. Shiloh

During the period before the monarchy, Shiloh was the spiritual center of the nation, the place where the tabernacle was set up (Josh 18:1). Housing the ark of the covenant, the menorah, the table of showbread, and everything needed for worship, the tabernacle was the epicenter of religious observance and sacrifices. Shiloh thus became the place of pilgrimage for the Israelites, where three times a year they brought their festival offerings.

According to 1 Samuel 1–3, the sanctuary at Shiloh played an important role in the early life of the prophet Samuel. His mother, Hannah, had been unable to have children, so she traveled to the tabernacle at Shiloh to pray for a son. Here she met the high priest, Eli, who told her, "Go in peace, the God of Israel grant the petition you have made to him" (1 Sam 1:17). In due time, Hannah conceived and gave birth to a son whom she named Samuel. She dedicated him to the Lord, as she had promised, and took him to Shiloh to live with Eli so that Samuel could devote his life to service at the sanctuary. Here she offered the beautiful Prayer of Hannah (1 Sam 2:1-10).

In later years, Samuel's prophetic ministry began with his call from the Lord while in the tabernacle. His humble words, "Speak, Lord, for your servant is listening," provide a sharp contrast to the corrupt ministry and blasphemy of Eli's sons, Hophni and Phinehas. Under Eli and his sons, the ark of the covenant was lost in battle with the Philistines at Aphek. This may also have been the occasion when the Philistines destroyed Shiloh and its sanctuary was reduced to ruins.

More than three hundred years later, the prophet Jeremiah used the example of Shiloh as a warning to the inhabitants of Judah and Jerusalem. Jeremiah spoke the word of the Lord: "Go now to my place that was in Shiloh, where I made my name dwell at first, and see what I did to it for the wickedness of my people Israel." God warned them that their Holy City, Jerusalem, could fall under divine judgment just as at Shiloh (Jer 7:12-14). The barren landscape of Shiloh today is a reminder that it is better for God's sanctuary to lie in ruins than for it to endure a corrupt priesthood and shameful worship.

Tel Shiloh is now an archaeological site. A glass and metal visitor's center stands amid the excavations on bedrock. The first floor is used for guiding and the second floor offers a media presentation of the site. Several altars have been excavated, indicating that Shiloh was a sacred place

The archaeological site of biblical Shiloh

during the Canaanite period, a status the Israelites adopted. Archaeologist debate about the exact site of the tabernacle, although most believe it stood on a level area near the summit of the hill. Several Byzantine churches have also been excavated at the site, built between the fourth and the sixth centuries, one of which has been reconstructed. The mosaic floors contain several Greek inscriptions, one referring to the site as the "village of Shiloh." Within the town, the modern synagogue is designed as a replica of the biblical tabernacle.

Meditation

- What do I want to remember about the excavations at Shiloh?

- How can I listen better as the Lord speaks to me in prayer?

Reading: 1 Samuel 3:1-10

Samuel was lying down in the temple of the Lord, where the ark of God was. . . .

Response: "Speak, Lord, for your servant is listening."

Hannah prayed and said,
    "My heart exults in the Lord;
    my strength is exalted in my God.
My mouth derides my enemies,
    because I rejoice in my victory.
There is no Holy One like the Lord,
    no one besides you;
there is no Rock like our God. R.

"Talk no more so very proudly,
    let not arrogance come from your mouth;
for the Lord is a God of knowledge,
    and by him actions are weighed.
The bows of the mighty are broken,
    but the feeble gird on strength.
Those who were full have hired themselves out for bread,
    but those who were hungry are fat with spoil.
The barren has borne seven,
    but she who has many children is forlorn. R.

"The LORD kills and brings to life;
    he brings down to Sheol and raises up.
The LORD makes poor and makes rich;
    he brings low, he also exalts.
He raises up the poor from the dust;
    he lifts the needy from the ash heap,
to make them sit with princes
    and inherit a seat of honor.
For the pillars of the earth are the LORD's,
    and on them he has set the world. R.

"He will guard the feet of his faithful ones,
    but the wicked shall be cut off in darkness;
for not by might does one prevail.
    The LORD! His adversaries shall be shattered;
the Most High will thunder in heaven.
    The LORD will judge the ends of the earth;
he will give strength to his king,
    and exalt the power of his anointed" (1 Sam 2:1-10). R.

Prayer: Speak to us, Lord, from the barren landscape of Shiloh. For you teach us that it is better for your sanctuary to lie in ruins than for it to endure a corrupt priesthood and shameful worship. Renew your people as we listen to your word, so that we may offer you a worthy sacrifice all the days of our lives.

Chapter V

Judea

Forming today's southern part of the Holy Land, between Samaria to the north and the Negev Desert to the south, Judea includes the major urban areas of Jerusalem, Bethlehem, Jericho, and Hebron. Judea is a mountainous region, part of which is considered a desert. It varies greatly in altitude, 3,346 feet above sea level at Mount Hebron to over 1,400 feet below sea level around the Dead Sea. Rainfall varies from about 24 inches around western Jerusalem, falling back to 16 inches in eastern Jerusalem, and dropping to about 4 inches in the Judean desert due to a rain-shadow effect. The climate, accordingly, moves between Mediterranean in the west and desert climate in the east, with a strip of steppe climate in the middle.

The name Judea originated from Judah, the son of Jacob, and his descendants, forming the Israelite tribe of Judah. After the division of Israel's monarchy, the southern kingdom was known as Judah or (in its Greek and Roman form) Judea. After the defeat by Babylon and the destruction of Jerusalem in 587 BC, the inhabitants gradually became known as Jews and their ethnic religion as Judaism. To refer to the religion of Israel as Judaism or to the people of Israel as Jews before this period of exile is anachronistic.

Judea was eventually wiped from the map, following its destruction by the Roman Empire after the first Jewish revolt in AD 70 and the second revolt in AD 135. The whole Roman province was then called Syria Palaestina, and eventually the name Palestine referred to the entire Holy Land. Many Jews departed into the Jewish diaspora, but there was never a complete Jewish abandonment of the area, and Jews remained an important minority in Judea through the centuries. Throughout the twentieth century, Jews from all over the world migrated to the land, and in 1948 the modern state of Israel was founded. The term Judea is now a geographical term revived by the Israeli government as part of the Israeli administrative district of Judea and Samaria for the territory generally referred to as the West Bank.

1. Ein Karem, Church of the Visitation

A few miles west of Jerusalem, picturesquely set within the folds of the Judean hills, lies the village of Ein Karem. Tradition tells us that here lived Elizabeth and Zechariah, along with their child John who would "prepare the way" for Jesus. In a valley on the south of the village is a freshwater spring known as Mary's Spring. The fountain gave the village its name, Ein Karem, which means "spring of the vineyard."

High above the village stands the Church of the Visitation, commemorating the meeting of Mary and Elizabeth. The Franciscan church, built in 1955, was designed by the architect Antonio Barluzzi. The mosaic on the

facade of the church depicts Mary traveling from Nazareth to Ein Karem. The verse beneath the image is in Latin: "And Mary arose in those days, and went into the hill country with haste, into a city of Judea" (Luke 1:39). Mary had been told by the angel that her aging relative Elizabeth was to have a child, so Mary went without hesitation, traveling an arduous journey of eighty miles to care for her.

The embrace of Mary and Elizabeth expresses the unity of God's saving plan. Elizabeth, representing the old covenant, is elderly and will have a son who will be the

Church of the Visitation on the hillside of Ein Karem

last great figure of ancient Israel; Mary, representing the new covenant, is young and will have a son who will usher in the new age of salvation. In Mary the new covenant reaches out to the old covenant, giving it ultimate meaning and preparing for its fulfillment. In Elizabeth the old covenant recognizes the new and gives honor to its coming.

Elizabeth praises Mary as "blessed" for two reasons: first, because she is the "mother of the Lord," and second, because she is a model of faith—"blessed is she who believed that there would be a fulfillment of what was spoken to her by the Lord." We honor Mary most often for the first reason; she is the divinely chosen mother of the Son of God. But for the adult Jesus, the second reason seemed even more important. When a woman in the crowd surrounding Jesus cried out, "Blessed is the womb that bore you and the breasts that nursed you," Jesus replied, "Blessed rather are those who hear the word of God and obey it!" (Luke 11:27-28). Truly Mary bore the word of God both in her womb and in her heart.

Mary's canticle of praise, the *Magnificat*, is inscribed on ceramic plaques in dozens of languages in the peaceful courtyard surrounding the church. In harmony with the flowers of the Judean hill country that spring day, Mary opened like a rose as her whole being unfolded in song. The musical words of her canticle sent forth the good news of God's salvation down through the ages as blossoms release their scent upon the wind. God is answering his ancient promises, lifting up the lowly and giving hope to all who wait. The mother of the Lord sings and all generations rejoice.

The frescoes inside the lower chapel show the annunciation to Zechariah while offering incense in the temple of Jerusalem (Luke 1:5-23), the joyful greeting of Mary and Elizabeth as John leaps with joy in the womb,

Fresco of the visitation of Mary to Elizabeth

and Elizabeth hiding her infant son from Herod's soldiers (Matt 2:16). A vaulted passage leads to an ancient well where tradition tells us that Mary met Elizabeth. On the right wall, a boulder set in a niche is known as the Stone of Hiding. According to an ancient tradition, the stone provided a hiding place for the baby John during Herod's Massacre of the Innocents.

An outside staircase leads to the upper church, filled with colorful frescoes honoring Mary whose inspired canticle proclaims, "From now on all generations will call me blessed" (Luke 1:48). In the center of the apse stands the glorified Mary; depicted to the left are shrines dedicated to her in various places throughout the world, and to the right are religious orders dedicated to her. On the right wall are five frescoes representing various titles of Mary. From left to right, the image of the Council of Ephesus honors Mary as the Theotokos (Bearer of God); Mary covering all people with her mantle reveres her as Refuge of Sinners; the Wedding Feast at Cana venerates Mary as Intercessor; the Battle of Lepanto, which saved Europe from the Ottoman Turks, pays tribute to Mary as Help of Christians; and the disputation of Duns Scotus honors Mary as the Immaculate Conception.

Meditation

- What emotions might Mary and Elizabeth have felt during their visit?
- For what blessings might I praise God in song?

Reading: Luke 1:39-45

Mary set out and went with haste to a Judean town in the hill country. . . .

Response: "The Mighty One has done great things for me, / and holy is his name."

And Mary said,
    "My soul magnifies the Lord,
and my spirit rejoices in God my Savior,
    for he has looked with favor on the lowliness of his servant." R.

"Surely, from now on all generations will call me blessed;
for the Mighty One has done great things for me,
    and holy is his name." R.

"His mercy is for those who fear him
    from generation to generation.
He has shown strength with his arm;
    he has scattered the proud in the thoughts of their hearts." R.

"He has brought down the powerful from their thrones,
    and lifted up the lowly;
he has filled the hungry with good things,
    and sent the rich away empty." R.

"He has helped his servant Israel,
    in remembrance of his mercy,
according to the promise he made to our ancestors,
    to Abraham and to his descendants forever." R.

And Mary remained with [Elizabeth] about three months and then returned to her home (Luke 1:46-56). R.

Prayer: Mighty God, who has done wondrous deeds throughout the old covenant and the new, may we always magnify your greatness with the Virgin Mary. As John the Baptist leapt for joy when he sensed the hidden Christ, so may your church rejoice to experience the presence of the same ever-living Lord.

2. Ein Karem, Church of St. John the Baptist

Although Mary visited Elizabeth in a cooler summer house, high on the hillside, John the Baptist was born in the home of Zechariah and Elizabeth within the village of Ein Karem. This tradition is marked by the Church of St. John the Baptist, a Franciscan church whose tall bell tower dominates the center of the village. The church is also called St. John Ba-Harim, meaning St. John in the Mountains, a reference to

Statue of the Baptizer in the Church of St. John the Baptist

the "hill country" of the gospel account. The canticle Zechariah sang after his son's birth can be found in multiple languages around the church's courtyard.

The church stands over the remains of Byzantine chapels, mosaic floors, and tombs, which can be seen from the grill beneath the porch and a gate within the church. Much of the church's foundation comes from the Crusader period. In the seventeenth century, the Franciscans recovered the ruins of the church and built the present structure with the help of the Spanish royal family. For this reason, the church is lined in blue and white azulejos, the famous tiles loved by Spaniards, and many of the paintings on the walls are created by Spanish artists. The ceiling and dome are supported by two rows of columns, and the dome contains stained glass scenes related to John the Baptist's life.

It is believed John was born in the cave on the left side of the church, called the Grotto of the Benedictus. The song of Zechariah begins in the traditional Jewish prayer style, the first few words of which are written atop the entrance to the cave: "Blessed be the Lord God of Israel, for he has visited and redeemed his people." A marble inscription under the altar is written in Latin: *Hic precursor Domini natus est* (Here was born the forerunner of the Lord). Here also, old Zechariah regained his power of speech when he obediently wrote on a writing tablet that the baby's name was to be John, reversing his earlier reluctance to believe God's word.

The birth, circumcision, naming, and manifestation of John are filled with echoes of the Old Testament. Like Abraham and Sarah (Gen 21:1-6), the elderly Zechariah and Elizabeth have a son in fulfillment of God's promises. Like their ancestors, they name their son and circumcise him on the eighth day after his birth. Yet, like the springtime emerging from winter, God is doing something new. The hillsides resound with new songs of God's salvation. Zechariah thought he was too old for dreaming, too old for raising a child, maybe even too old to sing. Because he opened his heart, God opened his mouth. This mistrusting, disbelieving old man now sang with full and confident voice and gained new strength to raise his son to be "the prophet of the Most High."

The grotto marking the birthplace of John the Baptist

Meditation

- What do I think I am too old for? How might God prove me wrong?

- Am I skeptical of God's promises? Can I trust in the unknown future God has planned for me?

Reading: Luke 1:57-66

Now the time came for Elizabeth to give birth, and she bore a son. . . .

Response: "The dawn from on high will break upon us."

Then . . . Zechariah was filled with the Holy Spirit and spoke this prophecy:
"Blessed be the Lord God of Israel,
  for he has looked favorably on his people and redeemed them." R.

"He has raised up a mighty savior for us
  in the house of his servant David,
as he spoke through the mouth of his holy prophets from of old,
  that we would be saved from our enemies and from the hand of all
  who hate us." R.

"Thus he has shown the mercy promised to our ancestors,
  and has remembered his holy covenant,
the oath that he swore to our ancestor Abraham,
  to grant us that we, being rescued from the hands of our enemies,
might serve him without fear, in holiness and righteousness
  before him all our days." R.

"And you, child, will be called the prophet of the Most High;
  for you will go before the Lord to prepare his ways,
to give knowledge of salvation to his people
  by the forgiveness of their sins." R.

"By the tender mercy of our God,
  the dawn from on high will break upon us,
to give light to those who sit in darkness and in the shadow of death,
  to guide our feet into the way of peace" (Luke 1:67-79). R.

Prayer: Lord God of Israel, who brought redemption to your chosen people after a long time of waiting, help us to live in trusting confidence, anticipating the fulfillment of your promises. May we be faithful to your new covenant, live as your children in freedom, and worship you in holiness.

3. Bethlehem, Church of the Nativity

It was foretold from of old that the Messiah would come from "the line of David" and that the birthplace of Israel's greatest king would be the birthplace of the King of Kings (1 Sam 16; Mic 5:1; Matt 2:4-6). Luke's gospel explains that a census of the empire had been ordered and that all were to return to the place of their family's roots. Joseph and Mary went from the town of Nazareth to the City of David called Bethlehem, because Joseph was descended from the house and family of David. Whether on donkey or on foot, the journey would have been exhausting.

The mother of Jesus, along with his relatives and Jewish Christian disciples, preserved the memory of his place of birth. Justin Martyr, writing in the middle of the second century, stated that Jesus was born in a cave and that its location is generally accepted by those living in the area. In the fourth century, the emperor Constantine ordered the construction of a magnificent basilica over the cave of Christ's birth. Its four rows of columns formed five aisles, at the eastern end of which was built an octagonal structure above the site of the grotto. Although devastated in the sixth century, the church was rebuilt by the emperor Justinian; this church still stands today, making it the oldest standing church in the Holy Land. It is said that the church was spared destruction from

Entrance to the Church of the Nativity through the Door of Humility

Cave of the Nativity marks the birthplace of Jesus

the Persians in 614 because the invaders saw the depictions on the walls of the Magi in Persian-style clothing.

Beneath the floor of the present church, visitors can see mosaic floors from the original church dedicated by St. Helena in 339. The walls of the Byzantine church were originally covered in white marble slabs. Traces of the holes used to attach the marble can be detected in the present plastered walls. The Greek iconostasis in the sanctuary dates from the eighteenth century. The columns and capitals, made of red stone from Bethlehem, are original from the Byzantine period. In the Crusader period, images of various saints were painted on the columns with a method using hot wax. The high walls of the nave are decorated with twelfth-century mosaics, some of which have been restored. These are divided into three bands, starting from the bottom: medallions of the ancestors of Jesus from the gospel genealogies; ecumenical and regional councils and synods of the church; and, at the top, a procession of angels dressed in white tunics. The tesserae of these mosaics are tilted downward in order to enhance the visual impact when seen from the observer below. The transepts and apses were also covered with mosaics of gospel scenes and the back wall held a mosaic image of the prophets holding messianic texts in a Jesse Tree, together creating a vision of unimaginable beauty throughout the church.

A stairway in the sanctuary descends to the Cave of the Nativity where a silver star, glistening with the reflections of dozens of oil lamps, marks the place honored as the birthplace of Jesus. The star is inscribed with the Latin words *Hic De Virgine Maria Jesus Christus Natus Est* (Here, of the Virgin Mary, Jesus Christ was born). A few feet away is the altar honoring the Adoration of the Magi and the site of the manger where the infant Jesus lay.

While the Son of God surely could have chosen whatever culture and economic strata he wanted to enter our world, we stand in wonder at the choice he made for himself, a choice that must have been for our benefit and our instruction. Since there was no room in the place for lodging travelers, Mary and Joseph withdrew to the place where animals are kept, perhaps underneath or in back of a house. The earliest tradition says the place of Jesus's birth was a cave, a natural area for keeping animals and their feed.

Bethlehem reminds us that God chooses the least likely people and places to bring us salvation. As David, the youngest son of Jesse, was

Grotto of St. Jerome adjoining the Cave of the Nativity

unexpectedly chosen to be king, so Jesus came to us as a tiny child born in an obscure village of the ancient world, laid in a lowly manger, and visited by simple shepherds. Childbirth in first-century Palestine would have been like delivery in some war-ravaged area of our world today. Emperors and their armies oppressed the people; corruption and extortion were a way of life. Because the spacious entry of the Church of the Nativity was reduced centuries ago to a small four-foot-tall opening to prevent looting on horseback, it seems appropriate that pilgrims should have to bow low to enter the place where God humbled himself to come among us.

Adjacent to the Church of the Nativity is the Church of St. Catherine of Alexandria. A statue of St. Jerome overlooks the courtyard. Although the Church of the Nativity is maintained by the Greek Orthodox, Roman Catholic, and Armenian Orthodox, the Franciscans possess this church. On the right side of the nave, steps lead down to a complex of subterranean chambers called the Grotto of St. Jerome. Here Jerome spent thirty years, much of the time translating the Scriptures from Hebrew and Greek into Latin, the most enduring and influential version of the Bible ever. Because this is part of the same underground complex as the adjoining Cave of the Nativity, from these caves emerged the word of Scripture and the Word made flesh.

St. Jerome is known for his ascetic lifestyle and his passionate involvement in doctrinal controversies. Paula, a noble Roman widow, and her daughter Eustochium worked with Jerome in making Bethlehem a great monastic center. The adjacent caves have been identified as the burial places of Jerome, his successor St. Eusebius, and Sts. Paula and Eustochium—although the remains of St. Jerome are now in St. Mary Major Basilica in Rome. Other parts of the cave structure include St. Joseph's Chapel, which recalls the dream in which an angel warned Joseph to take the Holy Family to Egypt, and the Chapel of the Holy Innocents, the burial place of infants killed by King Herod in his attempt to eliminate the newborn King.

Meditation

- What are my favorite memories and images of Christmas?

- What do I want to remember about these moments at the place of my Savior's birth?

Reading: Luke 2:1-7

She gave birth to her firstborn son and wrapped him in bands of cloth, and laid him in a manger. . . .

Response: In Bethlehem is born our Savior, Christ the Lord.

Let us rejoice in the Lord, for here our Savior is born to the world, here true peace has descended from heaven, here a light shines for us and for all the world. Here a child is born for us, a son is given to us, upon his shoulder dominion rest, and of his kingdom there will be no end. R.

Let us pray in solidarity with the Christians of this land, asking the Lord to make us attentive to their condition and their cry for justice. Let us ask for the gift of peace, converting our hearts to mercy and pardon, and be a joyful testimony of Christ's incarnation everywhere and to everyone. R.

Let us pray to the Child of Bethlehem for the children of this land. May we defend and respect their dignity, and may we commit ourselves to constructing a fairer and more peaceful world, where every child will be able to grow in age, in wisdom, and in grace. R.

Prayer: O God, who has made this holy site glow with the light of your incarnate Word, illumine our minds, make our hearts radiant, and shine through our deeds. Grant that we may share in the divinity of Christ, who here in Bethlehem humbled himself to share in our humanity.

4. Bethlehem, Milk Grotto

During Herod's Massacre of the Innocents, the Holy Family found refuge here before they fled into Egypt. The name is derived from a belief that, while Mary was nursing the baby Jesus, a drop of her milk fell on the stone floor of the cave and changed its color to white. The grotto has been a site of veneration since the fourth century, the first structure being built over it around 385. The current chapel was built by the Franciscans in 1872 on the site of the former Byzantine church.

The irregular grotto of soft white rock contains several images of Mary feeding Jesus from her breast. The images are a beautiful reflection on the humanity of Jesus and the intimate relationship between Mary and her child. Sacred to Christians and Muslims alike, this site is especially frequented by new mothers and couples who are trying to conceive. By mixing the soft white chalk with their drink, and praying through the intercession of Our Lady of the Milk, these visitors believe it will increase the quantity of their milk or enable them to have children. A room near the entrance features rows of framed letters and baby pictures sent from around the world, testifying to the effectiveness of the milk powder and prayer.

The monastery of the Sisters of Perpetual Adoration of the Blessed Sacrament is attached to the grotto. The red-and-white-clad nuns uninterruptedly pray for peace. The chapel contains the Queen of Peace tabernacle inspired by the book of Revelation. The closed tabernacle depicts earthly Jerusalem, with the twelve apostles and the twelve tribes of Israel surrounding the image of Jesus on the cross, while the open shrine represents the heavenly Jerusalem, brightly shining and flanked by a pair of olive trees. Their branches are filled with a variety of different crosses, symbolizing the various Christian professions emerging from the common trunk of Christianity. At the center of the open shrine, the monstrance depicts the Virgin Mary holding the eucharistic Christ in her hands.

Meditation

- How are women of today's world dehumanized and exploited?

- How does this place remind me of Mary's maternal love for me and all God's children?

Reading: Matthew 2:13-18

An angel of the Lord appeared to Joseph in a dream and said, "Get up, take the child and his mother, and flee to Egypt. . . ."

Response: Pray for us, O Holy Mother of God.

In this church dedicated to the Theotokos, the Bearer of God, we contemplate Christ at the breast of Mary. Let us commit ourselves to help ensure respect for the rights and dignity of all children, here in Bethlehem and throughout the world. R.

In this place we honor Mary's gift of maternal love for her son and all her children. We pray that Mary be a guide and mentor to every mother, so that they will be able to raise their children in holiness, giving them dignity, confidence, and compassion. R.

In this cave, Joseph stayed with Mary and Jesus in committed love and with selfless courage. We pray that Joseph be a teacher and model for all fathers, so that they will be able to offer their children affectionate guidance and provide them with tranquil care. R.

To this place of miracles, prayerful couples come every day to confide their hopes to the Mother of God. Through the intercession of Our Lady of the Milk, grant them healing from infertility and relief for their sufferings. R.

Here, where Mary is honored as Queen of Peace, may we welcome this great and indispensable gift of God's people. May our hearts be renewed with compassion and mercy, so that from the peace of every heart will spring the forgiveness that is able to establish a new civilization of love. R.

Prayer: O God, who bestowed on the human race the grace of eternal salvation through the fruitful virginity of Mary, accept our prayers we present to you through the powerful and loving intercession of Blessed

Image of Mary feeding the infant Jesus in the Milk Grotto

Mary. In this holy place, where Mary cradled her holy infant in her arms, help us listen to and follow her motherly invitation to always hear and fulfill your word.

5. Beit Sahour, Shepherds' Fields

To the east of the town of Bethlehem lie the fields in which the shepherds watched their flocks on that holy night when Christ was born. The sheep and goats grazed in the fields used for agriculture after the season of harvest and before the time for plowing and planting. The flocks fed on the stubble of the gathered wheat and barley and in the process fertilized the field for the next growing season. Throughout these fields there are traces of chapels and monasteries dating back to the fifth century which served pilgrims on their way to Bethlehem.

These fields first enter the Scriptures through the story of Ruth, a Moabite woman. She is celebrated for her devotion to her mother-in-law, Naomi, who came from Bethlehem and returned there after the death of her husband: "Where you go, I will go; / Where you lodge, I will lodge; / your people shall be my people, / and your God my God" (Ruth 1:16). Ruth met Boaz, a wealthy landowner of Bethlehem, while gleaning the barley left behind by the harvesters in the fields of this area. They married and Ruth became the great-grandmother of King David.

Shepherds' Fields reminds us of David, the shepherd king. When David was tending his flock near the town of Bethlehem, he was chosen as king and anointed (1 Sam 16:11). God said to David, "It is you who shall be shepherd of my people Israel" (2 Sam 5:2). At the time of Jesus, shepherds were people of low esteem. They were poor nomads, often looked upon with suspicion, holding no social or religious status in Israel. That they would be chosen as the first to hear the "good news of great joy" is surely an indication that God has lifted up the lowly. Jesus's birth among the poor anticipates his ministry to the poor outcasts of Israel's society. He, whose birth was first announced to shepherds in the fields, will become the Good Shepherd of the sheep.

Nestled in a natural glen is the Grotto of the Shepherds, a cave that has been converted into a chapel, its walls and altar of natural, uncut stone.

Shepherds receiving the message of Christ's birth

Chapel of the Angels in Shepherds' Fields

This grotto gives a good idea of the shelters used by the shepherds of the area. On the knoll above the cave is the Chapel of the Angels, designed by Antonio Barluzzi in the shape of a nomad's tent. A bronze angel hovers above the chapel door. Inside, the dome is studded with round glass blocks, which break up the sunlight streaming inside, calling to mind the divine glory that shone around the shepherds. These words are written in large, golden letters around the circumference of the church's dome: *Gloria In Altissimis Deo, Et In Terra Pax Hominibus Bonae Voluntatis* (Glory to God in the highest, and on earth peace to people of good will). The canticle of the angels, the Gloria, proclaims that heaven has touched earth in this wondrous birth. God in heaven is given glory; people on earth are brought peace.

The angel's announcement is the message of the entire gospel: the one born in Bethlehem is Savior, Messiah, and Lord. Yet the "sign"—a baby swaddled in bands of cloth and lying in a manger—is not what one would expect at the birth of such a child (Luke 2:11-12). Both the announcement of his sovereignty and the simplicity of the sign invite us to ponder the mystery of his humble birth. Three frescoes around the chapel help us reflect on the angel's announcement to the shepherds, the shepherds paying homage to Jesus, and the shepherds celebrating the birth of the Messiah. In all three paintings we can observe the shepherd's dog. At the appearance of the angels, the dog barks ferociously in fear; at the place of Jesus's birth, the dog sits with his eyes fixed on Jesus; as the shepherd joyfully returns from his visit, the dog runs with delight.

Meditation

- Why did God first proclaim to shepherds what kings and priests longed to hear?

- Is my life simple and humble enough to hear God's good news?

Reading: Luke 2:8-20

In that region there were shepherds living in the fields, keeping watch over their flock by night. . . .

Response: Glory to God in the highest, and on earth peace to people of good will.

Thus says the Lord God: I myself will search for my sheep, and will seek them out. As shepherds seek out their flocks when they are among their scattered sheep, so I will seek out my sheep (Ezek 34:11-12). R.

I will feed them with good pasture, and the mountain heights of Israel shall be their pasture; there they shall lie down in good grazing land, and they shall feed on rich pasture on the mountains of Israel (Ezek 34:14). R.

I will set up over them one shepherd, my servant David, and he shall feed them: he shall feed them and be their shepherd (Ezek 34:23). R.

They shall know that I, the Lord their God, am with them, and that they, the house of Israel, are my people, says the Lord God. You are my sheep, the sheep of my pasture and I am your God, says the Lord God (Ezek 34:30-31). R.

Prayer: Divine Shepherd, you chose David from among his sheep and made him shepherd of your people, and you promised to send the Messiah to rescue, heal, protect, and gather your flock. We rejoice with the angels and give you glory that you have chosen us to live in the era of the Good Shepherd who has laid down his life for us and for the world.

6. Hebron, Tomb of the Patriarchs and Matriarchs

Set in the Judean mountains south of Jerusalem and Bethlehem, Hebron has the highest elevation of any city in the Holy Land. Its central attraction for pilgrims is the Machpelah, the burial place of the Bible's patriarchs and matriarchs. Abraham's family tomb is of deep spiritual importance to Jews, Christians, and Muslims, all of whom honor Abraham as the father of faith, "the ancestor of all who believe" (Rom 4:11, 16). Abraham lived before the historical expression of each of these "Abrahamic" religions and is looked upon by all as their founding ancestor. Today the truth about God that was revealed to Abraham is dispersed to every corner of the world. When the spiritual descendants of Abraham look back to their origin, they discover that they are all offspring of the same father, members of the same family.

When Sarah, Abraham's wife, died, Abraham purchased land for the burial tomb of his family, the cave of Machpelah. He paid Ephron the Hittite the full market price—four hundred shekels of silver (Gen 23). After Abraham's

Herod's wall surrounding the Machpelah in Hebron

death, he too was buried here along with Sarah, as were his descendants, Isaac and Jacob, along with their wives, Rebekah and Leah. Although it is a small piece of real estate, its importance is monumental for the legacy of Abraham. God had promised that his descendants would become a thriving people with Canaan as their homeland, and from them all the peoples of the world would be blessed (Gen 12:1-3). The parcel of land was the first to be owned by Abraham, and thus the first step in fulfilling God's promise of the land for the divine mission of Abraham and his family. Centuries later, because of the importance of Hebron, David made the city his capital for the first seven and a half years of his reign (2 Sam 2:4, 11), and then all the tribal leaders met at Hebron to proclaim David king of all Israel (2 Sam 5:1-5).

In the first century BC, Herod the Great built an ornate wall enclosing the Machpelah, the Cave of the Patriarchs. The exterior walls are constructed with meticulously trimmed building stones, each laid without the use of mortar. Each stone is set back about a half inch on the one below it in order to avoid the impression of heaviness. Here we can get a sense of the magnificence of Herod's temple in Jerusalem before its destruction by the Romans. Later, a sixth-century Byzantine church was built inside the wall, which was converted by Muslims into a mosque in the seventh century, rebuilt as a church by the Crusaders in the twelfth century, then reconverted into a mosque by the sultan Saladin later in the same century. Although Herod left the interior open to the sky, today's vaulted ceiling, supporting pillars, capitals, and stained-glass windows, is from the Crusader church.

The enclosure now consists of three major rooms, each containing two domed monuments or cenotaphs, representing the tombs of the patriarchs and matriarchs. Their actual burial places are in the cave beneath, to which access is not permitted. In the center are the monuments of Abraham and Sarah; on the east side, those of Isaac and Rebekah; and on the west side are the cenotaphs of Jacob and Leah. The site is heavily guarded and hotly disputed, the scene of much bloodshed in recent years. For this reason, there are separate entries for Muslims and Jews, one leading to a mosque and the other to a synagogue. Christian pilgrims may enter from either entrance.

When Abraham died, Genesis records that his two sons, Ishmael and Isaac, who had been rivals since their births, stood side by side to bury their father in the Cave of Machpelah. Ishmael, who became the patriarch of the Muslim people, and Isaac, the son who inherited God's promises

Cenotaphs above the tombs of the patriarchs and matriarchs

made to the Israelites, shared their pain that day and recognized they were brothers, children of the same father. If there is ever to be peace between the offspring of Ishmael and Isaac, they must offer one another a reconciliation as profound as the moment when the two brothers came together to bury their father, Abraham. Could not their shared pain, the kind of grief that gives birth to forgiveness, be the spark that sets the world alight with new hope for peace four thousand years later?[1]

Meditation

- In what ways does the grief of burying a parent transcend sibling rivalries?

- In what way does this place of strife seem to also be a symbol of hope?

Reading: Genesis 25:7-11

[Abraham's sons] Isaac and Ishmael buried him in the cave of Machpelah. . . .

Response: "In you all the families of the earth shall be blessed" (Gen 12:3).

He is mindful of his covenant forever,
    of the word that he commanded, for a thousand generations,
the covenant that he made with Abraham,
    his sworn promise to Isaac,
which he confirmed to Jacob as a statute,
    to Israel as an everlasting covenant,
saying, "To you I will give the land of Canaan
    as your portion for an inheritance" (Ps 105:8-11). R.

Look to the rock from which you were hewn,
    and to the quarry from which you were dug.
Look to Abraham your father
    and to Sarah who bore you;
for he was but one when I called him,
    but I blessed him and made him many (Isa 51:1-2). R.

1. Stephen J. Binz, *Abraham: Father of All Believers* (Grand Rapids, MI: Brazos Press, 2011), 8–9.

Therefore the Lord assured him with an oath
>   that the nations would be blessed through his offspring;
that he would make him as numerous as the dust of the earth,
>   and exalt his offspring like the stars,
and give them an inheritance from sea to sea
>   and from the Euphrates to the ends of the earth (Sir 44:21). R.

And the scripture, foreseeing that God would justify the Gentiles by faith, declared the gospel beforehand to Abraham, saying, "All the Gentiles shall be blessed in you" (Gal 3:8). R.

Prayer: Lord God, your promises extend from Abraham to all the people of the world. We are grateful for the heritage of faith you have given us and for the blessings you have bestowed upon us. May we learn from the example of our ancestors so that we may leave a legacy to the generations who follow us.

7. *Bethany, Church of Martha, Mary, and Lazarus*

The town of Bethany lies on the eastern slope of the Mount of Olives. Here lived Martha, Mary, and their brother Lazarus. Jesus was a dear friend of this family. He would often spend his days teaching in Jerusalem, then retire for the evening to Bethany. While Jerusalem was a place of controversy and ultimate rejection, Bethany was a place of retreat and acceptance, from which Jesus returned revitalized to face the heat of Jerusalem.

The present Catholic church was built in 1954 by architect Antonio Barluzzi, who contrasted the sadness of death with the joy of resurrection by designing a crypt-like, windowless church, into which light floods from the large oculus in its dome. Above the main altar is a mosaic of Christ and his words to Martha, "I am the resurrection and the life." Further words of Jesus are written around the base of the dome: "Whoever believes in me, even if he dies, will live, and whoever lives and believes in me will never die."

The first church in Bethany, called the Lazarium, was built in the fourth century and was included in the notes of Egeria and the other early pilgrims. The church was built in Constantinian style with three naves, columns, and floor mosaics, and it contained the tomb of Lazarus. After it was destroyed by an earthquake, a fifth-century church was built further east. The Crusaders renovated and transformed the church along with a Benedictine monastery and a church directly over the tomb of Lazarus. The present Franciscan church sought to preserve remains of the three previous churches, and remnants may be seen in the courtyard and beneath the church entrance.

The three other mosaics in the church today commemorate events from the gospels that are set in Bethany. The first depicts the gracious hospitality of Martha and Mary when Jesus entered their village (Luke 10:38-42). Martha was busy with the domestic details while Mary sat at the feet of Jesus and listened. The words in Latin below the mosaic highlight Jesus's response to Martha: "The Lord said to her: Martha, Martha, you are anxious and troubled about many things." Jesus praises Mary for setting aside her culturally expected role and doing the one thing necessary for true discipleship and life's most necessary task, listening attentively to the word of the Lord.

The next mosaic presents the raising of Lazarus from the dead. Jesus, who is himself the resurrection and the life, demonstrates the truth of the words over the altar and around the dome. The words below the mosaic

Church of Martha, Mary, and Lazarus

address the reason for the miracle and Jesus's command: "'Father, that they may believe that you have sent me,' when he had said these things, he called out in a loud voice, 'Lazarus, come out!'" At his decree, the dead man came forth from the tomb, wrapped in strips of cloth. Like Lazarus, we too will experience death, but also like Lazarus, we will live again through the power of Christ's resurrection.

The final mosaic recalls Mary's anointing Jesus with perfumed nard. Passover was near and Jesus was particularly grateful for the hospitality of his friends at this time. Finding lodging in Jerusalem would have been difficult because of the many pilgrims coming for the feast. The version of the anointing from Mark's gospel is highlighted in the mosaic: "A woman with an alabaster jar of costly perfumed spikenard broke open the jar and poured it over his head" (Mark 14:3). The account in John's gospel, which is either a different anointing or a variation on the scene, tells us that Martha provided the practical hospitality of serving the meal, while Mary performed the impractical and extravagant gesture of pouring costly perfumed oil over his feet and drying his feet with her hair. The normal use of such perfume dictated that it be applied a few drops at a time. To use a pound at once was,

Jesus calls Lazarus forth from the tomb

in the eyes of many, irrational and foolish. No wonder the house was filled with the fragrance. But the extravagant scene represents in miniature what Jesus will do in the final days of his life. His love is lavish. He will pour out his lifeblood to anoint us with his grace. His action seemed foolish to many, but the extravagance of his divine love filled the whole world.

Meditation

- What aspects of the discipleship of Martha and Mary would I most like to imitate?

- What would happen if I loved extravagantly like Mary at the feet of Jesus?

Reading: John 12:1-8

Six days before the Passover Jesus came to Bethany, the home of Lazarus. . . .

Response: Teach us to befriend Jesus, our Lord.

St. Martha, who offered hospitality and attentive service to Jesus, show us how to make our homes welcome places to serve Jesus in all our guests and to see him in the face of those in need. R.

St. Martha, who was distracted and anxious with your many tasks, teach us how to be busy without worry so that we may be serene cooperators in the work of the gospel. R.

St. Lazarus, who was dearly loved by Jesus, show us how to be available to our friends in their needs and to be faithful to the gift of friendship. R.

St. Lazarus, who was raised by Jesus from death, instill in us the firm belief that Jesus is truly the resurrection and the life, and that those who die and believe in him will live. R.

St. Mary, who listened attentively at the feet of Jesus, teach us how to do the one thing necessary, which is listening to the word of God and pondering it in our hearts. R.

St. Mary, who wept at the feet of Jesus when he arrived in Bethany after the death of your brother, teach us how to both grieve and trust, knowing that the pain of death is the threshold to life. R.

Prayer: Lord Jesus, who came here to Bethany many times as guest of your friends Martha, Mary, and Lazarus, we come as pilgrims to reflect on the joyful commitment of friendship and the gift of extravagant love. Look upon our families with your blessing and help us to create homes filled with the affection, friendship, hospitality, and love that you experienced in Bethany.

8. Bethany, Tomb of Lazarus

The present Arab village is called al-Azariya, the place of Lazarus. The original village was probably a little farther up the hill to the west of the tomb of Lazarus. The prime focus in the early days of the church was not on the location of the family home but on the tomb, which would have been outside the village. The site of the tomb is mentioned by Eusebius, writing in about 290, before any church was built. The tomb of Lazarus was incorporated into subsequent Byzantine and Crusader churches, but beginning in the fourteenth century, the site of the tomb was occupied by the al-Uzair Mosque. So, in the middle of the sixteenth century, the Franciscans had to open up a new means of access, cutting two dozen steps down from the northern side, which is today's entrance to the tomb.

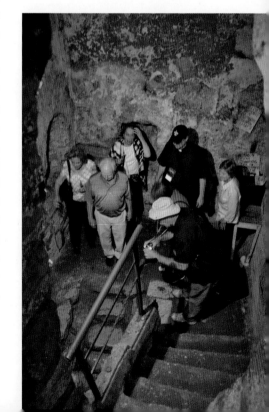

The steep, uneven steps lead to the atrium, where a walled door marks the original entrance. This atrium would have been the area from which Jesus called, "Lazarus, come out!" Three more steps descend to the burial chamber. Although the area is largely Crusader in design, the small inner chamber retains some of the tomb's original features. It is indeed a dark place, but one in which the light of life overcame the darkness for Lazarus, the friend of Jesus.

Descending to the tomb of Lazarus

John's gospel recounts how Martha and Mary sent for Jesus as Lazarus was dying. But Jesus delayed his coming and arrived in Bethany four days after Lazarus had been buried. When Martha and Mary went to meet Jesus, they each expressed a different face of grief. Martha expressed a composed and confident trust in Jesus, while Mary fell at the feet of Jesus and wept. Likewise, Jesus responded to Martha and Mary in quite different ways. With Martha, Jesus offered a statement of faith and expression of his own identity as the source of resurrection and life, while with Mary, Jesus was deeply moved and began to weep. The verbal reply that Jesus offered Martha and the emotional reply he offered Mary represent two necessary and complementary aspects of faith: the response of the mind and the response of the heart. Each of them serves as a consolation for those of us struggling with our own grief over the death of a loved one. The scene shows us that Jesus is the source of resurrection and life and that he is deeply, emotionally involved in our pain.

The raising of Lazarus is told briefly but powerfully. Jesus is weeping like Mary yet trusting like Martha. As Jesus prays, he knows that his petitions to the Father will be answered and that Lazarus will come to life. Then, at the dramatic climax, Jesus called Lazarus by name, and the dead man emerged from the tomb. The command of Jesus, "Unbind him and let him go," echoes the command spoken by Moses in the name of God: "Let my people go." God wants his people to be free from all bondage, even the final prison of death. Like the exodus from Egypt, the raising of Lazarus is a sign and foreshadowing of what God will do for Jesus and for all who belong to him.

Meditation

- What does the brief verse "Jesus wept" tell me about him?

- From what types of bondage does Jesus want to set me free?

Reading: John 11:17-44

When Jesus arrived, he found that Lazarus had already been in the tomb four days. . . .

Tomb of Lazarus in Bethany

Response: Lord, I believe you are the resurrection and the life.

Your dead shall live, their corpses shall rise.
    O dwellers in the dust, awake and sing for joy!
For your dew is a radiant dew,
    and the earth will give birth to those long dead (Isa 26:19). R.

The trumpet will sound, and the dead will be raised imperishable, and we will be changed. For this perishable body must put on imperishability, and this mortal body must put on immortality (1 Cor 15:52-53). R.

"Where, O death, is your victory?
    Where, O death, is your sting?"
The sting of death is sin, and the power of sin is the law. But thanks be to God, who gives us the victory through our Lord Jesus Christ (1 Cor 15:55-57). R.

We have been buried with him by baptism into death, so that, just as Christ was raised from the dead by the glory of the Father, so we too might walk in newness of life. For if we have been united with him in a death like his, we will certainly be united with him in a resurrection like his (Rom 6:4-5). R.

Prayer: Lord of life, who has always called your people out of bondage and darkness, you wept at the death of Lazarus, your friend. Help me to trust in you when I consider my own inevitable death and the death of those I love. Set us free from fear, anxiety, and finally, from the bonds of death itself. Make us realize that nothing we do is ever lost or wasted when done in union with you, our source of life eternal.

Chapter VI

Judean Wilderness and Dead Sea

The ancient Israelites were forged as a people by their experiences in the wilderness—forty years of wandering in the deserts of Sinai and Negev on their way to the Promised Land. Here they entered into covenant with God, learned to rely on God's provisions, and prepared to live in freedom. Grumbling and often rebelling against God, they gradually learned to trust in God and listen to his word.

The wilderness features frequently throughout the Old Testament. It was a place of escape and refuge, as in the case of the young David on the run from King Saul, and a place of recovery and restoration, as in the case of Elijah, running for his life then hearing God's gentle, whispering voice. The message of the prophet Isaiah, "Comfort, O comfort my people, / says your God," announced that the desert would be a place of preparation for the coming of the Lord: "In the wilderness prepare the way of the Lord, / make straight in the desert a highway for our God" (Isa 40:1, 3). The wilderness was a place of struggle, but ultimately a place of hope and rebirth.

The wilderness of Judea begins just east of Jerusalem. The eastern side of the Mount of Olives drops dramatically in elevation through pale chalky hills and narrow twisting canyons to the Jordan River Valley and the Dead Sea. Scant rainfall, steep slopes, and marginal soil makes agriculture impossible here, except in the rare oases. During the winter and spring, local shepherds still graze their flocks in this stingy landscape with its sparse desert vegetation. In biblical times, this wilderness was home to thieves, rebels, and ascetics.

Into this harsh and starkly beautiful landscape came John the Baptist. He appeared "in the wilderness of Judea," proclaiming his message of repentance. The people of Jerusalem and the whole Judean countryside as well as all the region around the Jordan were coming to him, confessing their sins, and being baptized by him in the river Jordan (Matt 3:1-6; Mark 1:4; Luke 23:2-3). Only John's gospel gives us a more precise location, saying that Jesus was baptizing "in Bethany across the Jordan" (John 1:28). John was making God's people ready for their redemption, preparing the way of the Lord. And when Jesus came to the Jordan, John declared of him, "Here is the Lamb of God who takes away the sin of the world!" (John 1:29). The end of exile and the restoration of God's people was at hand.

An experience of the desert is essential for any Holy Land pilgrimage. Here we encounter the landscape where the prophets heard God's voice—a place of both temptation and divine encounter. In the fourth and fifth centuries, men and women went out into the Judean desert to form some of the earliest monasteries. The Mar Saba monastery east of Bethlehem, the monastery of St. George of Khoziba in the Wadi Qelt, and the Monastery of Jesus's Temptation near Jericho are some of the few that still exist.

In the wilderness, we encounter the sounds of silence, a jarring contrast to the constant clamor that fills our lives. Spending time here in solitude strips us of every distraction and all sense of self-sufficiency. For our fathers and mothers of the desert, their monastic cells became places of struggle and testing, but also places where God met them and began to change them. They believed that God was revealed to them primarily through Scripture, which is why it had such a prominent place in their lives. Meditating on the Bible, soaking in its message and values, they embodied its wisdom and were transformed into the image of Christ.

Pilgrims who spend time in the desert, sensing its freedom from noise and distractions, find themselves returning home with a new desire and determination to listen hard for God's word in Scripture. Seeking a monastic cell in the midst of ordinary life, pilgrims learn to meditate on God's transforming Word, to encounter Christ there, and so become active contemplatives in the world.

1. The Road Connecting Jerusalem and Jericho

When Jesus told the parable of the Good Samaritan, he situated it on the road to Jericho: "A man was going down from Jerusalem to Jericho, and fell into the hands of robbers, who stripped him, beat him, and went away, leaving him half dead" (Luke 10:30). Travelers along this route, then as now, descend from Jerusalem's height, about 2,500 feet above sea level, to Jericho's depth, some 800 feet below sea level, an elevation difference of 3,300 feet. The descent produces distinctive environmental markers: after a short while, there are no more trees; then vegetation is reduced to steppe shrubs; and eventually, only desert plants find enough moisture to survive. The landscape alone made this a particularly parched and arduous trek.

In biblical times, the road between Jerusalem and Jericho was a major thoroughfare for trading caravans, military personnel, and the pilgrims who visited Jerusalem multiple times each year. Jesus was quite familiar with the road, having often walked it on the final stretch of the way from Galilee to Jerusalem along the Jordan Valley. In some of the more isolated terrain along the ancient road, people traveling alone were easy targets for outlaws, who found ample hiding places and escape routes into the desert where no one would pursue them. When Jesus told his parable, his listeners surely recognized the dangers that this journey posed. A person who was robbed and beaten on this road would have been in a truly vulnerable position, with no food or water to be found along the way and no shelter from the elements. The victim would be utterly exposed and isolated—desperate for help.

In the parable, a priest and a Levite saw the man who had been robbed but "passed by on the other side." The many priests and Levites living in Jericho and other areas used the road whenever they were rostered to serve in the temple. Given that this ancient road was only a few feet

Pilgrims adjust to the rigors of the Judean wilderness

wide at its dangerous points, the victim would have been near the feet of these religious officials. For his unlikely hero, Jesus chose a traveler from Samaria. As one whose people were at enmity with the Jews, this Samaritan would have been regarded as an alien in Judea. "Moved with pity," he tended the man's wounds, took him to an inn, and paid for his care. With this story, Jesus showed that loving one's neighbor requires expanding the definition of neighbor to include even an enemy.

Along the road to Jericho sits an ancient hostel for travelers, which existed in the time of Jesus. St. Jerome, in the fourth century, argued that this was the inn to which Jesus referred in the parable. In the sixth century, a monastery with pilgrim accommodations was erected on the site. Later the Crusaders established a fortress on a nearby hill to protect pilgrims against robbers. The remains of the monastery, just off the modern highway, became an Ottoman caravanserai and then served as a police post during the twentieth century.

The rocky desert terrain around where the Inn of the Good Samaritan now stands was notorious for robbers. The local name for the area, Ma'ale Adummim ("ascent of the red rocks"), came from patches of limestone tinted red by iron oxide, but also suggests bloody raids by bandits. In re-

cent years, the site has become a mosaic museum to display reconstructed mosaics discovered in excavated synagogues and churches.

Farther along the descent to Jericho, the turnoff to Wadi Qelt and a short hike offers pilgrims a remarkable view of this deep gorge along which the ancient road was built. Many claim this to be Psalm 23's "valley of the shadow of death." Clinging to the cliffside and defying gravity, the Monastery of St. George can be viewed. The monastery was founded in the fifth century when John of Thebes drew together a cluster of five Syrian hermits who had settled around a cave where they believed the prophet Elijah was fed by ravens (1 Kgs 17:1-7). But it is named after its most famous monk, St. George of Koziba, who came as a teenager from Cyprus in the sixth century to follow the ascetic life in the Judean desert.

Completely restored in the late nineteenth century, the monastery is inhabited by Greek Orthodox monks. Those hiking Wadi Qelt appreciate the desert beauty, pocked with caves that have offered habitation to monks and hermits for many centuries. The monastery welcomes visitors, but it requires walking down and up a steep and winding path. The three-level monastery encloses the Church of St. George and St. John, which contains a rich array of icons, paintings, mosaics, relics, and tombs. A small cave-chapel is dedicated to St. Elijah. The frescoed walls depict Elijah in a cave, fed by a raven.

Farther along the descent stands the sea-level marker along the highway. From here the road continues to descend toward the Jordan River. A left turn leads to Jericho, the lowest city in the world, and a right turn leads to the Dead Sea, the lowest landmark on earth.

Meditation

- What does the landscape of this road add to my appreciation of Jesus's parable?

- Who might Jesus use today as the hero of his parable in order to have a similar effect?

Reading: Luke 10:25-42

A man was going down from Jerusalem to Jericho, and fell into the hands of robbers. . . .

Monastery of St. George on the road from Jerusalem to Jericho

Response: Our help comes from the Lord, who made heaven and earth.

I lift up my eyes to the hills—
    from where will my help come?
My help comes from the LORD,
    who made heaven and earth. R.

He will not let your foot be moved;
    he who keeps you will not slumber.
He who keeps Israel
    will neither slumber nor sleep. R.

The LORD is your keeper;
    the LORD is your shade at your right hand.
The sun shall not strike you by day,
    nor the moon by night. R.

The LORD will keep you from all evil;
    he will keep your life.
The LORD will keep
    your going out and your coming in
    from this time on and forevermore (Ps 121). R.

Prayer: Compassionate Lord, you call us to love our neighbor even when our neighbor is an enemy. As you have been merciful to us, help us to extend mercy to others. Give us the grace to show compassion today to all those whom you put in our path.

2. Baptism Site on the Jordan River

The flowing water of the Jordan River is the lifeblood of the Holy Land. The word "Jordan" is derived from a Hebrew root meaning "to descend." The river begins in the high elevations of Upper Galilee and descends rapidly, flowing through the Sea of Galilee, then continuing to descend, finally flowing into the Dead Sea. Since the days of early Christianity, pilgrims have gone to the Jordan River to be baptized or to renew their baptism.

The baptismal site of Bethany beyond the Jordan (John 1:28) is near the southern end of the Jordan River on its eastern side, in today's country

The site of Jesus's baptism at the Jordan River

of Jordan. This site, known today as Al-Maghtas (Baptism), is the most likely site of John's baptism of Jesus. The baptismal site was not actually on the Jordan River, but at a stream, Wadi al-Kharrar, which flows into the river. John probably baptized in springs and brooks at least as much as he did in the more perilous Jordan River, which flowed more rapidly and widely at the time than it does today. The gospels also describe John's baptizing ministry at "Aenon near Salim" (John 3:23), "aenon" meaning natural fountain or spring.

Pilgrims as far back as 333 described visits to the baptism site of Bethany beyond the Jordan, and the sixth-century pilgrim Theodosius described a square-shaped church built on high arches to allow flood-waters to pass underneath. A monastery with four churches developed

between the fourth and sixth centuries on Tell Mar Elias (St. Elijah Hill), just above the springs that feed the stream. A hostel between the monastery and the river provided lodging for pilgrims, who would immerse themselves in the waters.

Since the site was abandoned after the 1967 Six-Day War, when both banks of the Jordan were heavily mined, excavations began only in 1996 after the peace treaty between Israel and Jordan. Al-Maghtas includes two principal archaeological areas: the monastery complex and an area close to the river with remains of churches, baptismal pools, and pilgrim dwellings. The two areas are connected by the Wadi al-Kharrar stream. Today, several new Christian churches have been built at the site, including the gold-domed Greek Orthodox Church of St. John the Baptist.

While the initial site of pilgrimage was on the eastern side of the Jordan River, focus shifted to the western side during the sixth century, when the place of baptism began to stretch over both banks of the river. The western part, known as Qasr el-Yahud, has also been developed for Christian baptisms and renewal services. Christians renew their baptisms today from both banks, divided only by the narrow river that serves as the international border.

Why did John the Baptist choose to locate his ministry here? First, the Jordan River and its tributaries provided the flowing water necessary for baptism in the Judean wilderness. Second, Bethany beyond the Jordan was strategically located along important east-west crossroads, providing heavy foot traffic and the ability to spread his message. Third, and most

important, here was the place where the Israelites crossed the Jordan River and entered the Promised Land under Joshua. John brought God's people into the wilderness, offered them a baptism of repentance, and prepared the way for the Lord's coming, in fulfillment of Isaiah's prophecy (Isa 40:3-5). What better location to call forth a renewed Israel after a long exile than at the place where God's people took their first steps toward their national identity in the land?

Repentance entails a radical conversion to a new way of life, a turning of the whole person away from sin and toward God. It demands an interior change of heart, a deeply rooted decision, and a consequent lifestyle of obedience to God. John's voice in the wilderness and his call to repentance was based on the reality that God's kingdom had drawn near. John was the forerunner of Christ, and his message prepared for the coming of God's universal salvation. Although Jesus had no need for personal repentance, he entered the baptism of John in solidarity with sinful humanity to offer repentance on behalf of all God's people. As Jesus descended into the deepest fissure in the earth, where the Jordan River nears the Dead Sea, he descended into the deep chasm of humanity's sin.

As Jesus came up from the water, the heavens opened, God's Spirit descended on him, and the voice of the Father spoke, "This is my Son, the Beloved." As readers of the gospel, we are privy to this exchange between the Father, Son, and Holy Spirit. Through our baptism, we have been united to Jesus, born to new life in him. We have been adopted as beloved sons and daughters of the Father, and the Holy Spirit now lives in us.

Meditation

- What does it mean to me to be a son or daughter of God?
- Why do I choose to be renewed in the faith of my baptism today?

Reading: Matthew 3:13-17

Jesus came from Galilee to John at the Jordan, to be baptized by him. . . .

Response: "I do."

Do you renounce sin, so as to live in the freedom of the children of God? R.

Pilgrims renewing their baptismal promises

Do you reject the lure of evil, so that sin may have no mastery over you? R.

Do you reject Satan, the author and prince of sin? R.

Do you believe in God, the Father almighty, creator of heaven and earth? R.

Do you believe in Jesus Christ, his only Son, our Lord, who was born of the Virgin Mary, suffered death and was buried, rose again from the dead, and is seated at the right hand of the Father? R.

Do you believe in the Holy Spirit, the Holy Catholic Church, the communion of saints, the forgiveness of sins, the resurrection of the body, and life everlasting? R.

Prayer: Father of life, who proclaimed Jesus as your Son at his baptism in the Jordan River, we want to live more fully as your children, to call you Abba, to confess Jesus as our Lord, and to live the good news of the kingdom. Having professed the faith of the church, we pray that you anoint us with the Holy Spirit and renew the grace of baptism within us today.

Each person may come to the water. The celebrant should sprinkle each with water, saying: "Be renewed in the faith of your baptism." *Each person makes the sign of the cross and responds,* "Amen."

3. Mount of Temptation

Towering from the northwest over the city of Jericho is the mountain where Jesus fasted for forty days and nights and where he was tempted by the devil. Halfway up to the top of the mount, clinging to its sheer face, is the Monastery of the Temptation or Qarantal. A steep path leads to the monastery from below or a cable car travels there from Tel Jericho. The lookout from the monastery offers spectacular views eastward of the Jordan Valley, the Dead Sea, and the mountains of Moab and Gilead across the river.

Immediately after his baptism, Jesus was led by the Spirit into the wilderness. While he fasted, the devil tempted him three times through visionary experiences. The devil sought to persuade Jesus to display his messianic power in spectacular ways. Jesus rebuffed each temptation with

Viewing the Mount of Temptation from Jericho

a quotation from the book of Deuteronomy, perhaps the book Jesus was using for his solitary reflection. His responses indicated that he would not use his identity as Son of God for his own selfish ends. Then the devil left and angels brought food to Jesus, who was famished. Unlike the Israelites, who were tested in the desert and often failed, Jesus emerged from the trial confirming his identity as God's faithful and obedient Son.

Monks have inhabited the mountain since the early centuries of Christianity, living in natural caves, which they turned into cells, chapels, and storage rooms. A sophisticated system of conduits stored rainwater and carried it to the caves. A Byzantine monastery was built in the fourth century, and the present monastery was reconstructed at the end of the nineteenth century. Within the monastery, a medieval cave-church built of masonry stands in front of a cave. The monastery also honors a stone on which, according to tradition, Jesus sat during his fasting and temptations.

Meditation

- Since Jesus faced temptations throughout his life, what might have been his greatest test?

- What temptations most test my identity as a child of God?

Reading: Matthew 4:1-11

Jesus was led up by the Spirit into the wilderness to be tempted by the devil. . . .

Response: "One does not live by bread alone, / but by every word that comes from the mouth of God."

Remember the long way that the LORD your God has led you these forty years in the wilderness, in order to humble you, testing you to know what was in your heart, whether or not you would keep his commandments (Deut 8:2). R.

No testing has overtaken you that is not common to everyone. God is faithful, and he will not let you be tested beyond your strength, but with the testing he will also provide the way out so that you may be able to endure it (1 Cor 10:13). R.

We do not have a high priest who is unable to sympathize with our weaknesses, but we have one who in every respect has been tested as we are, yet without sin. Let us therefore approach the throne of grace with boldness, so that we may receive mercy and find grace to help in time of need (Heb 4:15-16). R.

Whenever you face trials of any kind, consider it nothing but joy, because you know that the testing of your faith produces endurance; and let endurance have its full effect, so that you may be mature and complete, lacking in nothing (Jas 1:2-4). R.

Discipline yourselves, keep alert. Like a roaring lion your adversary the devil prowls around, looking for someone to devour. Resist him, steadfast in your faith, for you know that your brothers and sisters in all the world are undergoing the same kinds of suffering (1 Pet 5:8-9). R.

Monastery of the Temptation or Qarantal

Prayer: O God, whose word is our daily food, teach us that no temptation we will ever experience is beyond your power and grace. Through the example of your Son, show us how the devil's testing produces endurance and maturity, as we resist him, steadfast in our faith.

4. Jericho

Abundant springs in and around Jericho have attracted human habitation for thousands of years to this oasis in the midst of the wilderness. The city holds claim to being not just the lowest city on earth but also the world's oldest inhabited city. At a tell just north of today's Jericho, archaeologists have unearthed the remains of more than twenty successive settlements, the first of which dates back 11,000 years. In the Old Testament the city is frequently described as the "City of Palms." Still today it is characterized by its date palms, abundant fruit, flowers, and spices.

The Israelites conquered the town from its Canaanite inhabitants soon after crossing over the Jordan River into the land (Josh 6). Centuries later, the story began to be told of the prophet Elisha purifying the water of the city by throwing salt into the spring (2 Kgs 2:19-22). The wholesome spring, today called Elisha's Spring, still produces more than 1,000 gallons

Jericho, the oldest city in the world

of water per minute. In the final days of Jerusalem, when its walls had been breached by the armies of Babylon, King Zedekiah, the last king of the house of David, fled to Jericho, where he was captured, blinded, and led into captivity in chains (2 Kgs 25:5-7).

By the time of Jesus, Jericho had been rebuilt south of the ancient city. Because of its mild climate, Herod the Great constructed his winter palaces there and the area became a winter resort for the Jewish aristocracy of Jerusalem. Jesus often passed through Jericho as he traveled from Galilee along the Jordan River Valley, then turned westward to begin the steep ascent to Jerusalem. As Jesus approached Jericho for the last time, a blind man heard that Jesus was coming and shouted out, "Son of David, have mercy on me" (Luke 18:39). Unlike King Zedekiah, whose disobedience had lost him his sight and his kingdom, Jesus, the new Son of David, gave sight to the blind man and offered him a share in the kingdom of God. This is the gift that Jesus offers to us all: the ability to see the world with new eyes, to participate in the new life of God's kingdom.

Because he was the chief tax collector of Jericho, Zacchaeus was probably the most hated man in the region. Though wealthy and powerful, he felt empty. In the character of Zacchaeus, Jesus saw a man trapped in his own failure, desperately trying to be something better. And the enterprising Zacchaeus, urged on by the courage of desperation, climbed the sycamore tree and Jesus invited him to share in his life.

Upon meeting Jesus, Zacchaeus changed his life, and as evidence of his change, he promised to restore his ill-gotten gains fourfold and to give half his goods to the poor. Turning his life around, he experienced the kind of repentance and personal transformation that gives hope to us all. For Zacchaeus and so many others, Jesus came "to seek out and to save the lost."

Zacchaeus's sycamore tree in Jericho

Near the center of the city, pilgrims are shown a centuries-old sycamore tree that local residents say Zacchaeus climbed. Others claim that the tree is from the same generational line as the sycamore of Jesus's day. At a nearby Greek Orthodox monastery, the trunk of a dead sycamore behind a glass frame is also described as the tax collector's tree. Even if the tree is only for imaginative effect, this is the ideal place to reflect on the transforming encounter of Zacchaeus with Jesus.

Meditation

- What in the character of Zacchaeus would I like to imitate?

- What prevents me from encountering Jesus in the midst of the crowds?

Reading: Luke 19:1-10

[Jesus] entered Jericho and was passing through it. A man was there named Zacchaeus. . . .

Response: "The Son of Man came to seek out and to save the lost."

All the tax collectors and sinners were coming near to listen to Jesus. And the Pharisees and the scribes were grumbling and saying, "This fellow welcomes sinners and eats with them" (Luke 15:1-2). R.

Which one of you, having a hundred sheep and losing one of them, does not leave the ninety-nine in the wilderness and go after the one that is lost until he finds it? (Luke 15:4). R.

He calls together his friends and neighbors, saying to them, "Rejoice with me, for I have found my sheep that was lost." I tell you, there will be more joy in heaven over one sinner who repents than over ninety-nine righteous persons who need no repentance (Luke 15:6-7). R.

What woman having ten silver coins, if she loses one of them, does not light a lamp, sweep the house, and search carefully until she finds it? (Luke 15:8). R.

When she has found it, she calls together her friends and neighbors, saying, "Rejoice with me, for I have found the coin that I had lost." Just so, I tell you, there is joy in the presence of the angels of God over one sinner who repents (Luke 15:9-10). R.

While he was still far off, his father saw him and was filled with compassion; he ran and put his arms around him and kissed him. . . . "This son of mine was dead and is alive again; he was lost and is found!" And they began to celebrate (Luke 15:20, 24). R.

Prayer: Son of Man and Son of David, have mercy on us. You know our blindness, frailties, and failures, and you desire that we turn our hearts to you. Give us a restless enthusiasm to seek and follow you, so that we may experience your healing and saving presence.

5. Qumran

The words of Isaiah that inspired John the Baptist, "In the wilderness prepare the way of the Lord, / make straight in the desert a highway for our God" (Isa 40:3), also influenced the Jewish community of Essenes who established themselves as a monastic community in the desert, close to the shores of the Dead Sea. Disillusioned with the temple hierarchy in Jerusalem, they established themselves as an alternative community at Qumran in the second century BC, living there for several generations until they were removed by the Roman armies in AD 68.

Caves at Qumran that held the Dead Sea Scrolls

Model of jars and scroll fragments found in caves

The Essenes referred to their founding leader as the "Teacher of Righteousness." They devoted themselves to the close study of the Scriptures of Israel, especially the prophets, and must have understood themselves as forerunners of God's age of fulfillment. Through their lives of holiness and devotion to God, they prepared the way for the day of God's coming to his people.

The ruined site has been excavated and offers a strong sense of the community's life. It contains a tower, kitchen, dining hall, pottery workshop, and scriptorium or "writing room" where they copied Scriptures and the other literature of the community. Of special note is all the features connected with water: aqueducts, cisterns, and pools for purification baths form an elaborate system for water storage and ritual use. The cemetery contains more than a thousand graves, the bodies of which are mostly but not exclusively male, suggesting that at least most of the population had a rule of celibacy. While shared activities occurred within the compound, most of the members lived in tents and in the surrounding caves.

The residents of Qumran prepared for the onslaught of the Roman armies by hiding their precious library in the many caves to the west of the site. These documents, known collectively as the Dead Sea Scrolls, were preserved for two millennia in the dry caves and discoveries of them began in 1947. In time, a total of eleven caves yielded these treasures, which range from the twenty-five-foot-long Isaiah scroll to small fragments. The writings consist of nearly every book of the Hebrew Bible, commentaries on the biblical books, and literature defining the worldview and lifestyle of the community. The biblical texts are more than a thousand years older than the oldest of any previously existing manuscripts of the Bible in Hebrew. Yet comparisons indicate how little the sacred texts had been altered during that interval. This offers us assurance of the carefulness of those who transmitted the texts and great confidence that the biblical texts we have today are very close to the original texts.

Many have speculated that John the Baptist may have been a member of the Qumran community in his earlier life. Both were active in approximately the same area at the same time, and there are clear parallels between the ascetical lifestyle of John and that of the Essenes. Both emphasized the ritual use of water and believed they were preparing for the one coming in fulfillment of Isaiah. Yet, John's ministry went beyond that at Qumran, for he was acting as a prophet, announcing the arrival of the promised new age and its key agent in Jesus.

Although it remains unclear whether any New Testament writers were familiar with any of the Essene writings, there are many intriguing parallels between Qumran and the New Testament. For example, like the New Testament, the Essene documents emphasize the contrast between righteousness and lawlessness, light and darkness, and the Messiah and Beliar (Satan). They understood themselves as living in a new covenant with God, and they longed for the corrupt temple in Jerusalem to be replaced by a people endowed with God's spirit of holiness—a belief similar to Jesus's understanding of himself as the temple's fulfillment and his followers' understanding of themselves as the Spirit-filled new temple. Yet, there are also significant differences between Qumran and Christianity, especially the fact that Qumran was an exclusive, separatist community, and Jesus was widely inclusive, giving his disciples a missionary mandate to all the nations.

Another site to explore the Dead Sea Scrolls is the Shrine of the Book, part of the Israel Museum in Jerusalem. Here fragments and facsimiles of the scrolls and early manuscripts of the Bible may be viewed, along with explanations of their historical importance.

Meditation

- How does the desert offer people the opportunity to draw closer to God?

- From what influences must I separate myself in order to follow Jesus Christ?

Reading: 2 Corinthians 6:14–7:1

What partnership is there between righteousness and lawlessness? Or what fellowship is there between light and darkness? . . .

Response: "In the wilderness prepare the way of the LORD" (Isa 40:3).

Happy are those
   who do not follow the advice of the wicked,
or take the path that sinners tread,
   or sit in the seat of scoffers;
but their delight is in the law of the LORD,
   and on his law they meditate day and night (Ps 1:1-2). R.

The wicked will not stand in the judgment,
   nor sinners in the congregation of the righteous;
for the LORD watches over the way of the righteous,
   but the way of the wicked will perish (Ps 1:5-6). R.

Depart, depart, go out from there!
   Touch no unclean thing;
go out from the midst of it, purify yourselves,
   you who carry the vessels of the LORD.
For you shall not go out in haste,
   and you shall not go in flight;
for the LORD will go before you,
   and the God of Israel will be your rear guard (Isa 52:11-12). R.

Do not quench the Spirit. Do not despise the words of prophets, but test everything; hold fast to what is good; abstain from every form of evil. May the God of peace himself sanctify you entirely; and may your spirit and soul and body be kept sound and blameless at the coming of our Lord Jesus Christ (1 Thess 5:19-23). R.

Prayer: Lord God, you brought your people into the desert to draw close to you and to be purified from the enslaving attractions of Egypt. Through our sojourn in the wilderness, may we be cleansed from the attractions of sin and long for the transforming gift of your word. Build us into your holy temple, filled with the gifts of the Holy Spirit.

Jesus in Jerusalem

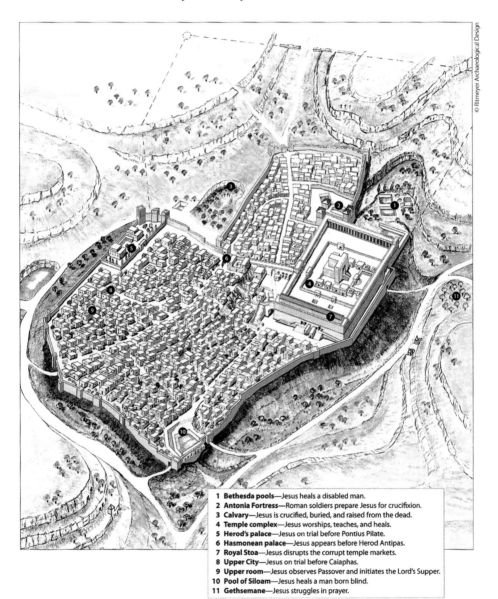

1 **Bethesda pools**—Jesus heals a disabled man.
2 **Antonia Fortress**—Roman soldiers prepare Jesus for crucifixion.
3 **Calvary**—Jesus is crucified, buried, and raised from the dead.
4 **Temple complex**—Jesus worships, teaches, and heals.
5 **Herod's palace**—Jesus on trial before Pontius Pilate.
6 **Hasmonean palace**—Jesus appears before Herod Antipas.
7 **Royal Stoa**—Jesus disrupts the corrupt temple markets.
8 **Upper City**—Jesus on trial before Caiaphas.
9 **Upper room**—Jesus observes Passover and initiates the Lord's Supper.
10 **Pool of Siloam**—Jesus heals a man born blind.
11 **Gethsemane**—Jesus struggles in prayer.

Image taken from The Baker Book of Bible Charts, Maps, and Time Lines, *© 2016 by John A. Beck. Published by Baker Books, a division of Baker Publishing Group. All rights reserved. Used by permission.*

Chapter VII

Jerusalem

The Jewish rabbinical tradition bestowed seventy names on Jerusalem, praising the city for its beauty and its perfection. The ancient name of the city, Urusalim, means "foundation of Shalem," the Canaanite patron god of the city. The popular meaning of Jerusalem, "the city of peace," comes from the Hebrew word "shalom," meaning peace, harmony, and wholeness. The city is also called "Zion" throughout the Bible. This poetic name for the city sometimes refers to the mount on which the temple rested but usually to the whole city and its people. Jerusalem is also called "the Holy City," "Salem" (Ps 76:2), "Mount Moriah," "Ariel" (Isa 29:1-2), and "City of David."

Jesus once called Jerusalem "the city of the great King" (Matt 5:35), recalling its long history as a royal city. Jerusalem came into prominence in biblical history when King David captured the city and made it his capital. Yet, David knew that the real king enthroned in Jerusalem was not himself but God. David's bringing the ark of the covenant into Jerusalem and his desire to build a temple to God there were expressions of his yearning to honor God as king. The psalms celebrate God's kingship and God's choice of Jerusalem. They proclaim Zion as the place where God exercises his sovereignty over heaven and earth.

Yet, Jerusalem was also the royal capital for Israel's human monarchs. God had installed his own king on Zion, and God's reign was expressed through the continuing dynasty of David. The kings reigning in Jerusalem were viceroys of God, anointed by God and charged with promoting God's reign of justice in the kingdom. The failure of the human kings to defend their people and to uphold honesty and social justice resulted eventually in the defeat of the kingdom and the destruction of its royal city Jerusalem.

Even in ruins, the city continued to be the focus of God's promises and the hopes of God's people. In exile the people of Judah began the practice of turning toward Jerusalem to pray. The prophets continued to speak of Jerusalem as the place where God's kingdom would be manifested. God's future Anointed One would bring about that final salvation for which all people yearned. The peoples of the earth would come to Zion to experience life as it was meant to be. God would establish a new Jerusalem more glorious than ever in which God would be king not only over Israel but over the whole world.

The New Testament writers, in proclaiming that the long-awaited Messiah had come to Jerusalem, evoked and reawakened all the ancient expectations that for so long had been associated with the Holy City. They knew that Jesus Christ and Jerusalem were inextricably linked and that what God had done in him had fulfilled the ancient prophecies about Jerusalem in unexpected ways and given new significance to the ancient city.

The climactic importance of Jerusalem for the life of Jesus reflects the centrality of the city within the whole history of salvation. The gospel writers interpreted Jesus's entry into Jerusalem as the coming of Zion's king. Humble and mounted on a donkey, Jesus came into God's own city as the divinely appointed ruler. Yet, by some perverse twisting of its destiny, this city of God had become the place where God's messengers could expect their fiercest opposition. The king was rejected and his only "throne" was an execution hill outside the city walls.

God would faithfully fulfill his promises toward Jerusalem, but it would not be through a physical restoration of the city or through its political independence. Paradoxically, it would be through the suffering and death of Israel's Messiah, then through the message of his resurrection going out to the ends of the earth. Jerusalem was no accidental backdrop to these events; Jerusalem was the one place where the true identity of Jesus could be revealed. Jesus said that Jerusalem would experience a fate similar to his own crucifixion, and these two tragedies were intrinsically linked. The Roman soldiers would eventually destroy Jerusalem, but first they would crucify the city's true king.

Yet, the resurrection of Jesus showed the way beyond Jerusalem's destruction. Jesus suffered in advance the fate of Jerusalem; likewise, Jesus was the first to experience the victory of resurrection for all believers. When the earthly Jerusalem lay in ruins, the saving news of resurrection continued to go out from Jerusalem to the ends of the earth. This work of

God's Spirit confirmed that God's saving plan had taken a new direction and that the exclusive focus on the historical Jerusalem was being eclipsed by the long-anticipated emphasis on universal salvation.[1]

1. The Center of God's Saving Will

For the ancient Israelites, Jerusalem was situated at the center of the world. "This is Jerusalem," wrote Ezekiel, "I have set her in the center of the nations, with countries all around her" (Ezek 5:5). A conception of concentric circles, continually focusing more intensely on Jerusalem and its temple, became firmly established in the Jewish rabbinical tradition: the center of the world is Israel, the center of Israel is Jerusalem, the center of Jerusalem is the Temple Mount, and the center of the Temple Mount is the temple. And within the temple, the holy of holies is where God came to dwell among his people.[2]

For both the ancient prophets of Israel and for the New Testament writers, Jerusalem was the central place of salvation history. For the ancient prophets, the movement of saving history was toward the Holy City, swirling centripetally toward the center. For the New Testament writers, however, saving history was moving centrifugally away from Jerusalem, outwardly to the entire world. The saving mystery of Jesus's death and resurrection dramatically reversed the direction of salvation's whirl, and the universal gospel began to expand its reach to all people.

Paul, the Jew educated in Jerusalem, tried to help his Gentile converts understand their spiritual debt to Jerusalem. Yet, Paul also understood the dangers of overfocusing on the earthly city. Paul urged his Jewish and Gentile converts to focus on the "Jerusalem above," for this transformed city of God is "mother" to all believers (Gal 4:26). The writer of Hebrews also called believers to set their sights on the heavenly Jerusalem, where Christ now reigns. This is the city that will endure, the goal of life's pilgrimage, the object of Christian hope. Knowing that the earthly Jerusalem would be destroyed, he said: "Here we have no lasting city, but we are looking for the city that is to come" (Heb 13:14). Finally, expressing

---

1. Stephen J. Binz, *Jerusalem, The Holy City* (New London, CT: Twenty-Third Publications, 2005), 1–11.
2. *Mishnah Kelim* 1.6-9; *Midrash Tanhuma, Kedoshim* 10.

the culmination of saving history, the book of Revelation affirmed the ancient prophecies that had foretold Jerusalem's future glory by describing the city "coming down out of heaven from God" (Rev 21:2, 10). This New Jerusalem pictorially expresses all that God has now achieved in and through Christ, the completeness of God's dwelling with his people.

Both the ancient Scriptures and the ancient city point the way toward Jesus the Messiah. Like the ancient sacrifices, temple, priesthood, and law, the City of David was destined to be eclipsed by the inauguration of God's new covenant in Christ. In light of the new, the former reality is seen as a shadow of the greater reality that was revealed in Christ. The resurrection of Jesus transformed all ancient reality; the historical city lost its saving significance for the present, but finds its eternal fulfillment in the risen Christ.

This New Testament understanding of the city in no way denigrates Jerusalem's vital role within salvation history. The Old Testament experiences of God's people in Jerusalem were not made invalid by the coming of God's Messiah. God truly dwelt among the people of Israel in the city of Jerusalem, yet that experience was localized in a way that is no longer relevant because of the resurrection and the coming of the Spirit. In the Old Testament that ancient city expressed God's eternal desire to dwell among his people and to form a community of peace around himself. Yet Jerusalem's role was inherently preparatory for the full accomplishment of that desire in Christ.

The history of Jerusalem did not end with its physical destruction by the Romans. In the early centuries of Christianity, pilgrims began traveling to the city to see the place of the Savior's death and resurrection. Christians already spoke of holy Scriptures and holy people; now holiness was attributed to a place: the "saving cave," the "most holy cave," the "most marvelous place in the world."[3] In describing the tomb of Christ as a sacred cave, Eusebius accented its character as a place of divine-human encounter. The sanctification of place was inevitable for a religion founded on the belief that God had become flesh in human history. By exposing to sight the tomb of Christ, Constantine unveiled the center of God's saving action in the world. Eusebius said that at this very place, "a new Jerusalem was constructed."[4]

---

3. Eusebius of Caesarea, *Vita Constantini* 3.31.
4. Eusebius of Caesarea, *Vita Constantini* 3.33.

As early as the third century, Origen knew of a tradition that the body of Adam, the original human being, was buried where Christ was crucified. Just as Paul had drawn a parallel between the first Adam and Christ, the second Adam (Rom 5), Christians of later generations would extend this parallel to the place of Christ's crucifixion "at the very center of the earth."[5] The tomb of Adam, the place of death's beginning, and the tomb of Christ, the first fruits of new life, come together at this place. In time, the new Christian "temple" at the place of Christ's crucifixion and resurrection would be viewed, like the Jewish Jerusalem, as the center of the earth. As the Temple Mount was the center of Jewish Jerusalem, Constantine's grand basilica to the Savior's victory over death became the center of the new Jerusalem. The mount of Calvary was the new place of sacrifice, and the tomb of Christ the new holy of holies.

Ezekiel had not only spoken of the departure of God's glory from Jerusalem; he had also prophesied its return. In Eusebius's *Life of Constantine*, he associates the new Jerusalem centered on the Church of the Anastasis (Resurrection) with the return of God's glory to the city. The magnificent beauty of Constantine's basilica indicates that the new Christian Jerusalem has begun to clothe itself in the biblical images of the everlasting, heavenly Jerusalem to come. From that most marvelous place in the world flows a river that brings salvation to all (Ezek 47:1-12).

2. City of Beauty and Sorrow

A Jewish guide relays to me a tale that the rabbis tell about Jerusalem: "Ten portions of beauty, God gave to the world; nine to Jerusalem and one to the remainder. Ten portions of sorrow, God gave to the world; nine to Jerusalem and one for the rest of mankind."

No other city in history has been as beloved and fought over as Jerusalem. The settlement on which the modern Jerusalem rests has been occupied for five millennia. It has been built, besieged, destroyed, and rebuilt over and over again throughout its history. Among its conquerors are pharaohs, Jebusites, Israelites, Babylonians, Persians, Greeks, Romans, Arabs, Crusaders, Ayyubids, Mamluks, and Ottomans.

---

5. Cyril of Jerusalem, *Catechetical Lectures* 13.28.

Coins issued by the Roman emperor to celebrate the capture of Judea and Jerusalem in AD 70

Model of a portion of the Arch of Titus commemorating the fall of Jerusalem and the destruction of the temple

Billions of people today revere Jerusalem as a holy city. The fact that Jerusalem is sacred to the three major monotheistic religions is both its blessing and its curse. Their common history goes back four thousand years to Abraham, the patriarch of Judaism, Christianity, and Islam. In an ideal world, the children of Abraham—Jews, Christians, and Muslims—would find common ground in their historical roots and in the one God they worship. They would seek to create that justice which is the highest aspiration of each religion and live together in the peace of the one God. But this world is not the kingdom to come and Jerusalem is at the vortex where bitter history, politics, and religion meet. In reality, the frailty of humanity is nowhere more apparent than here.

Jerusalem must be experienced with all the senses. Its sights, sounds, smells, and textures are like nowhere else on earth. Arab men with heads wrapped in keffiyas, Jewish men wearing skullcaps, women in head scarves, Franciscans in brown habits, children with every imaginable hue of skin and facial features—all reflect the diverse global roots of the people who inhabit the city. Jutting up from the cityscape are Christian crosses, Islamic crescents, and Jewish menorahs and stars of David. The Arabic chant from the mosques, the sound of church bells, and the Jewish chanted prayers create a dissonant harmony. Smells of coffee, produce, spices, and incense waft from the shops and houses into the cobbled streets.

When viewing Jerusalem from the hills that surround the city, the pilgrim knows that the atmosphere of the city is saturated with prayers and dreams. Here the memories of past centuries and the hopes of future ages force people to confront the big questions about God and human purpose.

For religious Jews, Jerusalem is not just a city that holds ancient memories; it is the focus of future promises. As envisioned by the ancient prophets, Jerusalem will be the center of God's rule on earth. God's people will be redeemed through the coming of the messiah who will make his appearance in Jerusalem.

One rabbi compared the world to a human eye: "The white of the eye is the ocean which surrounds the whole world; the iris is the inhabited land; the pupil is Jerusalem." Jerusalem is the center of the Jewish world. Their Sabbath prayers facing Jerusalem express a deep longing for the restoration of the city. Year after year, Jews the world over conclude their traditional Passover meal with the longing words, "Next year in Jerusalem."

Christianity inherited the recognition of Jerusalem as a holy city from the Scriptures of ancient Israel. In addition, Christianity honors Jerusalem as the place where Jesus lived, died, rose from the dead, ascended to heaven, and sent the Holy Spirit. It seems natural that the faith founded on the belief that God had become flesh would honor the places where those incarnate events occurred.

In the fourth century, with the discovery of the tomb of Christ, the emperor Constantine transformed Jerusalem into a Christian city. He designed the Basilica of the Resurrection (today's Church of the Holy Sepulcher) as the new temple. Christians constructed shrines throughout the city to mark the places that have a special connection to Jesus. Pilgrims traveled to Jerusalem from places far and wide in a stream of pilgrimage that continues to the present.

Like Christians, Muslims consider themselves as inheritors of the faith of Abraham. A few years after the death of Mohammed in 632, Muslim armies conquered Jerusalem because they wanted to bring the land of Abraham's migration under Islamic control. They quickly transformed Christian Jerusalem into a Muslim city. In 691 the reigning Caliph commissioned Byzantine architects to build the Dome of the Rock. It was to be built on the site formerly occupied by the temple and was to be taller than the dome of the Holy Sepulcher. Muslims viewed the shrine as expressing the triumph of Islam over Judaism and Christianity. The site eventually came to be designated as the goal of Muhammad's night journey where he joined earlier prophets, including Jesus, for prayer, and where he was briefly taken up into heaven.

All the great religions insist that the test of true spirituality is practical compassion. From the beginning of its biblical history, the test of Jerusalem's authenticity as God's city was its efforts to establish justice within its walls. The city could not be considered holy unless it was willing to be fair and compassionate to its inhabitants, especially those who are poor and vulnerable.

It was not enough that people were able to experience God's transcendence in Jerusalem. The experience of God must always be incarnated in the treatment of God's children with compassion. Vertically oriented worship of God must be accompanied by horizontally oriented justice and forgiveness of people. The holiness of God must give rise to a deep understanding of the sacredness of humanity. Yet sadly, some of the worst atrocities in Jerusalem have occurred through the centuries when people have tried to gain access to God there, while neglecting the quest for justice and peace.

Though God certainly expresses the divine presence on high mountains, quiet deserts, and isolated caves, biblical history demonstrates that the populated city most fully expresses God's ideal for divine dwelling with humanity. By grace, God has been involved in the all-too-human city of Jerusalem. For thousands of years, this city has exerted an influence on people's imagination and aspirations out of all proportion to its physical size or its political significance. It has ignited passion and excited controversies, sometimes of worldwide proportion. Its future does not seem to be any less significant for the billions of people of the three monotheistic religions.

The New Testament vision of our ultimate future, the New Jerusalem, is not a pie-in-the-sky utopia. Because it is a graced perfection of the earthly Jerusalem, it offers a blueprint of the type of society we must seek to create in this world. It is a city not divided by race, stratified by ability, or segmented by nationalism. It is a community where justice reigns, where forgiveness is plentiful, and where peace flourishes for all. This urban vision is applicable to all societies throughout the world, but it must also pertain to the earthly Jerusalem today. It would be ironic and tragic if there, of all places, this biblical vision went unheeded.

As pilgrims following in the way of Jesus, we will forever be debtors to Jerusalem. For as long as history and earthly reality are important, Christians will be connected to Jerusalem and rooted in its soil. So, let us pray that all the sons and daughters of Abraham might create a city that is both holy and peaceful. Let us heed the words of the ancient psalmist: "Pray for the peace of Jerusalem" (Ps 122:6).

3. The Hills, Valleys, Walls, and Gates of Jerusalem

Although the modern city of Jerusalem extends far beyond the city of ancient times, we will focus on the primary topographical and structural elements in order to form a mental schema of the city in the biblical periods and the biblical parts of the city today. Our understanding of the primary hills, valleys, walls, and gates of the city will help us better understand the sacred geography as we explore it as pilgrims. Refer to the diagram "Basic Layout of Jerusalem."

Basic Layout of Jerusalem

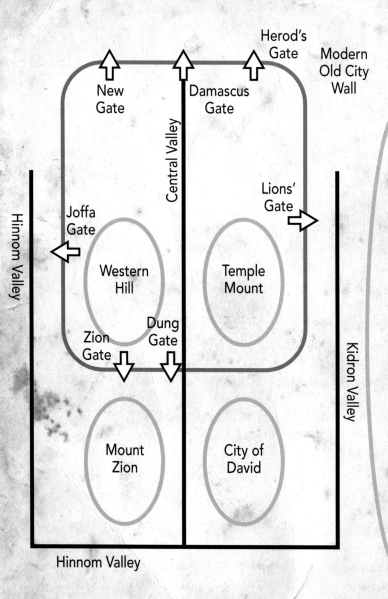

Excerpt from The Holy Land for Christian Travelers, *© 2017 by John A. Beck. Used by permission of Baker Books, a division of Baker Publishing Group.*

Locating Jerusalem's five hills will enable us to locate sites from the various periods of Jerusalem's history. The original city began on the southeastern hill or ridge called the City of David. As we will explore later, this was the city David captured and made his capital. The first expansion of the city began under Solomon when he built the temple on the Temple Mount, the northeastern hill. A few centuries later, under King Hezekiah, the walls of the city were greatly expanded to include Mount Zion and the Western Hill. The northern border to the city ran approximately from Joffa Gate to Lion's Gate. After the Babylonian exile, the city contracted again to the two eastern hills, but by the time of Jesus, the city had expanded again and grown larger than it had been in any era of the Old Testament. Although the fifth hill, the Mount of Olives, was never enclosed within the city walls, it has a prominent role in the city's history and offers a commanding view of the entire city today. The four gospels record events from the life of Jesus that occurred on each of these five hills of Jerusalem.

The five hills of the city are defined and separated by the three valleys. The most prominent is the Kidron Valley, which separates the walled city from the Mount of Olives. The steep gorge provided Jerusalem with natural defenses on its east side. In biblical times, it was sometimes called the King's Valley and the Valley of Jehoshaphat. The Old Testament mentions the valley as the place where God's judgment will be delivered, and Jesus uses it as the backdrop for his teaching on the temple's destruction and God's judgment at the end of time. During his final week, Jesus would have crossed this valley numerous times, passing from Bethany and the Mount of Olives into the city and back again.

The Central Valley, also called the Tyropoeon Valley or Valley of the Cheesemakers, is the valley that divides the eastern hills of the city from the western hills. Because it runs directly through the city, this valley has been progressively filled in with masonry and rubble and is the least noticeable of Jerusalem's valleys. At the time of Jesus, the valley was so pronounced that the western hills were connected to the Temple Mount with bridges.

The Hinnom Valley runs from the western side of the Old City and forms the city's southern defense. It meets and merges with the Kidron Valley near the city's southeastern corner. Although much of the valley forms a city park today, in the biblical era it witnessed some of the Bible's most dreadful events. At the time of the kings, God's people worshiped pagan deities there, even offering their own sons and daughters as burned offerings to Molech and other Canaanite gods (2 Kgs 23:10; Jer 7:31-34).

In the New Testament, "Gei-hinnom" became Gehenna in Greek and describes a place of sin and evil. Based on the hellishness associated with this place, Jesus himself used the word to describe the opposite of life in God's kingdom (Mark 9:43-48). The valley is also the place where Judas Iscariot took his own life. Before his death, Judas had returned the thirty pieces of silver, his payment for the betrayal of Jesus to the chief priests of the temple. Since it was "blood money," they could not add it to the temple treasury, but used the money to buy the potter's field as a place to bury foreigners. This part of the valley was thereafter known as Akeldama, the "Field of Blood" (Matt 27:3-10). The site is today marked by the Greek Orthodox Monastery of St. Onuphrius.

After becoming familiar with the hills and valleys of Jerusalem, let's look at the modern walls of the Old City, as shown on the diagram. These were completed by the Turkish sultan Suleiman the Magnificent in 1541. Notice that the present walls of the city do not include the City of David or Mount Zion. The walled section of the city has thus shifted northward from its borders during much of the biblical period. The walls of the city were destroyed and restored many times over its long history. Yet, when new walls were erected, there was often no need to quarry new stones. Rather the stones of earlier walls were reshaped and relocated to become parts of new and restored walls. So, touch any stone in the present walls of the city and you are quite probably touching a stone present during Scripture's saving events. Pilgrims may ascend the city wall near the Jaffa Gate and walk along its ramparts, traveling either northward to Herod's Gate or southward to the Dung Gate. In addition to the terrific views, plaques are positioned along the walks to help identity landmarks and offer explanations.

The walled city is divided into four "quarters" of unequal size, named for the dominant ethnic or religious identity of its residents. The Muslim Quarter, to the northeast, is the largest and most populous of the four. It includes the Temple Mount, with the Dome of the Rock and Al-Aqsa Mosque, the Pools of Bethesda, and part of the Via Dolorosa. The Christian Quarter, to the northwest, contains the rest of the Via Dolorosa and the Church of the Holy Sepulcher. It also includes the headquarters of several Christian denominations. The Jewish Quarter, to the southeast, adjoins the Western Wall, which is Judaism's holiest place. Because of its destruction during the wars of the twentieth century, this quarter is more modern, with

The walls surrounding Jerusalem today

plazas, parks, and reconstructed synagogues. The Armenian Quarter, to the southwest, surrounds the Armenian Orthodox Cathedral of St. James.

In addition to the hills, valleys, and walls of Jerusalem, the city gates are the final components to consider in order to understand Jerusalem's geography. There are currently eight gates in the city walls, seven of them are used today and one is sealed. The only gate on the west side of the Old City is Joffa Gate, which used to lead from Jerusalem to the port city of Joppa. At this gate begins the principal road from west to east in the Old City, leading directly to the Temple Mount. On the north side are New Gate, opened in 1889 to allow easier access to the Christian Quarter; Damascus Gate, beginning the principal north-south road through the city; and Herod's Gate, which today connects the Muslim Quarter with the Arab neighborhoods outside the wall. On the east is found Lion's Gate, often called St. Stephen's Gate, leading toward the Mount of Olives, and the walled-up Golden Gate, built over the ruins of the gate through which Jesus entered. On the south side are Dung Gate, which today leads inwardly to the Western Wall and the Jewish Quarter and outwardly

to the ancient City of David, and also Zion Gate, which leads from the Armenian Quarter to the sites on Mount Zion.

This overview of Jerusalem's topography is meant to orient the pilgrim with a simple schema. Yet this overly simple layout does not account for the vast variation in the hills, valleys, walls, and other structural details of the city. To make this basic layout come alive, look over the city from the Mount of Olives or begin exploring each part of the Holy City with a map or a guide.

4. Panorama of the City

Standing on the Mount of Olives, overlooking the ancient hills, valleys, walls, and gates of Jerusalem, enables the modern pilgrim to capture the feeling of expectancy sensed by our spiritual ancestors as they came over the crest of the Mount of Olives and gained their first view of the city.

Dominating the view is the golden Dome of the Rock, an Islamic shrine built over the jutting bedrock that served millennia ago as the sacrificial altar of the Canaanite city called Urusalim. To this rock Jews believe Abraham brought his son to be sacrificed, and around this rock King Solomon built his temple. In the courts of the later temple of Herod, Jesus taught and was challenged by the religious leaders of his day.

Jutting southward from the Temple Mount is the narrow spur called the City of David, the small city that David conquered and made his capital. Behind the City of David to the west stands the higher Mount Zion, the most prominent feature of which is Dormition Abbey, with its domed bell tower, a conical dome, and corner towers, resembling a fortress. Both of these southern hills—the City of David and Mount Zion—were enclosed by walls during the time of Jesus, but lie south of the city walls today. Behind the Dome of the Rock and on a hill to the west stands the gray-domed Church of the Holy Sepulcher. Although it is enclosed within the city walls today, this area was north of the city walls in the days of Jesus.

This landscape holds four thousand years of sacred history. It testifies to the works of God on behalf of his people through the ages. This "city of the great King" symbolizes and synthesizes the promises God has given to the world and the hopes of God's people everywhere.

Overlooking Jerusalem from the Mount of Olives

Two other sites will help pilgrims gain an overview of the ancient city. First, at the Israel Museum in the new city, a model of Jerusalem from the Second Temple period has been constructed. On a scale of 1:50, the replica shows the walls, towers, palaces, houses, marketplaces, and the impressive temple from the time of Jesus. Second, the Tower of David Museum, located at Jaffa Gate, presents the four-thousand-year-old history of Jerusalem using models, dioramas, film, and explanations in Hebrew, Arabic, and English. The citadel itself is a fascinating archaeological site, and its towers offer a 360-degree view of the city. The museum also stages unique performances at night within the citadel courtyard.

Meditation

- In what ways is Jerusalem the central site for both the Old and New Testaments?

- What thoughts come to my mind when I hear the name Jerusalem?

Reading: Isaiah 2:2-4

In days to come / the mountain of the Lord's house / shall be established as the highest of the mountains. . . .

Response: "Pray for the peace of Jerusalem" (Ps 122:6).

Jerusalem, place where Abraham was willing to offer his beloved son in sacrifice to God. R.

Jerusalem, City of David, the shepherd king, singer of Israel's psalms of praise. R.

Jerusalem, city of unity for the twelve tribes, capital of the united kingdom of Israel. R.

Jerusalem, site of the glorious temple, built by Solomon for the worship of God. R.

Jerusalem, city destroyed by the invading armies of Babylon and Rome, lamented by your people from age to age. R.

Jerusalem, city of Jesus, who celebrated your feasts and entered in messianic triumph on Palm Sunday. R.

Jerusalem, city of the cross, of the passion, death, and burial of Jesus. R.

Jerusalem, city of the resurrection, the ascension, and the descent of the Holy Spirit. R.

Jerusalem, great desire of devoted pilgrims in every age. R.

Jerusalem, sacred city for Jews, Christians, and Muslims. R.

Jerusalem, city of peace, sign of God's *shalom* for all the people of the world. R.

Prayer: Lord God, though all creation reveals your presence, you chose Jerusalem as the place of your dwelling. In its history of tragedy and triumph, you show your judgment and your salvation to the world. In this holy city, you prepared your people for the fullness of your coming among us. Lead us through the sacred texts of Scripture to experience this city of your Messiah, and establish your rule over our lives and lead us to the eternal Jerusalem, where you reign as King forever.

Chapter VIII

Mount of Olives

This hill, also called Mount Olivet, faces Jerusalem on the eastern side of the Kidron Valley, offering an unrivaled vista of the city and its environs. It takes its name from the groves of olive trees that covered its slopes from ancient times. It is first mentioned in the Bible when King David fled over the Mount of Olives to escape when his son Absalom rebelled: "David went up the ascent of the Mount of Olives, weeping as he went, with his head covered and walking barefoot" (2 Sam 15:30).

The Mount of Olives is one of three hills on a mountainous ridge. The hill to the north is Mount Scopus, which served as the base of the Roman army during the siege of Jerusalem and today is the site of Hebrew University. The hill to the south is the Mount of Destruction, named for the scandal created when King Solomon built pagan temples there for the gods of his foreign wives (1 Kgs 11:7-8). The mount was known for idol worship throughout the monarchy until the sites were finally destroyed by King Josiah (2 Kgs 23:13-14).

According to Jewish tradition, based on the final chapter of Zechariah, the Messiah will appear on the Mount of Olives and the resurrection of the dead will begin there. For this reason, Jews have always sought to be buried on the slopes of the mount and the hillside is covered by thousands of graves. The tradition further states that the Messiah will descend the Mount of Olives and enter Jerusalem through the Golden Gate, the blocked-up double gate in the eastern wall of the Temple Mount. Many of these grave markers have small stones upon them, a Jewish custom for honoring the grave and remembering the person's life.

Until the destruction of the temple, many Jews would sleep under the olive trees during times of pilgrimage to avoid the crowded city. Jesus knew the Mount of Olives well, often traveling there with his disciples and teaching them on this hill, while overlooking the city. During his triumphal entry to Jerusalem on Palm Sunday, Jesus went down the mount, weeping over the city's future destruction. He prayed there with his disciples before his betrayal and arrest. Finally, he ascended into heaven from the mount. By the sixth century, the Mount of Olives had twenty-four churches, surrounded by monasteries containing large numbers of monks and nuns. The churches there today testify to the many acts associated with Jesus on the mount.

1. Bethphage, Sanctuary of the Palms

A village made famous by a donkey, Bethphage commemorates the beginning of Jesus's messianic entrance into the Holy City. Jesus sent two of his disciples into the village, where he had made prior arrangement to borrow the animal on which he would ride into the city. The small Franciscan church was built in 1883 over the ruins of a Crusader church. Behind the altar is a fresco depicting Jesus riding a donkey to the temple, accompanied by his disciples. Around the walls, colored in shades of brown, frescos portray preparations for the procession. The main feature of the church is a cube-shaped stone from the Crusader church. The drawings on it depict two disciples bringing Jesus an ass and her foal, a crowd of people holding palms, the meeting of Jesus and Martha, the raising of Lazarus in nearby Bethany, and an inscription reading "Bethphage."

The Palm Sunday processions, celebrated in churches throughout the world, began here. Since the Byzantine period, the Christians of Jerusalem have come to the Mount of Olives to reenact the Messiah's entry into the city. The annual procession today begins at Bethphage, descends the Mount of Olives, crosses the Kidron Valley, and enters St. Stephen's Gate. The way is filled with crowds carrying banners, holding branches of palm and olive, and singing "Hosanna to the Son of David."

Jesus's entry into Jerusalem was a visual teaching and an enacted parable of the upside-down values of the kingdom. The familiar scene of a conquering king parading gloriously into a city is reversed, becoming a scene embodying the humble dignity that typifies God's kingdom. The king is dressed not in royal splendor or military trappings but in the simple dress of a Jewish teacher. He is meek and humble, not bellicose and splendorous. He rides not a mighty warhorse, but a young donkey. Jesus's royal authority is clearly in view as he triumphantly approaches

Sanctuary of the Palms at Bethphage

the majestic city and its stately temple. Yet, this is a king like no other. The mixed signals perplex the citizens and pilgrims of the city.

As he enters Jerusalem, Jesus acts out the prophecy of Zechariah in order to dramatize the kind of Messiah he is. The prophet had announced a king riding into Jerusalem, "triumphant and victorious," yet "humble and mounted on a donkey" (Zech 9:9-10). This royal ruler, for whom the people rejoice and shout for joy, is further described by the prophet as banishing the implements of war and commanding "peace to the nations."

The residents of the city and the pilgrims who came for the feast spread their cloaks along the road and placed branches from the trees to carpet the way, literally giving Jesus the royal treatment. They shouted "Hosanna to the Son of David," a cry of praise hailing Jesus as David's Son, the Messiah. The acclamation from Psalm 118:25-26 continued with the shout, "Blessed is the one who comes in the name of the LORD!" The people of Jerusalem were accustomed to crowds of high-spirited pilgrims entering the city for the feasts, but when Jesus made his entrance, "the whole city was in turmoil" (Matt 21:10). People were asking about the identity of the one who entered with such a flourish.

Meditation

- What might Jesus have wished the crowds to understand about himself by entering Jerusalem in such a manner?

- What is the meaning of the words shouted by the people as they greeted Jesus?

Reading: Matthew 21:1-11

When they had come near Jerusalem and had reached Bethphage, at the Mount of Olives, Jesus sent two disciples. . . .

Response: "Blessed is the one who comes in the name of the Lord!"

Open to me the gates of righteousness,
    that I may enter through them
    and give thanks to the Lord.
This is the gate of the Lord;
    the righteous shall enter through it.
I thank you that you have answered me
    and have become my salvation. R.

The stone that the builders rejected
    has become the chief cornerstone.
This is the Lord's doing;
    it is marvelous in our eyes.
This is the day that the Lord has made;
    let us rejoice and be glad in it. R.

Save us, we beseech you, O Lord!
    O Lord, we beseech you, give us success!
Blessed is the one who comes in the name of the Lord.
    We bless you from the house of the Lord. R.

The Lord is God,
    and he has given us light.
Bind the festal procession with branches,
    up to the horns of the altar.
You are my God, and I will give thanks to you;
    you are my God, I will extol you.
O give thanks to the Lord, for he is good,
    for his steadfast love endures forever (Ps 118). R.

Prayer: Son of David, the city trembled at your entry and acknowledged you as the one who comes in the name of the Lord. Enter our lives today and reign as our King and Lord. Hosanna in the highest heaven!

2. Chapel of the Ascension

The ascension of Jesus is commemorated at a twelfth-century octagonal chapel on the top of the Mount of Olives. The distance between this shrine and the city of Jerusalem is "a sabbath day's journey" (Acts 1:12), about half a mile, the maximum distance a Jew was allowed to travel on the Sabbath. An earlier shrine of the fourth century consisted of a circular colonnade, which was open to the sky. A rough piece of bedrock marks the place where an early tradition says Jesus left this world to return to the Father. The site was captured by the Muslim sultan Saladin when he defeated the Crusaders and, since Muslims also believe in the ascension of Jesus, it was converted into a mosque.

Although pilgrims may pray in the Chapel of the Ascension on any day, the liturgy is celebrated here only on Ascension Thursday. The iron hooks embedded in the walls surrounding the chapel are for tents set up for multiple liturgies. The Acts of the Apostles specifies that forty days separated the resurrection and ascension (Acts 1:3), marking a period of transition between the earthly and heavenly ministry of Jesus. The ascension

Chapel of the Ascension at the top of the Mount of Olives

Stone inside the Chapel of the Ascension commemorates Jesus's return to the Father

represents Jesus leaving this world and entering the presence of God. It expresses the reality that Jesus is not only risen, but now reigns in power and glory with the Father.

Before ascending into heaven, Jesus instructed his disciples to pray for the power of the Holy Spirit. After the Ascension, the church awaits the coming of the Holy Spirit at Pentecost with a nine-day period of prayer, the original novena. This anointing with God's Spirit includes various gifts given to each believer. Followers of Jesus are challenged by the angels not to "stand looking up toward heaven" (Acts 1:11), but to prepare for missionary discipleship. Through the gifts of the Holy Spirit and the ongoing spiritual presence of the Lord, we are called to be the church, to be witnesses to the gospel in every place and to everyone.

Meditation

- Do I seek Jesus by gazing to heaven or by doing his work on earth?
- What is the task of disciples between the time of his ascension and his return in glory?

Reading: Acts 1:6-12

They returned to Jerusalem from the mount called Olivet, which is near Jerusalem, a Sabbath day's journey away. . . .

Response: God mounts his throne to shouts of joy.

Clap your hands, all you peoples;
     shout to God with loud songs of joy.
For the LORD, the Most High, is awesome,
     a great king over all the earth. R.

God has gone up with a shout,
     the LORD with the sound of a trumpet.
Sing praises to God, sing praises;
     sing praises to our King, sing praises. R.

For God is the king of all the earth;
     sing praises with a psalm.
God is king over the nations;
     God sits on his holy throne (Ps 47). R.

Prayer: Ascended Lord, send your Holy Spirit to us so that we may understand your word and proclaim it through our lives. Empower us to be your witness and to continue your work in the world today. Come, Holy Spirit, come.

3. Eleona (Church of Pater Noster)

When we look today at the enormous stones that remain from the foundation walls of the Temple Mount, we can imagine what a magnificent structure the temple must have been and why the Galilean disciples of Jesus looked back in awe as they left the Temple Mount. But the response of Jesus, "Not one stone will be left here upon another," must have been devastating to those devoted Jews who looked toward the temple as the hub of God's radiating presence. Walking up the Mount of Olives with his closest disciples, Jesus halted at the grotto of Eleona (Greek for "olive grove"). In this cave, near the summit of the mount, Jesus instructed

*Remains of the ancient
Eleona Church*

Cloister containing the Lord's Prayer in multiple languages

them about the destruction of Jerusalem and future events, the so-called Olivet discourse (Matt 24, Mark 13, and Luke 21).

At the time of Jesus, the Eleona cave would have been a secluded and sheltered place for a small group to gather. The bishop and historian Eusebius wrote that "in that cave the Savior of the universe initiated his disciples in ineffable mysteries."[1] When the emperor Constantine built a three-level church on the site in 330, it was known simply as the Eleona. Recounting the Holy Week liturgies, the pilgrim Egeria related that on Tuesday of Holy Week, late at night, everyone goes "to the church that is on Mount Eleona. When they have come to that church, the bishop enters into the cave in which the Lord was accustomed to teach the disciples, and he takes the gospel book, and, standing, the bishop himself reads the words of the Lord that are written in the Gospel according to Matthew, where he says, 'See, let no one lead you astray' (Matt 24:4); and the bishop reads through that whole discourse."[2]

The Olivet discourse, in each version of the gospels, is written in language called "apocalyptic," as in the book of Revelation. It uses mysterious language to describe the course of history and offers a highly symbolic depiction of a climactic transformation of the world. Jesus compares the threat of wars, earthquakes, and famines to the labor pains that a woman endures in giving birth to a child. The metaphor emphasizes that the coming period of testing is integral to God's plan that will lead to the glorious return of Christ. Like the passion of Jesus, the suffering of Christians will end in glory. Jesus also says that "this good news of the kingdom will be proclaimed throughout the world" (Matt 24:14) before the end will come, tempering the excessive enthusiasm and speculation of many in the early church. The future fullness of God's kingdom, the glorious revelation of Jesus, and the vindication of God's faithful ones is God's to bring. The task of disciples is to pray for the coming of the kingdom and to stay awake, alert, and ready.

By the Middle Ages, the site was also associated with Jesus's teaching on prayer (Luke 11:1-13), and the Crusaders constructed the Church of Pater Noster (Latin for "Our Father"). Pilgrims of the time reported seeing the words of the Lord's Prayer inscribed in Hebrew and Greek on marble plaques. The present church and cloister, along with the first Pater

---

1. Eusebius of Caesarea, *Vita Constantini* 3.43.
2. *Itinerarium Egeriae* 33.2.

Noster plaques, were completed in 1874 by Aurélie de Bossi, the Princess de la Tour d'Auvergne. Later she added a convent for Carmelite Sisters and prepared her own tomb for the church.

The cloisters of the present church and walls throughout the grounds hold colorful ceramic plaques with the Lord's Prayer inscribed in many different languages. Notice the prayer in Braille just outside the doors of the church. Pilgrims may pray the Our Father together, each in a language they know.

Meditation

- What do I think of when I pray "thy kingdom come"?

- Why does Jesus tell us to stay awake and keep alert?

Reading: Matthew 24:1-14

When he was sitting on the Mount of Olives, the disciples came to him privately. . . .

Response: Keep me safe, O God; you are my hope.

If anyone says to you, "Look! Here is the Messiah!" or "There he is!"— do not believe it. For false messiahs and false prophets will appear and produce great signs and omens, to lead astray, if possible, even the elect (Matt 24:23-24). R.

The sign of the Son of Man will appear in heaven, and then all the tribes of the earth will mourn, and they will see "the Son of Man coming on the clouds of heaven" with power and great glory. And he will send out his angels with a loud trumpet call, and they will gather his elect from the four winds, from one end of heaven to the other (Matt 24:30-31). R.

If the owner of the house had known in what part of the night the thief was coming, he would have stayed awake and would not have let his house be broken into. Therefore you also must be ready, for the Son of Man is coming at an unexpected hour (Matt 24:43-44). R.

"Lord, when was it that we saw you hungry and gave you food, or thirsty and gave you something to drink? And when was it that we saw you a stranger and welcomed you, or naked and gave you clothing? And when was it that we saw you sick or in prison and visited you?" And the king will answer them, "Truly I tell you, just as you did it to one of the least of these who are members of my family, you did it to me" (Matt 25:37-40). R.

Prayer: Glorious Son of Man, you urge us to stay awake, alert, and ready for your coming in any disguise. We pray for the coming of your kingdom, that God's will be done on earth as it is in heaven. Come, Lord Jesus.

4. Dominus Flevit

Midway down the slope of the Mount of Olives stands the small chapel called Dominus Flevit (Latin for "the Lord wept"), built to recall the lament of Jesus over Jerusalem, the city of peace. Jesus loved this city and its temple, but he knew it was bringing destruction upon itself because of its refusal to obey its God. The words of Jesus over the city echo those of Isaiah, Jeremiah, and other prophets down through the centuries who

Dominus Flevit commemorates Jesus's lament over Jerusalem

warned Jerusalem's inhabitants of destruction and pleaded for their repentance. According to Luke's account, Jesus wept as he saw the city, just as many other leaders and prophets before him had wept over Jerusalem.

The chapel, according to the design of Antonio Barluzzi, is shaped in the form of a teardrop, with tear-catching vials on the four corners of its dome. Looking outward from its window, the pilgrim beholds a wondrous view of the walled city and its Temple Mount. The church was built inside the ruins of a fifth-century church and has incorporated some of its remains. An elaborate mosaic floor from the ancient church has been preserved next to the entrance. At the foot of the altar, a mosaic of a hen gathering her chicks under her wings recalls the sorrowful words of Jesus: "Jerusalem, Jerusalem, the city that kills the prophets and stones those who are sent to it! How often have I desired to gather your children together as a hen gathers her brood under her wings, and you were not willing!" (Luke 13:34).

In the days of Jesus, the temple towered over the walls of the city as Israel's expression of God's presence, the place where the ancient covenant was renewed each day through praise and sacrifice, the place where God's glory dwelt and where God's name was honored. But Jesus knew that his efforts to bring about repentance and forgiveness for God's people would end in his own death. He knew further that this city of peace would not know peace because it could not recognize the call to return to God.

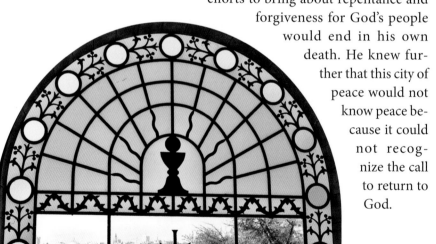

Window behind the altar looks over the city of Jerusalem

The destruction of Jerusalem at the hands of the Romans—described by Jesus as setting up ramparts, hemming in on every side, crushing to the ground, and not leaving one stone upon another—occurred forty years after Jesus's utterance. Like the prophets who warned Jerusalem of its destruction by the Babylonians in the sixth century BC, Jesus portends the imminent destruction of the city of peace.

Meditation

- What does Jesus's saying about the hen who "gathers her brood under her wings" tell me about him?

- Can I imagine Jesus weeping over my city and my world?

Reading: Luke 19:41-44

As Jesus came near and saw the city, he wept over it. . . .

Response: If you had only recognized on this day the things that make for peace!

"The wall of Jerusalem is broken down, and its gates have been destroyed by fire." When I heard these words I sat down and wept, and mourned for days, fasting and praying before the God of heaven (Neh 1:3-4). R.

Let my eyes run down with tears night and day,
    and let them not cease,
for the virgin daughter—my people—is struck down with a crushing blow,
    with a very grievous wound (Jer 14:17). R.

We look for peace, but find no good;
    for a time of healing, but there is terror instead.
We acknowledge our wickedness, O LORD,
    the iniquity of our ancestors,
    for we have sinned against you (Jer 14:19-20). R.

Prayer: Lord of the future, as you wept over Jerusalem you expressed a profound understanding of human sin. As you teach us to repent and trust in you, forgive the sins of your people. Show us the things that make for peace and how to place our hope in the new and eternal Jerusalem where every tear will be wiped away.

5. *Basilica of the Agony*

Knowing that he would soon be betrayed and arrested, Jesus went with his disciples across the Kidron Valley to the foot of the Mount of Olives. He could have chosen to continue walking up the mount, over its top, and into the desert to escape his betrayer and the soldiers. But Jesus stopped that evening at an olive grove called Gethsemane where he prayed and agonized over his pending passion. Since it was the eve of Passover, the moon was full, casting shadows from the olive branches that surrounded him. The gnarled and ancient olive trees there today look as though they could have been the silent witnesses to Jesus's sorrowful prayer to the Father that fateful night.

Gethsemane is accentuated by the haunting beauty of the Basilica of the Agony. The dim interior evokes the grief of that terrible night. The architect, Antonio Barluzzi, evoked the nighttime of the agony by leaving the interior in semi-darkness, relieved only by subdued natural light filtered through violet-blue alabaster windows. The somber blue of a star-studded night sky is re-created in the ceiling domes, the stars being framed by olive branches reminiscent of the view that Jesus and his disciples had in the Gethsemane garden that night.

The focus of the church is the flat outcrop of worn rock, surrounded by a metal crown of thorns. A long Christian tradition identifies this as the Rock of Agony where Jesus fell prostrate in prayer: "My Father, if it is possible, let this cup pass from me; yet not what I want but what you want." Behind the rock is the altar, the base of which forms a cup, referring to the prayer of Jesus that the cup of suffering pass from him. The protrusion of rock extends to the outside of the church as well, to be venerated by those who are unable to touch the stone inside the church.

Large mosaics are seen in each of the three apses. In the center, Christ in agony collapses on the rock while being consoled by an angel. The three disciples overcome by sleep are seen behind the olive trees to the right. Beneath are the words of the gospel in Latin describing the scene: "And an angel appeared to him from heaven, comforting him. He was in such agony and he prayed so fervently that his sweat became like drops of blood falling on the ground" (Luke 22:43-44). In the apse of the left aisle, the mosaic presents the kiss by which Judas identified and betrayed Jesus.

Ancient olive trees growing in Gethsemane

The dim interior of the Basilica of the Agony

Rock of Agony where Jesus fell prostrate in prayer

The three disciples stand to the left and the guards to the right, holding a torch. In the right apse is the scene of Jesus's arrest as told in John's gospel. When Jesus identified himself with the words "I am," the guards stepped back and fell to the ground. On the left, the three disciples are depicted at the moment when Peter was prepared to draw his sword to defend Jesus. Jesus is shown with arms open, ready to accept his fate (John 18:1-11).

A Byzantine and later a Crusader church were built on this same site where it is believed that Jesus prayed to the Father hours before his crucifixion. Parts of the mosaic floor of the original Byzantine church were discovered and are now preserved under glass inserts throughout the church. The architect decided to copy this fourth-century mosaic design in the floor of the modern church, to suggest a spiritual continuity through the ages.

The narrative of the agony in the garden alternates between the emotional suffering of Jesus and his call to the disciples to be watchful, attentive, and prayerful. The writer offers a sharp contrast between the awful struggle of Jesus and the weariness and inattentiveness of his closest followers. Gethsemane reminds us of the choice Jesus made to abandon

Façade of the basilica with mosaic of Christ the mediator

himself to the Father's will and to pour out his whole self for us. It encourages us not to grow weary and yield to selfish temptations. It urges us to watch and pray, for we don't know when our greatest test of faith will come. In our life's agonies, we can turn to our Father who turns the darkness into light and defeat into victory.

On the façade of the church, the triangular area over the great portal displays a mosaic of Christ depicted as the mediator between God and humanity, on whose behalf he gives his very heart which is being received by an angel. On the left, a group of the powerful and wise acknowledge the shortcomings of their might and learning; on the right, a throng of lowly people, in tears, look to him with confidence. Both groups are kneeling in prayer before Jesus, who receives the prayers of all humanity with open arms and commends them to the Father, the beginning and end of all things. Below the mosaic, statues of the four evangelists are separated by three arches. Between the mosaic and the statues are the Latin words from Hebrews, which clarify the meaning of the scene: "He offered prayers and supplications with loud cries and tears and he was heard because of his reverence" (Heb 5:7).

Meditation

- What are some of the emotions Jesus must have experienced at Gethsemane?

- How can I stay more watchful and trustful as I anticipate the struggles of life?

Reading: Matthew 26:36-46

Then Jesus went with them to a place called Gethsemane. . . .

Response: Let not my will but yours be done.

Why are you cast down, O my soul,
    and why are you disquieted within me?
Hope in God; for I shall again praise him,
    my help and my God (Ps 42:11). R.

Do not cast me away from your presence,
    and do not take your holy spirit from me.

Restore to me the joy of your salvation,
>   and sustain in me a willing spirit (Ps 51:11-12). R.

For my enemies speak concerning me,
>   and those who watch for my life consult together.
They say, "Pursue and seize that person
>   whom God has forsaken,
>   for there is no one to deliver" (Ps 71:10-11). R.

The snares of death encompassed me;
>   the pangs of Sheol laid hold on me;
>   I suffered distress and anguish.
Then I called on the name of the LORD:
>   "O LORD, I pray, save my life!" (Ps 116:3-4). R.

Prayer: Lord Jesus, you experienced distress, rejection, and loneliness in this place of agony and betrayal. Be with us in our dark nights of weariness, indifference, and fear. Taught by the weakness of your disciples, may we learn to conform our will to the will of the Father with a life dedicated to prayer and vigilance.

6. *Tomb of the Virgin Mary*

At the annunciation, the angel greeted Mary as "full of grace." At the visitation, Elizabeth addressed Mary as "mother of my Lord," a royal accolade for the queen mother, heard in the courts of Jerusalem and other royal cities of the ancient world. In her own canticle, Mary sang, "Surely, from now on all generations will call me blessed." In the nativity, the simple maiden gave birth to the Son of God, the Lord and Savior of the world. "More honorable than the cherubim, more glorious than the seraphim," the liturgy of the Orthodox and Eastern Catholic Churches sings her praises throughout the ages.

Sacred tradition tells us the holy body of Mary was carried in procession by the apostles through Jerusalem and laid in a tomb near the Garden of Gethsemane. The apostles sealed the tomb with a large stone and remained there praying and chanting the psalms. Thomas the apostle was not present at the death and burial of Mary, and when he arrived late on the third day, he asked that he might be permitted to look once

more upon her body and bid her farewell. When the apostles opened the tomb for him, they found only the grave wrappings and were thus convinced of the bodily assumption. This was confirmed by the message of an angel and by her appearance to the apostles.[3]

At the foot of the Mount of Olives, a large crypt containing the empty tomb of the Virgin Mary is all that remains of the fifth-century Church of the Assumption. Entering through the facade of a twelfth-century

Crusader-era entrance to the fifth-century Church of the Assumption

Crusader basilica, pilgrims find a wide stairway that leads to the crypt. Partway down, on the right, is a niche dedicated to Mary's parents, Sts. Anne and Joachim, and on the left, a niche dedicated to Mary's husband, St. Joseph. The smell of incense fills the dark and gloomy crypt, filled with an abundance of candles, gold and silver lamps, and icons. The Greek Orthodox and the Armenian Orthodox share possession of the crypt, with the Syriac, Coptic, and Ethiopian Orthodox sharing minor rights. A *mihrab* pointing toward Mecca was installed after Saladin's conquest in the twelfth century, since Muhammad saw a light over Mary's tomb during his night journey to Jerusalem, making the crypt holy also to Muslims.

Turning right at the bottom of the stairway, a shrine houses a stone bench on which Mary's body was laid. Pilgrims may enter to venerate the tomb, and they may touch the stone through three holes in the front of the shrine. The idea of isolating the tomb in the middle of the crypt was suggested by the tomb of Christ where, a century earlier, Constantine's engineers had cut away the surrounding rock to isolate the holy sepulcher. An octagonal-shaped church was built on the upper level in the fifth century. During the Crusader period, a larger church was built on the upper level and a monastery was added—the Abbey of St. Mary of the

3. Stephen J. Binz, *Transformed by God's Word* (Notre Dame, IN: Ave Maria Press, 2016), 207.

Valley of Jehoshaphat—which was protected by a wall. Today's entrance and staircase were part of this Crusader church.

The book of Revelation introduces the "woman clothed with the sun" as the ark of the covenant in heaven. As the visionary sees the ark revealed when God's heavenly temple is opened, the heavenly woman is seen as "a great portent appeared in heaven." As the ark was the bearer of God's presence in ancient Israel, Mary is the ark of the new covenant, the eternal bearer of God's presence in her son. Mary is the Theotokos, the one who gave birth to God on earth, and her holy body was not left to the vicissitudes of the transitory world, but was incomparably exalted by its glorious ascent to heaven. The commemoration of Mary's assumption into heaven is a celebration of our human nature, for in Mary, human nature has reached its goal.

Meditation

- How does the face of Mary in icons lead me to her son?

- How does Mary evoke in me a desire to share in divine life?

Reading: Revelation 11:19–12:6

Then God's temple in heaven was opened, and the ark of his covenant was seen. . . .

Response: Glorious things are said of you, O Virgin Mary.

Virgin Mother of God, assumed into heaven as the beginning and image of the church's coming to perfection, be a sign of sure hope and comfort to your pilgrim people. R.

The crypt containing the empty tomb of the Virgin Mary

Queen of heaven and earth, exalted over all the earth, may all people glorify Christ the King, whose kingdom will endure forever. R.

How lovely and beautiful are you, O Virgin Mary, you have left this world to be joined with Christ. Rightly he would not allow you to see the corruption of the tomb, since from your own body you marvelously brought forth your incarnate son, the Author of all life. R.

The angels rejoice and the archangels sing your praises, O Virgin Mary. Adorned with heavenly power you shine forth among the saints. R.

Prayer: O God, who looking on the lowliness of the Blessed Virgin Mary raised her body and soul into heaven, grant through her prayers that we be saved by the mystery of our redemption. As your only begotten Son was born of her according to the flesh and as she was crowned in heaven with surpassing glory, grant that we too may merit to be exalted by you on high.

Chapter IX

The City of David and Temple Mount

The City of David is the narrow eastern ridge sloping southward from today's Temple Mount. Outside the present walls of the city, this was the original city of Jerusalem, the heart of Israel's monarchy from the time of King David to the conquest of the Babylonians. Although this ridge is far from the highest mountain around, it possessed the natural defenses of the Kidron Valley to the east, the Hinnom Valley to the south, and the Central (Tyropoeon) Valley to the west. And, most important, it had fresh water gushing at its foot.

When David decided to conquer the city from the Jebusites to use as his own royal capital, it was already well-fortified. Knowing that the city was dependent on its one source of water, the Gihon Spring, which lay outside the walls of the city, David hatched a clever plan. Since a water channel was cut into the rock to create a large reservoir pool and a large tower protected access to the water source during times of siege, David and his men climbed through the water system to enter the city and took it by surprise (2 Sam 5:8). Having conquered the city, David built his royal palace on the upper part of the ridge, and he brought the ark of the covenant into the city, amplifying its status as the religious center of the united kingdom (2 Sam 6:1-19).

A visit to the City of David begins at a high observation point overlooking biblical Jerusalem. Constructed in the eighteenth century BC as the fortified city of Salem on the ridge above the spring, here Abraham met with Melchizedek, king and priest of Salem (Gen 14:18-20). At the summit of the excavated area is a massive stepped-stone structure, dating from before the tenth century BC, which served as a retaining wall either for David's palace or for the Canaanite fortress that preceded it. Excavators unearthed bullae (clay seals) bearing names of officials mentioned in the Bible. Moving along the excavated slope, visitors continue underground to the Gihon Spring and then either follow the Canaanite tunnel or trek through the knee-deep water in King Hezekiah's water tunnel from the eighth century BC, one of the wonders of early engineering (2 Chron 32:2-4, 30). After reaching the Pool of Siloam, visitors may walk northward toward the Temple Mount along the ancient roadway built by King Herod.

The son of David, King Solomon, built the first temple of Jerusalem on Mount Moriah, just north of the City of David. David had bought the Jebusite threshing floor on the windy hilltop where Abraham had prepared to sacrifice Isaac many centuries before, and he "built there an altar to the Lord" (2 Sam 24:25). Solomon's lavish temple, built of stone and timber with an exterior of white marble and a gold-plated facade, was to provide a fitting resting place for the ark of the covenant. Built around 950 BC, it served as the central place for offering sacrifice to God. It stood for several centuries, until invading Babylonians destroyed it and took many of the Jews into exile. The Mishnah says the ark of the covenant was hidden in an underground chamber, but what became of it is unknown.

Fifty years later, the Jews were allowed to return from Babylon. They rebuilt the temple, completing it in 515 BC, but were disappointed that it didn't approach the magnificence of Solomon's temple. The temple Jesus knew was rebuilt by Herod the Great in a project he began around 20 BC. He began his grandiose project by extending the Temple Mount on the north, south, and west to create a vast platform bordered by a retaining wall of huge limestone blocks. This is the platform that still exists in ruined form today. Although the temple had already been rebuilt once, Herod's temple is still known in Jewish tradition as the Second Temple.

1. The Temple Mount

The vista of Jerusalem's Temple Mount looks quite different today than it did when Jesus entered the city from the Mount of Olives. The remains of the temple platform are dominated by the Dome of the Rock, a golden-domed shrine sacred to Islam. The whole area of the Temple Mount, known to Muslims as Haram esh-Sharif or the Noble Sanctuary, including all its minor domes, shrines, colonnades, and fountains, is regarded as a mosque, Islam's third holiest site, after Mecca and Medina.

The Dome of the Rock is an octagon structure, built in 691, over the "foundation rock." In Jewish tradition, the rock is the place where Abraham came to sacrifice his son Isaac. According to Muslim tradition, the rock is the place where Muhammad ascended to paradise and then back to Mecca after his night journey on the winged steed called Al-Burak. In constructing the shrine, the caliph wanted to stress the superior truth of Islam over both Judaism and Christianity and to outshine the splendor of the Byzantine churches. As of this writing, only Muslims may enter the shrine and non-Muslims may not pray publicly anywhere on the mount.

Herod's Temple Complex

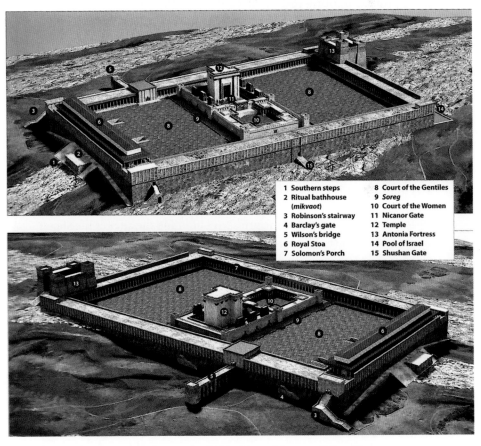

1 Southern steps	8 Court of the Gentiles
2 Ritual bathhouse	9 *Soreg*
(*mikvaot*)	10 Court of the Women
3 Robinson's stairway	11 Nicanor Gate
4 Barclay's gate	12 Temple
5 Wilson's bridge	13 Antonia Fortress
6 Royal Stoa	14 Pool of Israel
7 Solomon's Porch	15 Shushan Gate

Image taken from The Baker Book of Bible Charts, Maps, and Time Lines,
© 2016 by John A. Beck. Published by Baker Books, a division of Baker Publishing Group.
All rights reserved. Used by permission.

On the southern side of the Temple Mount today, the silver-domed Al-Aqsa Mosque, meaning "the farthest mosque," also commemorates the night travel of Muhammad, who according to the tradition was transported from Mecca to Jerusalem and back. Initially built in 705, the present structure dates to 1035. During the twelfth century, the Crusaders used the mosque first as their royal palace, then as the headquarters of the new Knights Templar. The Dome of the Rock was converted to a church and crowned with a cross. However, the Temple Mount was immediately reverted to Muslim devotion after the defeat of the Crusaders.

During the life of Jesus, this Temple Mount was crowned by the gleaming structure of the temple, constructed by Herod the Great. The temple stood as the dominant symbol of Israel's relationship with God. The historian Josephus said, "It appeared from a distance like a snow-clad mountain; for all that was not overlaid with gold was of purest white."[1] Its sacrifices, rituals, and feasts were central to that tradition to which Jesus belonged. Yet, like the prophets of Israel before him, Jesus challenged those who would pay attention only to the outward forms of worship without making their daily lives a means to honor God.

Although Jesus was the true king of Israel in the line of David, he came in humility and peace to the royal city. He traveled down the Mount of Olives, across the Kidron Valley, and up to the temple through the Golden Gate. Many events from the life of Jesus, especially during his final week, took place within the area of the temple. Since he was not a Jewish priest, Jesus would not have entered the temple itself. Surrounding the temple were four courts: the court of the priests (containing the altar of sacrifice), the court of Israel (for Jewish men only), the court of the women, and, on a lower level, the court of the Gentiles. Notices warned Gentiles not to enter the higher courts on the pain of death. Jesus spent much of his time teaching around the porticos, the covered and columned galleries around the edges of the Temple Mount.

The day after his triumphal entry into the city, Jesus entered the temple area and began to challenge the temple system and its leaders. Like the prophets before him, Jesus condemned the corruption of the temple through symbolic actions. Overturning the money changers and upsetting the business of those selling animals for sacrifice, Jesus proclaimed that the temple was to be open for all peoples and that sacrifice was no

---

1. Josephus, *War*, V.5.6.

Dome of the Rock on the Temple Mount

substitute for the work of justice. The meaning of Jesus's prophetic action can be discerned through the writings of the prophets. Jesus is bringing about the time, as prophesied by Zechariah, when all nations will worship God in Jerusalem and when "there shall no longer be traders in the house of the LORD of hosts on that day" (Zech 14:21). Quoting a passage from Isaiah, "My house shall be called a house of prayer / for all peoples" (Isa 56:7), Jesus indicates God's will that the temple be a sacred place where both Jews and Gentiles could worship God with reverence. Jesus also alludes to the words of Jeremiah, "Has this house, which is called by my name, become a den of robbers in your sight?" (Jer 7:11), as a description of the corrupt practices of the temple leadership. "A den of robbers" is where bandits take refuge and store what they have dishonestly obtained. Jeremiah was warning that God would destroy the temple because of those who try to hide their greed and injustices within its walls.

The prophetic action of Jesus on the Temple Mount caused the chief priests and scribes to fear him. They sought a way to put him to death because he was a threat to their religious authority as well as to their income and lifestyle. The scene points to the judgment Jesus will bring on the temple through his saving death.

Meditation

- What is the symbolism expressed in Jesus's prophetic action of cleansing the temple?

- How can I make my body a temple of God's Spirit and my actions a sacrifice to the Father?

Reading: Mark 11:15-19

[Jesus] entered the temple and began to drive out those who were selling and those who were buying. . . .

Response: Glorious things are spoken of you, O city of God.

Great is the LORD and greatly to be praised
    in the city of our God.
His holy mountain, beautiful in elevation,
    is the joy of all the earth,
Mount Zion, in the far north,
    the city of the great King (Ps 48:1-2). R.

We ponder your steadfast love, O God,
    in the midst of your temple.
Your name, O God, like your praise,
    reaches to the ends of the earth (Ps 48:9-10). R.

Walk about Zion, go all around it,
    count its towers,
consider well its ramparts;
    go through its citadels,
that you may tell the next generation
    that this is God,
our God forever and ever.
    He will be our guide forever (Ps 48:12-14). R.

On the holy mount stands the city he founded;
    the LORD loves the gates of Zion
    more than all the dwellings of Jacob.
Glorious things are spoken of you,
    O city of God (Ps 87:1-3). R.

Prayer: Most High God, you founded Zion on the holy mountain, not as a distant and exclusive abode, but as your universal dwelling place and a house of prayer for all peoples. May the sacrifices we offer be true expressions of inner faith so that we may bear the fruit of holiness and justice in your kingdom. Change the hearts of your people and bring all peoples of the world into the unity of your kingdom.

2. The Western Wall

Since the destruction of the temple by the Romans in AD 70, all that remains of the great complex built by Herod the Great is part of the retaining wall of the Temple Mount. Jewish pilgrims from around the world come to this Western Wall (in Hebrew, HaKotel) to lament the destruction of the temple, to remember their history, and to pray that God continue to listen to their petitions. For observant Jews, it is considered an outdoor synagogue and the world's most sacred place. Christians pray here in solidarity with their elder brothers and sisters in Judaism because of the history of salvation we share. After pilgrims pray at the wall and insert prayer petitions between the stones, it is proper to take a few steps backward upon leaving the wall rather than turning their back to it.

The Western Wall, foundation wall of the Temple Mount

Prayers of people from all nations offered at the Western Wall

Prayer at the site of the Western Wall started after the destruction and was discussed in texts beginning in the third century. For much of the two thousand years since the temple destruction, Jews were forbidden to approach the site and were harassed if they did so. After the Six-Day War in 1967, the holy site was returned back to Jewish control. The area in front of the wall, consisting of Arab housing and mosques, was razed to create today's plaza, stretching from the wall to the Jewish Quarter.

The visible wall contains twenty-five levels of stones, with another fifteen levels buried under the ground. The prayer area in front of the wall is divided into separate sections: a small section for women on the south side, a larger section for men in the middle, and a continuation of the men's prayer area through a covered passageway to the north. Orthodox Jewish men, fully bearded and garbed in black, are a common sight. They often read and pray from the Torah while rocking back and forth, a traditional method of increasing concentration and emotional intensity. Observant Jews pray three times a day, often with phylacteries tied around their forehead and wrist, while wearing white and blue prayer shawls.

In addition to viewing the wall above ground, visitors are allowed to tour the Western Wall Tunnel that reveals the hidden Herodian foundation excavated below ground. The tunnel starts at the Western Wall and extends to the wall's northern end at today's Via Dolorosa. The sights in the tunnel include the biggest stone in the wall, weighing 570 tons, with a length of 44 feet, height of 10 feet, and depth of 12–16 feet. It ranks as one of the heaviest objects ever lifted by human beings without powered machinery. The tunnel also includes a place of prayer opposite the foundation stone, the location of the wall closest to the former holy of holies, part of the quarry in which stones were prepared for the wall, and an ancient water reservoir called the Struthion Pool and its water channel.

The book of Lamentations was written out of the ashes and ruins of the temple's destruction by the Babylonians. The lament for the city and its temple is somber and is recited in the mournful cadence of a funeral dirge. The fractured images of Jerusalem's intense suffering are expressed through the image of the city personified as a woman—the ravaged, abandoned, and uncomforted daughter Zion. Both the people and the architecture express total suffering: the roads mourn, the gates are deserted, the priests groan, the maidens grieve. God's people through the ages have expressed the pains of tragedy and the grief of loss through these words.

Meditation

- What joins my prayer to that of the Jewish people?
- What prayer petition would I want to insert between the stones of the Western Wall?

Reading: Lamentations 1:1-11

How lonely sits the city / that once was full of people! . . .

Response: Cry aloud to the Lord, O wall of daughter Zion.

All who pass along the way
    clap their hands at you;
they hiss and wag their heads
    at daughter Jerusalem;
"Is this the city that was called
    the perfection of beauty,
    the joy of all the earth?" (Lam 2:15). R.

But this I call to mind,
    and therefore I have hope:
The steadfast love of the LORD never ceases,
    his mercies never come to an end;
they are new every morning;
    great is your faithfulness (Lam 3:21-23). R.

For the Lord will not
    reject forever.
Although he causes grief, he will have compassion
    according to the abundance of his steadfast love;
for he does not willingly afflict
    or grieve anyone (Lam 3:31-33). R.

How the gold has grown dim,
    how the pure gold is changed!
The sacred stones lie scattered
    at the head of every street.
The precious children of Zion,
    worth their weight in fine gold—
how they are reckoned as earthen pots,
    the work of a potter's hands! (Lam 4:1-2). R.

But you, O LORD, reign forever;
    your throne endures to all generations.
Why have you forgotten us completely?
    Why have you forsaken us these many days?
Restore us to yourself, O LORD, that we may be restored;
    renew our days as of old—
unless you have utterly rejected us,
    and are angry with us beyond measure (Lam 5:19-22). R.

Prayer: Faithful God, you allow your people to be afflicted with suffering
and grief, yet you offer the comforting hope of your merciful presence. Do
not forget your afflicted people or ignore the cries of your suffering children. Give us confidence in your faithfulness and trust in your promises.

3. Jerusalem Archaeological Park

The Jerusalem Archaeological Park is a dedicated zone of ongoing
excavations on the south and southwest sides of the Temple Mount, built
during the time of Herod the Great. These discoveries—including the
Robinson arch structure, a paved street, a flight of stairs leading to the

Image of the southwestern side of the Temple Mount in the time of Jesus

temple, and its gateways—show us the busiest and most commercial area of Jerusalem during the time of Jesus. Surely Jesus, his family, and his disciples walked frequently through this district.

Walking to the observation area below the southwestern corner of the Temple Mount, the visitor can see the massive size of the stones forming the foundation wall. The top stone of the southwest corner bore an inscription that read in part, "to the place of trumpeting." Here the priests would blow the shofar, the ram's horn, to signal the beginning of the Sabbath and other feast days. Looking downward to the street below, the visitor sees this very stone with its top carved into a gentle curve. It was toppled from the heights by the Roman troops in the destructive fury of AD 70. The street itself, a thirty-two-foot-wide thoroughfare, dates to the decades of Herod's temple. It was paved with large slabs up to a foot thick and lined with shops. Since some of the massive stones have been left exactly where they fell, here is graphic evidence of Jesus's prophetic words, "Not one stone will be left upon another."

Halfway up the wall are remains of Robinson's arch, which was part of a wide pathway that led the pilgrims from the street level, up through a staircase, across over the street, then into the southwestern entrance of

the Temple Mount. This was one of the several bridges that led into the temple. When Edward Robinson first noted the arch back in 1842, it was at ground level. Everything below it was the rubble of destruction, and the street level has only recently been uncovered. A building with four commercial shops was below the arch on the opposite side of the street from the wall of the Temple Mount.

Walking eastward to the south side of the foundation wall, the visitor reaches the excavated steps that led up to the gates used by most pilgrims to enter and exit the temple complex. This staircase consists of alternating broad and narrow steps, encouraging a more deliberate and reverential approach to the holy site. Although many of the steps have been repaired, they are a sure link to the days of Jesus. Jewish society converged here in the first century, especially during the three major pilgrimage festivals each year.

At the top of the stairs, the pilgrims reached a street, built with large paving stones. Then crossing the street, the worshipers entered into the Hulda Gates, which brought them through a tunnel and up into the grounds of the Temple Mount. Looking eastward along the wall, visitors may see the outlines of the triple-arched gate, although the gate is filled in. The ornate capitals that once were part of the gates were smashed during the Roman destruction, but excavators found many of the fragments that once decorated these gates. Further to the west along the wall was a double-arched gate, although only half of one arch is visible today. The rest is hidden by a medieval structure extending southward from the wall. This section still has a decorated lintel stone on top of the arch.

Dozens of ritual baths were part of the installations around the entry, so the pilgrims could purify themselves before entering the area of the temple. Because of the laws regarding purity, there was much demand for these *mikvot*. Some of the larger ritual baths include a divider separating the entrance route from the exit.

Jesus and his disciples must have entered the Temple Mount often through the Hulda Gates. On these steps he taught and healed. Jesus's parable of the Pharisee and the tax collector speaks of two men who "went up to the temple to pray." Although they each would have cleansed themselves in the ritual baths, only one was interiorly prepared to encounter God. The parable and these temple steps encourage us to make ourselves ready with humble trust and a contrite spirit as we approach the courts of our God in prayer.

Meditation

- What emotions do I feel as I imagine myself preparing to enter God's temple?

- What must I do to prepare myself to enter into God's presence?

Reading: Luke 18:9-14

"Two men went up to the temple to pray. . . ."

Response: "Enter his gates with thanksgiving, / and his courts with praise."

Make a joyful noise to the LORD, all the earth.
    Worship the LORD with gladness;
    come into his presence with singing. R.

Know that the LORD is God.
    It is he that made us, and we are his;
    we are his people, and the sheep of his pasture. R.

Enter his gates with thanksgiving,
    and his courts with praise.
    Give thanks to him, bless his name. R.

For the LORD is good;
    his steadfast love endures forever,
    and his faithfulness to all generations (Ps 100). R.

Prayer: Lord Jesus, you are the temple destroyed in hatred but raised up again in sacrificial love. Cleanse us from sin and give us hearts like the tax collector so that we may stand in your presence and give you joyful praise.

4. Pool of Siloam

Located on the southern slope of the City of David, the Pool of Siloam was a rock-cut pool fed by the waters of the Gihon Spring. When fortifying the city in preparation for the Assyrian invasion, King Hezekiah ordered the construction of a tunnel from the Gihon Spring to the Siloam Pool, which is today commonly known as Hezekiah's Tunnel. In an amazing feat, one group of workers began digging at the spring in the Kidron

Valley and another group started working from the Central Valley at the opposite side near the pool. After tunneling through solid rock for more than 1,700 feet, they met in the middle, more than 100 feet underground. By expanding the walls of the city to the west and enclosing the Central Valley, the springwater was able to be channeled into the pool within the city walls. Second Chronicles praised the king for this achievement: "Hezekiah closed the upper outlet of the waters of Gihon and directed them down to the west side of the city of David. Hezekiah prospered in all his works" (2 Chr 32:30).

As a freshwater reservoir, the pool would have been a major gathering place for Jews making religious pilgrimages to the city. The pool remained in use during the time of Jesus, about 700 years after Hezekiah, but was demolished and covered after the Roman destruction of Jerusalem in AD 70. In the years following, winter rains washed alluvium from the hills down to the pool until it was completely covered by layers of silt. Yet, the Pool of Siloam was rediscovered in 2004, leading to extensive excavations revealing that the pool was 225 feet wide and that steps existed on at least three of its sides. Portions of the pool remain unexcavated, as the land around it is otherwise occupied.

According to John's gospel, Jesus encountered "a man blind from birth." Jesus spat on the ground, made mud with his saliva, and spread the mud on the man's eyes. "Go, wash in the pool of Siloam," he said (John 9:1, 6-7). The man did as he was told, and he was able to see and to witness to the divine work revealed in Jesus. Since the man was blind from birth, receiving his sight was a new birth, coming from darkness to light, born anew through water and the Spirit. While the anointed king Hezekiah used the Pool of Siloam to provide flowing water for his people, Jesus the Messiah used the pool to open the eyes of the blind and to give them living water. The blind man is all of us who have walked in darkness and have been given the light of life. As we encounter Jesus, we must make a decision: either remain in the darkness or receive his salvation and walk in the light.

Meditation

- What do I want to receive from Jesus, the light of the world?

- In what ways have I experienced Jesus as the source of living water?

Reading: John 9:1-11

As [Jesus] walked along, he saw a man blind from birth. . . .

Response: The Lord is my light and my salvation.

Everyone who drinks of this water will be thirsty again, but those who drink of the water that I will give them will never be thirsty. The water that I will give will become in them a spring of water gushing up to eternal life (John 4:13-14). R.

Let anyone who is thirsty come to me, and let the one who believes in me drink. As the scripture has said, "Out of the believer's heart shall flow rivers of living water" (John 7:37-38). R.

I am the light of the world. Whoever follows me will never walk in darkness but will have the light of life (John 8:12). R.

Excavated Pool of Siloam at the foot of the City of David

Walk while you have the light, so that the darkness may not overtake you. If you walk in the darkness, you do not know where you are going. While you have the light, believe in the light, so that you may become children of light (John 12:35-36). R.

Prayer: Lord Jesus, you are the source of life-giving water. Open our hearts so that the waters of life may flow through us, healing, quenching, and giving us abundant new life. You are the light of the world, leading us out of darkness and into the light of life. Open our eyes so that we may see and believe. Continue to re-create us so that we may be bearers of light to others.

Chapter X

Mount Zion

Mount Zion is today's name for Jerusalem's highest hill, just south of the Old City walls and west of the City of David. Throughout biblical history, Mount Zion referred to different places within the city of Jerusalem. Originally Zion was the eastern fortress that David captured from the Jebusites and made his capital. After Solomon built the temple, the Temple Mount came to be called Mount Zion. Only in the Christian period, following the Roman destruction of Jerusalem, did the name refer to its present location on the highest part of Jerusalem's western hill. Here, several events central to the early church took place: the Last Supper, the appearance of Jesus before the high priest Caiaphas, the descent of the Holy Spirit at Pentecost, the Council of Jerusalem, and the falling asleep of the Virgin Mary before her assumption to heaven. So, Psalm 48, describing Mount Zion as God's "holy mountain, beautiful in elevation," has been sung about different mountains in Jerusalem in various ages of biblical history.

The southwestern hill, today's Mount Zion, was incorporated within the walls of Jerusalem in the eighth century BC by King Hezekiah. Parts of this Broad Wall have been excavated. The Central Valley divides the City of David from Mount Zion, although this valley is much less pronounced today than in biblical times because it has been filled in with the debris of the ages. The Hinnom Valley borders Mount Zion on its western and southern sides.

In the days of Jesus, Mount Zion was densely populated and enclosed within the city walls. It is the place where Christians returned after the city's destruction and where the church began to grow within the city. Here early pilgrims mentioned a Roman-era synagogue-church that belonged to an early Jewish-Christian congregation. It came to be known as the Church of the Apostles on Mount Zion. In the early fifth century, the Byzantine basilica Hagia Sion (Holy Zion) was built, which came to be known as the Mother of All Churches. The relics of St. Stephen were transferred here on December 26, 415. In the Crusader era, a monastic order was established on the site, known as the Abbey of Our Lady of Mount Zion, with a church built on the ruins of the earlier demolished Byzantine church. The area is today occupied by the Church of the Dormition and the Cenacle (or Upper Room).

As the Mount of Olives is the location of many Jewish tombs, Mount Zion is the site of numerous Christian burials. The Catholic cemetery holds the tomb of Oskar Schindler, a German industrialist credited with saving the lives of 1,200 Jews during the Nazi era by employing them in his enamelware and ammunitions factories in occupied Poland. The Protestant cemetery also contains the graves of many notable Christians of the city since the mid-nineteenth century.

1. Church of St. Peter in Gallicantu

After the arrest of Jesus in Gethsemane, he was taken to the house of Caiaphas, the high priest of Jerusalem. Here Jesus was interrogated by Caiaphas and mocked and beaten by the guards. Peter had followed the arresting party "at a distance" and sat with them around a fire in the courtyard while Jesus was interrogated inside the house. Here Peter denied his master three times.

The house of Caiaphas and Peter's denials are commemorated at the Church of St. Peter in Gallicantu, owned and maintained by the Assumptionist Fathers from France. Gallicantu means "cock-crow," and today a golden rooster is mounted in the center of the church's roof, recalling the words of Jesus at the supper that Peter would refute their relationship three times before the cock would crow.

The church was rebuilt in 1931 on the ruins of a fifth-century Byzantine church and a twelfth-century Crusader church. Sculpted bronze doors, depicting Jesus at the Last Supper predicting to Peter his triple denial, lead into the church's upper level. The stained-glass window under the dome shines light on the mosaics of Peter's life and Christ's passion that decorate the walls of the sanctuary. The lower church features three icons showing Jesus looking upon Peter after his third denial, Peter remorseful over his sin, and the risen Christ confirming Peter's mission. The lowest level reveals a guardhouse with handles carved into the rock

House of Caiaphas enclosed by St. Peter in Gallicantu

to which prisoners were chained. The most revered part of the church is the deep pit in which Jesus was held captive the night before his death. Byzantine crosses engraved in the stone reveal the veneration of early pilgrims.

While Jesus was on trial in the house of Caiaphas, Peter also found himself on trial. The judges were not the high priest and religious authorities of Jerusalem but a servant girl and bystanders around the fire that night. Peter's courtroom was the high priest's courtyard, where he testified that he was neither a friend nor disciple of Jesus. In this moment of trial,

Bronze doors of the church showing Jesus predicting Peter's triple denial

"I do not know him"—the moment of Peter's denial

Peter denied his relationship with Jesus, a bond that had been the deepest commitment of Peter's life. Although Peter had promised his fidelity to Jesus at the Last Supper—"Lord, I am ready to go with you to prison and to death!" (Luke 22:33)—he crumpled under his first significant challenge.

The crow of the rooster pierced the darkness of those early hours and startled Peter with the enormity of his denial. He had denied Jesus three times, one denial for each failure to stay awake and pray in Gethsemane. Luke's gospel heightens the impact of the scene by mentioning that, at Peter's final denial, Jesus turned and looked straight at Peter (Luke 22:61). Presumably the interrogation had just concluded and Jesus was being led down from the chambers where he had been humiliated and condemned.

While Peter "went out and wept bitterly," Jesus was being locked away in a deep dungeon where he would spend the night in torturous loneliness. The exterior mosaic of the church depicts Jesus being lowered with ropes into this pit and is captioned by a verse from the psalms: "You have put me in the depths of the Pit" (Ps 88:6). The whole of this psalm could have served as the prayer of Jesus that night.

The courtyard outside contains a bronze sculpture freezing the moment of Peter's denial: "I do not know him." Beyond the courtyard is a flight of old stone steps dating from the first century. These stairs, built into the steep eastern slope of Mount Zion on which the church is built, were likely trod by Jesus on his way to and from Gethsemane the night of his Last Supper and arrest.

Meditation

- How would the crow of the rooster be a reminder to Peter for the rest of his life?

- When my relationship with Jesus has been on trial, have I been a courageous or cowardly disciple?

Reading: Luke 22:54-62

Then they seized [Jesus] and led him away, bringing him into the high priest's house. . . .

Response: "Let my prayer come before you; / incline your ear to my cry."

O LORD, God of my salvation,
    when, at night, I cry out in your presence,
let my prayer come before you;
    incline your ear to my cry.
For my soul is full of troubles,
    and my life draws near to Sheol. R.

I am counted among those who go down to the Pit;
    I am like those who have no help,
like those forsaken among the dead,
    like the slain that lie in the grave,
like those whom you remember no more,
    for they are cut off from your hand. R.

You have put me in the depths of the Pit,
    in the regions dark and deep.
Your wrath lies heavy upon me,
    and you overwhelm me with all your waves.
You have caused my companions to shun me;
    you have made me a thing of horror to them. R.

Your wrath has swept over me;
    your dread assaults destroy me.
They surround me like a flood all day long;
    from all sides they close in on me.
You have caused friend and neighbor to shun me;
    my companions are in darkness (Ps 88). R.

Prayer: Merciful Lord, you have offered me the privilege of being your disciple and walking the way of your passion. Give me strength in times when I am tempted to deny you and forgiveness for my times of failure.

2. *The Cenacle, Upper Room*

The gospels relate that Jesus celebrated the Last Supper with his disciples in an "upper room" (see Mark 14:15; Luke 22:12), and the Acts of the Apostles describes the "upper room" as the place where the apostles

The Crusader-era Cenacle or Upper Room

and Mary, the mother of Jesus, gathered, "devoting themselves to prayer" (Acts 1:13-14). This upper room on Mount Zion, placed at Jesus's disposal for the celebration of the new Passover, became, after his passion and resurrection, the center of early Christianity in Jerusalem. Also called the Cenacle ("supper room"), this Upper Room has been revered since the early centuries as the place of Jesus's paschal meal and the institution of the Eucharist, certain resurrection appearances to the apostles, the gathering of the disciples after the ascension of Jesus, and the descent of the Holy Spirit at Pentecost.

Beginning in the fourth century, pilgrims reported a structure on Mount Zion commemorating the founding events in the Upper Room. Basing his writing on documents of the second century, Bishop Epiphanius (310–403) wrote: "Hadrian found the temple of God destroyed and the whole city devastated, with the exception of some houses and a certain small church of the Christians, which had been constructed in that place where the disciples, when they had returned after the Savior had ascended from the Mount of Olives, went to the upper room."[1] Of course, formal churches would not be built until the time of Constantine, so places of worship for Jewish Christians of the second and third centuries would have often looked like synagogues. The anonymous pilgrim from Bordeaux reported seeing such a synagogue here in the year 333.

The building has experienced numerous cycles of destruction and reconstruction, culminating in the Gothic structure that stands today, built by the Crusaders. Within the Crusader church, the Cenacle was formed by four chapels, two below and two above. Steps led from the lower to the "upper room," where the institution of the Eucharist and the descent of the Holy Spirit were represented in mosaics. Although much of the Crusader church was soon destroyed, the Cenacle remained.

The Franciscans took possession of the Cenacle in the fourteenth century, but after a difficult existence were expelled in 1551. The Upper Room was transformed into a mosque and access to Christians was forbidden. This situation lasted until the twentieth century when it was partially reopened for Christian pilgrims to visit, but celebration of the Eucharist or other devotions were prohibited. Architectural evidence of the period of Muslim control includes the elaborate mihrab pointing in the direction of Mecca, the Arabic inscriptions on its walls, and the minaret and dome

---

1. Epiphanius, *On Weights and Measures*, 14.

Chapel of St. Francis Ad Coenaculum near the Upper Room

atop the roof. The Cenacle, with its Tomb of David on the first floor, is currently managed by the State of Israel.

Jesus first went to the upstairs room on the first day of the feast of Unleavened Bread, the day the lambs were slaughtered in the temple and brought to each home for the Passover meal that evening. The owner of the room is not known, but this is not surprising in a culture that placed such emphasis on hospitality and where all families opened their doors to pilgrims and strangers for the feasts. The gospels do not elaborate on the traditional rituals of the meal or the recounting of the story of Exodus; only those parts of the Seder meal given radically new significance by Jesus are highlighted. The unleavened bread of the Passover is identified as the body of Jesus, and the ritual cup of wine is identified as the blood of Jesus, the blood of the covenant by which disciples of Jesus renew their committed partnership with God.

Those of us who return in mind and heart to the Upper Room week after week, to do again what Jesus did there, share in the paschal mystery which joins us in the new covenant. Although this room is empty today, the events that took place in this upstairs room continue to live at the heart of the Christian faith. What happened here is now renewed over and over again throughout the world as the crucified and risen Lord gathers us as his people in the Holy Spirit.

Since the liturgy is not permitted inside the Upper Room, the Franciscans returned to within a few yards of the Cenacle in 1936, building the Chapel of St. Francis Ad Coenaculum, allowing for services to be held near the Upper Room. At the front of the church stands a life-size bronze of the Last Supper in which Jesus holds up a large round of bread that, in fact, is the chapel's tabernacle.

Meditation

- In what sense is the Eucharist my nourishment for pilgrimage?

- In what ways is the Holy Spirit like a mighty wind, a gentle breath, and a penetrating fire?

Reading: Mark 14:22-26

While they were eating, [Jesus] took a loaf of bread, and after blessing it he broke it, gave it to them, and said, "Take; this is my body.". . .

Response: "Come Holy Spirit, fill the hearts of your faithful people."

O Christ, who sends your Holy Spirit upon our gifts of bread and wine so that they may become for us your sacred body and blood, may we always be nourished by the bread of life and the cup of our salvation. R.

O Christ, who told your apostles, "Do this in memory of me," send forth ministers of the new covenant through the laying on of hands in ordination, so that they may renew your holy sacrifice at the altar. R.

O Christ, who said to your apostles, "Receive the Holy Spirit; whose sins you shall forgive, they are forgiven," may we experience the healing and reconciling power made present through your Holy Spirit in the church. R.

O Christ, who promised that the Holy Spirit would teach us everything and remind us of all that you told us, safeguard the apostolic faith you have given to the apostles and entrusted to your church. R.

O Christ, who poured forth the Holy Spirit on your church at Pentecost, send forth your Spirit upon us to create us anew and enkindle in us the fire of your divine love. R.

Prayer: Come Holy Spirit, send forth your bright rays to confirm the hearts of those born again by your grace. Send your gifts across the face of the earth and fill the hearts of believers with the same fervor at work when the gospel was first proclaimed to the world.

3. Abbey of the Dormition

The summit of Mount Zion is crowned by the Benedictine abbey and church commemorating the place of the Virgin Mary's dormition or "falling asleep," a Christian term for the temporary state of earthly death. The traditions of Jerusalem tell us that Mary was taken to the home of John, the beloved disciple, to whom Jesus had entrusted his mother at the cross. Other traditions relate that Mary accompanied John to live in Ephesus for a time, but the earliest traditions all locate the end of Mary's life in Jerusalem. At the time of her death, the apostles of the Lord, who were preaching throughout the world, returned to Jerusalem and gathered at her bedside.

The woman who welcomed the actions of God's Spirit in her life at the annunciation, the mother who trusted Jesus to bring forth the new wine at Cana, the woman who watched Jesus beneath the cross and was given by Jesus to be the mother of his disciples, the woman who prayed for the

Life-size statue of Mary at her deathbed

coming of the Holy Spirit upon the apostles, this holy woman continued through her death to show the way to life. Her connection to her son was so intimate during his earthly life that she shared with him the experience of death and burial, and then was raised by him and brought to heaven to share in his glory.

The circular Church of the Dormition is a fortresslike building, with a conical roof and four corner towers. Nearby soars the bell tower of the Benedictine monastery. In the Byzantine era, the basilica Hagia Sion (Holy Zion) was built on this summit, a church which came to be known as the Mother of All Churches. In the Crusader era, a monastic community was established on the site, known as the Abbey of Our Lady of Mount Zion, with a church built on the ruins of the earlier demolished Byzantine church. The present complex was built by order of Kaiser Wilhelm II and completed in 1910, responding to a request to have a German Catholic church in the city following the kaiser's support for the construction of the Lutheran Church of the Redeemer in 1898.

The church is built on two levels, with the main altar and monastic choir on the upper of these, and the crypt with its Marian shrine on the lower. Light from several large windows pours into the upper level, brightening the mosaic of Mary and the infant Jesus high above the altar. Underneath her image are pictures of eight Old Testament prophets and the Latin prophecy from Isaiah: "Behold, a virgin shall conceive, and bear a son, and shall call his name Immanuel" (Isa 7:14). Six side chapels are decorated with mosaics, from left to right: the first depicts St. Boniface in the center, with St. Lioba and St. Mauritius; the center left portrays John the Baptist standing on the banks of the Jordan river; the first on the left of the center highlights Mary and the child Jesus surrounded by Bavarian bishops; the first on the right of the center depicts the family tree of Jesus; the center right shows Mary and child greeting pilgrims, including St. Willibaldus, the first English pilgrim to Jerusalem; and the chapel on the far right portrays St. Benedict, the founder of the Benedictine order.

In contrast to the luminous upper church, the circular crypt seems totally shrouded. In the center is a simple bier on which rests a life-size statue of Mary, fallen asleep in death. The figure is made of cherry wood and ivory. Her eyes are closed and her hands crossed. We can imagine the apostles gathered around her in prayer. The dome above the statue is adorned with mosaic images of Old Testament women: Eve, Miriam, Jael, Judith, Ruth, and Esther. Around the walls are several chapels, donated and designed by different countries. The reclined image of Mary

Fresco of Christ receiving the soul of Mary into glory

is facing a fresco showing Mary at her deathbed. Like the statue, Mary is lying in death. The apostles are shown gathered around her, while the presence of Christ, hidden from their physical sight, is shown in glory. He is holding the holy soul of Mary in his arms. She is wrapped in a burial cloth and presented as if she were a newborn child. The parallel between Christ holding the childlike soul of Mary and the many images of Mary holding Christ in her own arms indicates a purposeful reversal of roles.

We know that on that future day of days, Christ will come from heaven to raise us and transform us fully into his likeness. Then our perishable, mortal bodies will put on imperishability and immortality. Even now, we can sing a taunting victory song over the fallen enemy: "Where, O death, is your victory? / Where, O death, is your sting?"(1 Cor 15:55). Mary is the icon and model of what God will do for those who wait in faith, hope, and love. As the mother of Christ and of his disciples, she is the archetype and the supreme realization of our final glory. The tradition of the early church assures us of the glorious death and assumption of Mary, body and soul, into heaven. Rather than experience bodily corruption and await the final resurrection, Mary experienced the glorified life immediately after her death because of her singularly important role in God's plan for the world's salvation.

Meditation

- Imagine Mary surrounded by the apostles at her death. How does being a member of the communion of saints put my life in perspective?

- What graces might God wish me to receive through the intercession of Mary today?

Reading: 1 Corinthians 15:50-58

This perishable body must put on imperishability, and this mortal body must put on immortality. . . .

Response: May your mother intercede for us, Lord.

As Mary welcomed the actions of the Holy Spirit into her life at the annunciation, may we learn to listen to God's word and let it be done in our lives. We pray. R.

As Mary cradled you as an infant and guided your childhood, may we be guided by you throughout our lives and embraced in your arms when our life is done. We pray. R.

As Mary trusted you to bring forth the new wine at Cana, may we always follow her motherly invitation to do whatever you tell us to do. We pray. R.

As Mary stood beneath your cross and was given by you to be the mother of your disciples, may we trust in her maternal care and call upon her in our needs. We pray. R.

As Mary prayed for the coming of the Holy Spirit in the Upper Room, may we open our lives to receive spiritual gifts and be your witnesses. We pray. R.

As Mary died and was brought to heaven to share in your glory, may we be surrounded at death by the prayers of the saints and await your coming with joyful hope. We pray. R.

Prayer: Lord Jesus Christ, who dwelt in the ever-virginal womb of Mary, without you our humanity is trapped in sin and destined for eternal death. Through the intercession of Mary, shelter of orphans and guide for travelers, whom the grave could not contain, give us unshakable hope in the life of the world to come.

Chapter XI

The Via Dolorosa

The traditional route of Jesus, from the place of his trial and condemnation to his crucifixion and burial, is called the Via Dolorosa—the Way of Sorrow. It winds through the northern parts of the Old City, beginning in the Muslim Quarter near St. Stephen's Gate (Lion's Gate) and winding westward, through the Christian Quarter to the Holy Sepulcher. Via Dolorosa is the route and also the name of the principal street followed, a narrow marketplace crowded with traders and shoppers, similar to the busy scene on the first Good Friday.

On Friday afternoons, the Franciscan friars lead a procession along the Via Dolorosa, ending at the tomb of Christ. Many other pilgrims, individually or in groups with guides, follow the same route throughout the week. The devotion is also known as the Way of the Cross, the Via Crucis, and the Stations of the Cross. It commemorates the key events from Christ's final walk through the streets of Jerusalem, carrying the cross. The devotion originated in medieval Europe when wars prevented pilgrims from visiting the Holy Land. European artists installed sculptures or paintings along a processional route, either outdoors or inside of churches, depicting scenes of Christ's journey to Calvary. The Via Crucis meant walking the route, stopping to pray at each station. Today, fourteen stations are on display in nearly all Catholic churches.

Scholars debate the historical route Jesus followed on his way to Calvary. The primary difficulty in determining the path of Jesus is that the site of Pontius Pilate's praetorium, where Jesus was condemned to death, is unknown. The Via Dolorosa assumes it was at the Antonia Fortress, a vast military garrison built by Herod the Great north of the Temple Mount, with a commanding view of the temple complex. The first station stands on what is believed to be this site. Other scholars believe Jesus was condemned by Pilate at Herod the Great's palace, the citadel, the remains of which are just inside the present Jaffa Gate. Although scholars disagree on the path Jesus took on Good Friday, processions in the fourth and fifth centuries from the Mount of Olives to Calvary followed more or less along the route taken by modern pilgrims, except there were no individual stations. Although the exact route is uncertain, the Via Dolorosa is hallowed by the footsteps of pilgrims throughout the centuries.

1. St. Stephen's Gate

The eastern gate of Jerusalem is known by different names. Christians often refer to it as St. Stephen's Gate because of the tradition that the first Christian martyr was stoned to death just outside this gate. It is also called Lions' Gate because of the four stone lions, two on the left and two on the right, that decorate the gate's facade. According to the legend, they were integrated into this structure following the dream of Sultan Suleiman, in which two lions were about to devour him as a punishment for not fortifying the city for protection. The sultan interpreted the dream as a sign from above and ordered a wall be built around the city in the sixteenth century. The gate is also named Bab Sitna-Mariam (Arabic for St. Mary's Gate) because of the tradition that the Virgin Mary was born nearby and because her tomb is in the valley below.

Stephen is first mentioned in the Acts of the Apostles as one of seven deacons appointed by the apostles to distribute food and charitable aid to poorer members of the community in the early church. He is described as full of faith and the Holy Spirit, performing miracles among the people. Put on trial, he made a long speech before the Sanhedrin, recounting Israel's history of disobedience and resistance to God's work. Like Jesus, Stephen was accused of blasphemy, and false witnesses testified against him; like Jesus, he was condemned to death and taken outside the city to be executed; like Jesus, he prayed for forgiveness for his slayers; and, as Jesus delivered over his spirit to the Father, so Stephen in his final moments committed his spirit to Jesus. The parallels are made explicit in order to make the point that disciples are called to follow in the footsteps of Jesus as his witnesses in the world.

St. Stephen is known as the first martyr of the church because he died as a consequence of his bold profession of the Christian faith. He faced his death, in imitation of Jesus, with courage and compassion. The word

St. Stephen's Gate, also called Lions' Gate

Lions placed on the gate's façade following the dream of Sultan Suleiman

"martyr" derives from the Greek word for witness. Stephen gave witness to the Lord's death and resurrection in a supreme manner by giving his life to the end. He is the first in a long line of martyrs in the church, a heavenly assembly whose numbers continue to grow today.

Although the Acts of the Apostles recounts the martyrdom of Stephen, it does not indicate the exact location of his death or his burial. One tradition places the events at Jerusalem's northern gate, while another from the twelfth century locates the martyrdom at the eastern gate. In 415 a priest named Lucian had a dream that revealed the location of Stephen's remains at Beit Jamal. After that, his relics were taken in procession to the Church of Hagia Sion on December 26. In 439, the relics were translated to a new church north of the Damascus Gate built by the empress Aelia Eudocia in honor of St. Stephen. Although this church was destroyed in the twelfth century, a twentieth-century French Catholic church, Saint-Étienne, was built in its place. The Greek Orthodox Monastery of St. Stephen, built down the hill from St. Stephen's Gate, commemorates his martyrdom. The rock floor of a chapel at the base honors the place on which St. Stephen's body lay after being stoned.

Meditation

- How can I be a more fervent witness to Jesus Christ by imitating his life and death?

- Who are the martyrs of the church that I most admire?

Reading: Acts 7:54–8:3

Then they dragged [Stephen] out of the city and began to stone him. . . .

Response: St. Stephen, pray for us.

St. Stephen, first martyr of the church, who suffered and died outside the gate of Jerusalem for preaching the name of Jesus Christ. R.

St. Stephen, who saw the heavens opened and Jesus standing at the right hand of the power, praying that Jesus might receive his spirit. R.

St. Stephen, who so closely imitated Jesus in his love even for enemies and cried for God's forgiveness of his persecutors. R.

St. Stephen, whose appearance cast forth sparks not of anger but of love, to set on fire the hearts of his oppressors, which were harder than the stones they threw. R.

St. Stephen, whose fortitude is admired by all, by whom so many miracles are wrought, and who converts many to the faith of Christ. R.

Prayer: Lord Jesus, you called St. Stephen to serve your church, filled him with your grace, and gave him wisdom and power through your Holy Spirit. Continue to raise up ministers in your church to preach, heal, and suffer in imitation of you.

2. Church of St. Anne

Just inside St. Stephen's Gate and on the north side of the Temple Mount, pilgrims enter the property administered by the Missionaries of Africa (White Fathers), containing the Pools of Bethesda and St. Anne's Church. Although the Bible says nothing about the birthplace of Mary, an ancient tradition, recorded in the *Protoevangelium of James* in about 150, places the house of her parents, Anne and Joachim, close to the temple. This writing expands backward in time the infancy accounts of Matthew and Luke, and presents a narrative concerning the birth and upbringing of Mary herself.

The Crusader Church of St. Anne and its central altar

Since at least the fifth century, pilgrims have frequented this site identified as the place where the Pool of Bethesda was located as well as the church dedicated to "Mary where she was born." The present Church of St. Anne was built in the twelfth century over the cave of Mary's birth. It is the finest example of Crusader architecture in the Holy Land, with strong lines, thick walls, and simple dignity. The church is renowned for its remarkable acoustics and reverberating echoes, making it ideal for chant and melodic prayer.

The central altar, designed by the French sculptor Philippe Kaeppelin, incorporates scenes from the life of the Virgin Mary. The front of the altar depicts Mary giving birth to Jesus, his descent from the cross into Mary's arms, and the annunciation to Mary. The left end of the altar shows St. Anne teaching the young Mary, and the right end shows Mary being presented in the temple. A flight of steps leads to the crypt, where a small chapel honors the place where St. Anne gave birth to her holy daughter, Mary.

Unlike other churches in Jerusalem, this church was not destroyed after the Muslim conquest. Instead, it was turned into an Islamic law school by the sultan Saladin, whose name appears in the Arabic inscription still

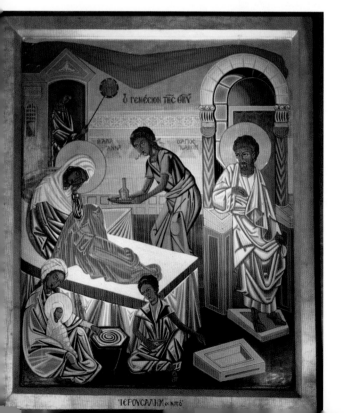

Icon of St. Anne giving birth to the infant Mary

St. Anne and her young daughter, the Virgin Mary

above the church's main entrance. After a few centuries, the building was abandoned. At the end of the Crimean War, the Sultan of Istanbul in 1856 offered the site to the French government in gratitude for its help during the war. France undertook extensive restoration, returning St. Anne's as closely as possible to the original basilica.

The Christian tradition so honors the Blessed Virgin Mary, the Theotokos, that there is a tendency to overlook Joachim and Anne, the parents of the flesh-and-blood Mary and, therefore, the grandparents of Jesus Christ. In their old age, Joachim and Anne prayed for a child, and an angel said to Anne, "The Lord has heard your prayer, and you shall conceive and bring forth, and your offspring shall be spoken of throughout the entire world." Anne accepted the words and replied, "As the Lord my God lives, if I give birth to male or female, I will bring it as a gift to the Lord my God; and it shall minister to him holy things all the days of its life."[1]

So we remember here the grandparents of Jesus and honor the dignity and wisdom of the elders who are so exalted throughout the Scriptures. Parents and grandparents are the bearers of tradition, and Israel's Torah gives them the responsibility of keeping the faith alive: "Take care and watch yourselves closely, so as neither to forget the things that your eyes have seen nor to let them slip from your mind all the days of your life;

---

1. *Protoevangelium of James* 4,1.

make them known to your children and your children's children" (Deut 4:9). Paul writes that just as grandparents have a responsibility to impart their faith and show affection to their grandchildren, so too grandchildren have a duty to show respect and care for their grandparents' physical needs. Paul exhorts, "If a widow has children or grandchildren, they should first learn their religious duty to their own family and make some repayment to their parents. . . . And whoever does not provide for relatives, and especially for family members, has denied the faith and is worse than an unbeliever" (1 Tim 5:4, 8).

The Scriptures honor the elders by name. Paul praises the faith of Timothy's grandmother and mother: "I am reminded of your sincere faith, a faith that lived first in your grandmother Lois and your mother Eunice and now, I am sure, lives in you" (2 Tim 1:5). Likewise, Luke's infancy narrative presents two elderly figures, Simeon and Anna, who were in the temple when Mary and Joseph brought Jesus to Jerusalem to present him to the Lord. The elderly Simeon took the child Jesus in his arms and gave praise to God for showing him the Messiah before his death, and the eighty-four-year-old Anna "began to praise God and to speak about the child to all who were looking for the redemption of Jerusalem" (Luke 2:38).

Meditation

- What might grandparents today learn from the grandparents of Jesus?
- In what ways are grandparents the bearers of the Christian tradition?

Reading: Luke 2:25-38

Now there was a man in Jerusalem whose name was Simeon. . . .

Response: God's salvation is near to those who fear him.

My mouth is filled with your praise,
    and with your glory all day long.
Do not cast me off in the time of old age;
    do not forsake me when my strength is spent (Ps 71:8-9). R.

O God, from my youth you have taught me,
  and I still proclaim your wondrous deeds.
So even to old age and gray hairs,
  O God, do not forsake me,
until I proclaim your might
  to all the generations to come (Ps 71:17-18). R.

As for mortals, their days are like grass;
  they flourish like a flower of the field;
for the wind passes over it, and it is gone,
  and its place knows it no more (Ps 103:15-16). R.

But the steadfast love of the LORD is from everlasting to everlasting
  on those who fear him,
  and his righteousness to children's children,
to those who keep his covenant
  and remember to do his commandments (Ps 103:17-18). R.

The LORD bless you from Zion.
  May you see the prosperity of Jerusalem
  all the days of your life.
May you see your children's children.
  Peace be upon Israel! (Ps 128:5-6). R.

Prayer: God of our ancestors, who bestowed on Ss. Anne and Joachim the grace of begetting the holy Virgin Mary, the mother of your incarnate Son, hear the prayers of all grandparents. May they hand on the gift of faith to their children and their children's children, and having completed your work on earth, enjoy the grace of eternal life with you forever.

3. Bethesda Pools

In the days of Jesus, the Pools of Bethesda (sometimes called Beth-zatha) were just north of the temple, near the gate where the sheep were sold and brought to the temple to be sacrificed. This is the setting for the account of Jesus healing the paralyzed man as told in John's gospel. These pools were originally two reservoirs filled with water to serve the temple, whose sacrificial rites required large amounts of water to preserve the cleanliness

Excavations of the Bethesda Pools with the Church of St. Anne behind

of the site. The northern pool was constructed in the eighth century BC and the southern pool in the second century BC. By the time of Jesus, this double-pool complex was surrounded by colonnaded walkways on its four sides, with a fifth colonnade across the middle of the dike dividing the two pools. This explains the reference in the gospel to the "five porticoes."

In Jesus's days, the waters were thought to have curative powers at certain times of the day when intermittent springs bubbled up into the pools. The sick, blind, and lame would sit or lie along the five porticoes; and when the waters stirred, they would try to enter the waters to be cured. A verse was added to the gospel text in the second century explaining what some of the Jews believed in Jesus's day: "For an angel of the Lord went down at certain seasons into the pool, and stirred up the water; whoever stepped in first after the stirring of the water was made well from whatever disease that person had" (John 5:4; not included in most texts). When Jesus encountered the paralyzed man who had been waiting at the pool since before Jesus was born, he asked him, "Do you want to be made well?" But the man gave the excuse, "I have no one to put me into the pool when the water is stirred up." He thought that Jesus would help him into the water, because by himself he could never reach the water before someone else stepped down ahead of him.

Jesus cured the man immediately with his powerful word, telling him to pick up his mat and walk. But Jesus does not want us to focus on won-

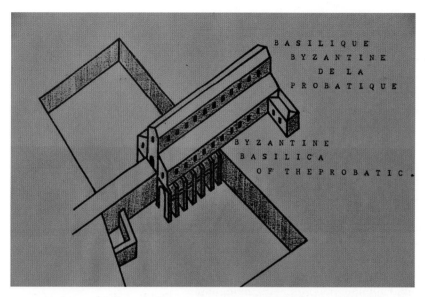

Drawing of the northern and southern pools with the Byzantine basilica built over them

ders alone, so he followed the physical cure with spiritual encouragement. As with many of Jesus's miracles, the man's ability to walk becomes an invitation to a more total restoration. Jesus wants complete healing for us, an end to any obstacles that separate us from God.

After the time of Jesus, the Pools of Bethesda were enshrined by the Romans as a place of healing, and they built a temple to Asclepius, the god of healing, on the site. By the fifth century, a large Byzantine basilica covered the area of today's ruins. The central nave of the church was built over the dike, while its flanking aisles extended over the pools, supported by deep arches, which can be seen rising from the ruins today. In the twelfth century, a Crusader chapel was built within the larger basilica. A stairway led down to a corner of the northern pool, permitting pilgrims to commemorate the healing miracle.

The healing pools remind us that God heals in many ways, through many means. He is the ultimate source of healing, regardless of his instruments: the medical profession, intercessory prayer, psychological or physical therapy, or shrines and miracles. For the afflicted, Jesus and the Holy Spirit "become in them a spring of water gushing up to eternal life" (John 4:14).

Meditation

- What is the difference between a physical cure and complete healing?

- In what ways might God desire to heal me? Am I willing to ask for that healing?

Reading: John 5:2-9

Now in Jerusalem by the Sheep Gate there is a pool. . . .

Response: O Lord, be gracious to me and heal me.

I sought the LORD, and he answered me,
  and delivered me from all my fears.
Look to him, and be radiant;
  so your faces shall never be ashamed.
This poor soul cried, and was heard by the LORD,
  and was saved from every trouble (Ps 34:4-6). R.

When the righteous cry for help, the LORD hears,
  and rescues them from all their troubles.
The LORD is near to the brokenhearted,
  and saves the crushed in spirit.
Many are the afflictions of the righteous,
  but the LORD rescues them from them all (Ps 34:17-19). R.

The LORD sustains them on their sickbed;
  in their illness you heal all their infirmities.
As for me, I said, "O LORD, be gracious to me;
  heal me, for I have sinned against you" (Ps 41:3-4). R.

Bless the LORD, O my soul,
  and do not forget all his benefits—
who forgives all your iniquity,
  who heals all your diseases,
who redeems your life from the Pit,
  who crowns you with steadfast love and mercy,
who satisfies you with good as long as you live
  so that your youth is renewed like the eagle's (Ps 103:2-5). R.

Chapel of the Flagellation on the Via Dolorosa

Prayer: Lord Jesus, you desire us to be completely restored to life in its fullness. Reach into those areas of our lives that are broken and failing, and speak your powerful words of healing. May our healing be for your greater glory and praise, now and forever.

4. Chapels of Flagellation and Condemnation

The Franciscan complex marking the beginning of the Way of the Cross includes a friary, two chapels with a courtyard between them, a center of biblical and archaeological study (Studium Biblicum Franciscanum), and the Terra Sancta Museum. Entering from the street, visitors encounter the Chapel of the Flagellation on the right, which may serve as the place to pray the first station of the cross. The Chapel of the Condemnation and Imposition of the Cross, on the left, may serve as the location of the second station.

The Chapel of the Flagellation memorializes Jesus being condemned to death, scourged and mocked by the Roman soldiers, and crowned King of the Jews with a crown of thorns. The first chapel was built in 1839 and rebuilt according to the design of Antonio Barluzzi in 1929. The stained-glass windows behind the altar and on either side of the sanctuary depict Pilate washing his hands, Jesus being scourged, and Barabbas expressing joy at his release. On the ceiling above the altar, a mosaic on a golden background depicts the crown of thorns pierced by stars.

The round bronze marker for the first station is on the other side of the Via Dolorosa, at today's Umariya Elementary School, which covers the remains of the Antonia Fortress, thought to be the site of Pilate's praetorium where Jesus was tried for blasphemy. The remains of the fortress explain why Christ's condemnation, scourging, and beginning of the Way of the Cross are remembered here, and the fact that the fortress contained prison cells explains the ready presence of Barabbas and the two thieves for judgment and execution with Jesus.

The Chapel of the Condemnation is topped by five white domes and honors the traditional site where Jesus took up the cross after his sentence. An earlier chapel was constructed here in the thirteenth century,

and the new church was built on its ruins in 1904. The location is based on the finding of large Roman surface stones believed to be part of the Stone Pavement (*Gabbatha* in Aramaic, *Lithostrotos* in Greek) on which sat Pilate's judgment seat (John 19:13). Although archaeologists today have determined that these stones were part of the Roman pavement of Hadrian from the second century, it is possible that it contained stones recovered from the ruins of the Antonia Fortress. These pavement stones form the floor at the back of the chapel today. Above the altar is an image of Pilate washing his hands while Jesus is being given the cross. On the wall opposite the door features a scene of Jesus's mother Mary watching him take up his cross, while Mary Magdalene tries to comfort her and John lifts his cloak to shield her from seeing Jesus with his cross.

This Chapel of the Condemnation is just inside the wall of the Via Dolorosa. The bronze marker for the second station is located below the white domes of the chapel and outside the wall on the street . This chapel and the Chapel of the Flagellation are two of the several chapels associated with the stations along the Via Dolorosa. Some of these other chapels, however, are not often open to pilgrims. For this reason, the Way of the Cross is best walked along the streets, stopping at the round marker and bronze relief marking each of the stations.

Meditation

- How does following the Way of the Cross prepare me to take up the cross and follow Jesus?

- Am I able to see Jesus's suffering in the least of my brothers and sisters?

Reading: John 19:1-7
Pilate took Jesus and had him flogged. . . .

Response: How great are the works of the Lord.

Let the same mind be in you that was in Christ Jesus,
who, though he was in the form of God,
    did not regard equality with God
    as something to be exploited,

Chapel of the Condemnation on the Via Dolorosa

but emptied himself,
    taking the form of a slave,
    being born in human likeness. R.

And being found in human form,
    he humbled himself
    and became obedient to the point of death—
    even death on a cross. R.

Therefore God also highly exalted him
    and gave him the name
    that is above every name,
so that at the name of Jesus
    every knee should bend,
    in heaven and on earth and under the earth,
and every tongue should confess
    that Jesus Christ is Lord,
    to the glory of God the Father (Phil 2:5-11). R.

Prayer: Lord, Jesus Christ, have mercy on me, a sinner. You took on the intense pain of scourging and the humiliation inflicted by the soldiers. Yet you endured in noble silence so that through your passion, we might be healed and forgiven. Give us a holy grief for all you have endured for us.

5. *Way of the Cross*

The Via Crucis, Via Dolorosa, or Way of the Cross developed from the desire of early Christians to follow in the footsteps of Jesus on his way to crucifixion. In fourth-century Jerusalem, Christians processed with candles from Gethsemane to Calvary before dawn on Good Friday. The stations developed gradually as a standard devotion among European Christians. Some of the stations are explicitly from the biblical accounts of the passion; others derive from popular traditions and attempts to fill in the details not mentioned in the texts. By the sixteenth century a Way of the Cross with fourteen stations was in use.

The Via Dolorosa assumes that the trial, mockery, and imposition of the cross took place at the Antonia Fortress just north of the temple. The first two stations are within the grounds of this former fortress, a massive bastion that served as the headquarters of the Roman garrison. The next stations are marked along the road leading west, and the final five stations are within the Church of the Holy Sepulcher. Like other condemned prisoners, Jesus was forced to carry the cross, or at least its crossbeam, to his place of execution. Although the site of Golgotha is today within the present walls of Jerusalem, during Jesus's time it was outside the city gates.

In the days of Jesus, the street he walked was a busy thoroughfare, teeming with merchants and shoppers, donkeys and carts, beggars and soldiers, much like it is today. Rubbing shoulders with the life of the street is part of experiencing the Way of the Cross. It is a path that often intersects the journey of our own lives. Each of us has had, or will have, our way of the cross—down a hospital hallway to surgery, to divorce court, to the bedside of a dying spouse—and having followed the way of Jesus will give us strength and hope for our journey.

Each station is designated with a round bronze marker, indicating the station in Roman numerals, and a bronze sculpture depicting what is commemorated there. Participants are encouraged to stop at each of the stations for meditation, which includes a Scripture and prayer. Each station concludes with a verse of Stabat Mater, a thirteenth-century hymn describing the sorrows of Mary at the cross.

The Way of the Cross follows along the "Sorrowful Way"

First Station—*The innocent Jesus accepts the unjust sentence of death pronounced against him by Pilate.*

V. We adore you Lord Jesus Christ and we bless you.

R. Because by your holy cross you have redeemed the world.

Reading: John 19:13-16

When Pilate heard these words, he brought Jesus outside and sat on the judge's bench at a place called The Stone Pavement, or in Hebrew Gabbatha. Now it was the day of Preparation for the Passover; and it was about noon. He said to the Jews, "Here is your King!" They cried out, "Away with him! Away with him! Crucify him!" Pilate asked them, "Shall I crucify your King?" The chief priests answered, "We have no king but the emperor." Then he handed him over to them to be crucified.

Prayer: Lord Jesus, by your condemnation, you free us from the sentence our sins deserve. As we follow along the Way of the Cross, help us to embrace the inevitable suffering and death of our own lives. May we bear the cross of our lives with the love and conviction you brought to your passion. May we walk with you all the days of our lives.

At the cross her station keeping,
Stood the mournful Mother weeping,
Close to Jesus to the last.

Second Station—*Jesus takes the cross upon his shoulders out of love for us.*

V. We adore you Lord Jesus Christ and we bless you.

R. Because by your holy cross you have redeemed the world.

Reading: Isaiah 53:3-6

He was despised and rejected by others;
    a man of suffering and acquainted with infirmity;
and as one from whom others hide their faces
    he was despised, and we held him of no account.
Surely he has borne our infirmities
    and carried our diseases;

yet we accounted him stricken,
struck down by God, and afflicted.
But he was wounded for our transgressions,
crushed for our iniquities;
upon him was the punishment that made us whole,
and by his bruises we are healed.
All we like sheep have gone astray;
we have all turned to our own way,
and the LORD *has laid on him*
the iniquity of us all.

Prayer: Lord Jesus, it was our sin and our guilt which you bore. Through your suffering, borne in love, you heal us and make us whole. Remove the spirit of selfishness from us and fill our hearts with sacrificial love for one another.

While she waited in her anguish,
Seeing Christ in torment languish,
Bitter sorrow pierced her heart.

Third Station—*Wearied by the agony at Gethsemane, tortured by the scourging and the crowning with thorns, Jesus falls for the first time beneath the weight of the cross.*

V. We adore you Lord Jesus Christ and we bless you.

R. Because by your holy cross you have redeemed the world.

Reading: Lamentations 3:14-24

I have become the laughingstock of all my people,
the object of their taunt-songs all day long.
He has filled me with bitterness,
he has sated me with wormwood.
He has made my teeth grind on gravel,
and made me cower in ashes;
my soul is bereft of peace;
I have forgotten what happiness is;
so I say, "Gone is my glory,
and all that I had hoped for from the LORD*."*

The thought of my affliction and my homelessness
  is wormwood and gall!
My soul continually thinks of it
  and is bowed down within me.
But this I call to mind,
  and therefore I have hope:
The steadfast love of the LORD *never ceases,*
  his mercies never come to an end;
they are new every morning;
  great is your faithfulness.
"The LORD *is my portion," says my soul,*
  "therefore I will hope in him."

Prayer: Lord Jesus, you fell in order to sustain us when we fall. Help us remember our weakness and dependence on you and support us with your care. When we stumble and fall, help us to rise again, trusting in your unfailing love.

With what pain and desolation,
With what noble resignation,
Mary watched her dying Son.

Fourth Station—*Jesus meets Mary, his sorrowful mother.*

V. We adore you Lord Jesus Christ and we bless you.

R. Because by your holy cross you have redeemed the world.

Reading: Luke 2:33-35
And the child's father and mother were amazed at what was being said about him. Then Simeon blessed them and said to his mother Mary, "This child is destined for the falling and the rising of many in Israel, and to be a sign that will be opposed so that the inner thoughts of many will be revealed—and a sword will pierce your own soul too."

Prayer: Lord Jesus, your passion and death pierced the heart of your sorrowful mother, Mary. Her dedication to your Father's will and her constant love for you shows us the way. Help us to imitate her faith, now and at the hour of our death.

Ever-patient in her yearning
Though her tear-filled eyes were burning,
Mary gazed upon her Son.

Fifth Station—*Simon from Cyrene helps Jesus carry his cross.*

V. We adore you Lord Jesus Christ and we bless you.

R. Because by your holy cross you have redeemed the world.

Reading: Luke 23:26

As they led him away, they seized a man, Simon of Cyrene, who was coming from the country, and they laid the cross on him, and made him carry it behind Jesus.

Prayer: Lord Jesus, Simon reminds us that authentic discipleship means taking up our cross and following in your steps. Help us to realize that we cooperate in your redeeming love as we offer our suffering in union with yours.

Who, that sorrow contemplating,
On that passion meditating,
Would not share the Virgin's grief?

The Fourth Station along the Via Dolorosa

Sixth Station—*With tender compassion, Veronica (True Icon) wipes the face of Jesus and receives the imprint of his face.*

V. We adore you Lord Jesus Christ and we bless you.

R. Because by your holy cross you have redeemed the world.

Reading: 2 Corinthians 4:6-11

For it is the God who said, "Let light shine out of darkness," who has shone in our hearts to give the light of the knowledge of the glory of God in the face of Jesus Christ. But we have this treasure in clay jars, so that it may be made clear that this extraordinary power belongs to God and does not come from us. We are afflicted in every way, but not crushed; perplexed, but not driven to despair; persecuted, but not forsaken; struck down, but not destroyed; always carrying in the body the death of Jesus, so that the life of Jesus may also be made visible in our bodies. For while we live, we are always being given up to death for Jesus' sake, so that the life of Jesus may be made visible in our mortal flesh.

Prayer: Lord Jesus, as we gaze upon the image of your face, we see your suffering humanity and your divine love. Help others to see your image manifested in us, and help us to recognize you in the least of our brothers and sisters.

Christ she saw, for our salvation,
Scourged with cruel acclamation,
Bruised and beaten by the rod.

Seventh Station—*As the strength of Jesus fails him, Jesus falls for the second time beneath the cross.*

V. We adore you Lord Jesus Christ and we bless you.

R. Because by your holy cross you have redeemed the world.

Reading: Lamentations 3:52-58

Those who were my enemies without cause
*   have hunted me like a bird;*
they flung me alive into a pit
*   and hurled stones on me;*
water closed over my head;
*   I said, "I am lost."*

I called on your name, O LORD,
from the depths of the pit;
you heard my plea,
"Do not close your ear
to my cry for help, but give me relief!"
You came near when I called on you;
you said, "Do not fear!"
You have taken up my cause, O LORD,
you have redeemed my life.

Prayer: Lord Jesus, as you left the city through its ancient gate, the pain of rejection bore down upon you, yet you embraced the cross more tightly. Help us to face the struggles of life with love and imitate your obedient courage.

Christ she saw with life-blood failing,
All her anguish unavailing,
Saw him breathe his very last.

Eighth Station—*Jesus meets the daughters of Jerusalem who weep for him.*

V. We adore you Lord Jesus Christ and we bless you.

R. Because by your holy cross you have redeemed the world.

Reading: Luke 23:27-29

A great number of the people followed him, and among them were women who were beating their breasts and wailing for him. But Jesus turned to them and said, "Daughters of Jerusalem, do not weep for me, but weep for yourselves and for your children. For the days are surely coming when they will say, 'Blessed are the barren, and the wombs that never bore, and the breasts that never nursed.'"

Prayer: Lord Jesus, despite your great suffering, you expressed deep concern for the families of Jerusalem. The city of the next generation would be destroyed by invading armies and would lie in ruins. Help us to care for the next generation by word and example.

Mary, fount of love's devotion,
Let me share with true emotion
All the sorrow you endured.

Ninth Station—*Jesus falls for the third time beneath the cross.*

V. We adore you Lord Jesus Christ and we bless you.

R. Because by your holy cross you have redeemed the world.

Reading: John 12:23-26

Jesus answered them, "The hour has come for the Son of Man to be glorified. Very truly, I tell you, unless a grain of wheat falls into the earth and dies, it remains just a single grain; but if it dies, it bears much fruit. Those who love their life lose it, and those who hate their life in this world will keep it for eternal life. Whoever serves me must follow me, and where I am, there will my servant be also. Whoever serves me, the Father will honor."

Prayer: Lord Jesus, you fell to the ground so that we might rise to life. I detest all my sins because they have offended you, who are all good and deserving of all my love. Help me to avoid whatever leads me to sin.

Virgin, ever interceding,
Hear me in my fervent pleading:
Fire me with your love of Christ.

Tenth Station—*At Calvary, Jesus is stripped of his garments.*

V. We adore you Lord Jesus Christ and we bless you.

R. Because by your holy cross you have redeemed the world.

Reading: John 19:23-24

When the soldiers had crucified Jesus, they took his clothes and divided them into four parts, one for each soldier. They also took his tunic; now the tunic was seamless, woven in one piece from the top. So they said to one another, "Let us not tear it, but cast lots for it to see who will get it." This was to fulfill what the scripture says, "They divided my clothes among themselves, / and for my clothing they cast lots."

Prayer: Lord Jesus, you made yourself poor, so that we might be rich. You were stripped of your garments, so that we might receive the glorious garments of baptism. You emptied yourself so that we might be filled with eternal life.

Mother, may this prayer be granted:
That Christ's love may be implanted
In the depths of my poor soul.

Eleventh Station—*The executioners nail Jesus to the cross.*

V. We adore you Lord Jesus Christ and we bless you.

R. Because by your holy cross you have redeemed the world.

Reading: Luke 23:33-43

When they came to the place that is called The Skull, they crucified Jesus there with the criminals, one on his right and one on his left. Then Jesus said, "Father, forgive them; for they do not know what they are doing." And they cast lots to divide his clothing. And the people stood by, watching; but the leaders scoffed at him, saying, "He saved others; let him save himself if he is the Messiah of God, his chosen one!" The soldiers also mocked him, coming up and offering him sour wine, and saying, "If you are the King of the Jews, save yourself!" There was also an inscription over him, "This is the King of the Jews." One of the criminals who were hanged there kept deriding him and saying, "Are you not the Messiah? Save yourself and us!" But the other rebuked him, saying, "Do you not fear God, since you are under the same sentence of condemnation? And we indeed have been condemned justly, for we are getting what we deserve for our deeds, but this man has done nothing wrong." Then he said, "Jesus, remember me when you come into your kingdom." He replied, "Truly I tell you, today you will be with me in Paradise."

Prayer: Lord Jesus, you forgave your executioners and you promised paradise to the repentant criminal. Through your holy cross you forgive us and save us from the powers of sin and death. Help us to crucify our selfishness and live in your love.

At the cross, your sorrow sharing,
All your grief and torment bearing,
Let me stand and mourn with you.

Twelfth Station—*Darkness comes at midday and Jesus dies on the cross.*

V. We adore you Lord Jesus Christ and we bless you.

R. Because by your holy cross you have redeemed the world.

Reading: Matthew 27:45-56

From noon on, darkness came over the whole land until three in the after-noon. And about three o'clock Jesus cried with a loud voice, "Eli, Eli, lema sabachthani?" that is, "My God, my God, why have you forsaken me?" When some of the bystanders heard it, they said, "This man is calling for Elijah." At once one of them ran and got a sponge, filled it with sour wine, put it on a stick, and gave it to him to drink. But the others said, "Wait, let us see whether Elijah will come to save him." Then Jesus cried again with a loud voice and breathed his last. At that moment the curtain of the temple was torn in two, from top to bottom. The earth shook, and the rocks were split. The tombs also were opened, and many bodies of the saints who had fallen asleep were raised. After his resurrection they came out of the tombs and entered the holy city and appeared to many. Now when the centurion and those with him, who were keeping watch over Jesus, saw the earthquake and what took place, they were terrified and said, "Truly this man was God's Son!" Many women were also there, looking on from a distance; they had followed Jesus from Galilee and had provided for him. Among them were Mary Magdalene, and Mary the mother of James and Joseph, and the mother of the sons of Zebedee.

Prayer: Lord Jesus, as both priest and victim you offered your life in sac-rifice for all. As we stand on the hill of Calvary, we are grateful for your love which gave completely, even to death. Help us to give our lives for others so that we can love one another as you have loved us.

Fairest maid of all creation,
Queen of hope and consolation,
Let me feel your grief sublime.

Thirteenth Station—*The body of Jesus is taken down from the cross and received by his sorrowful mother.*

V. We adore you Lord Jesus Christ and we bless you.

R. Because by your holy cross you have redeemed the world.

Reading: John 19:31-40

Since it was the day of Preparation, the Jews did not want the bodies left on the cross during the sabbath, especially because that sabbath was a day of great solemnity. So they asked Pilate to have the legs of the crucified men broken and the bodies removed. Then the soldiers came and broke the legs of the first and of the other who had been crucified with him. But when they came to Jesus and saw that he was already dead, they did not break his legs. Instead, one of the soldiers pierced his side with a spear, and at once blood and water came out. (He who saw this has testified so that you also may believe. His testimony is true, and he knows that he tells the truth.) These things occurred so that the scripture might be fulfilled, "None of his bones shall be broken." And again another passage of scripture says, "They will look on the one whom they have pierced." After these things, Joseph of Arimathea, who was a disciple of Jesus, though a secret one because of his fear of the Jews, asked Pilate to let him take away the body of Jesus. Pilate gave him permission; so he came and removed his body. Nicodemus, who had at first come to Jesus by night, also came, bringing a mixture of myrrh and aloes, weighing about a hundred pounds. They took the body of Jesus and wrapped it with the spices in linen cloths, according to the burial custom of the Jews.

Prayer: Lord Jesus, you are the Lamb of God, pierced and slain, who takes away the sins of the world. By your wounds we are healed. The blood of the new and everlasting covenant is poured out to give us life. May we look to your empty cross as our sign of victory.

Virgin, in your love befriend me,
At the Judgment Day defend me.
Help me by your constant prayer.

Fourteenth Station—*The body of Jesus is laid in the rock-cut tomb and the stone is rolled across the entrance.*

V. We adore you Lord Jesus Christ and we bless you.

R. Because by your holy cross you have redeemed the world.

Reading: Mark 15:42-47

When evening had come, and since it was the day of Preparation, that is, the day before the sabbath, Joseph of Arimathea, a respected member of the council, who was also himself waiting expectantly for the kingdom of God, went boldly to Pilate and asked for the body of Jesus. Then Pilate wondered if he were already dead; and summoning the centurion, he asked him whether he had been dead for some time. When he learned from the centurion that he was dead, he granted the body to Joseph. Then Joseph bought a linen cloth, and taking down the body, wrapped it in the linen cloth, and laid it in a tomb that had been hewn out of the rock. He then rolled a stone against the door of the tomb. Mary Magdalene and Mary the mother of Joses saw where the body was laid.

Prayer: Lord Jesus, your sealed tomb could not contain the life within. The light of the world scatters the darkness of the sepulcher and the darkness of our lives. Be with us at the hour of death and deepen our faith in the resurrection of the body and the life of the world to come.

Savior, when my life shall leave me,
Through your mother's prayers receive me
With the fruits of victory.

6. Church of the Holy Sepulcher

Called the Church of the Anastasis (Greek for Resurrection) by Orthodox Christians, the church contains the two holiest sites in Christianity: the place where Jesus was crucified and the empty tomb where he was buried and resurrected. Its two gray domes and cutoff belfry mark its location in Jerusalem's Christian Quarter. Inside the church, its perplexing composite of chapels is enveloped with the devotional adornment of various historical periods and several Orthodox and Catholic rites. It bears the scars of fires and earthquakes, deliberate destruction and reconstruction down through the centuries. Although it can seem dreary and dark, the saving events that occurred in this space have brought light to all the world. It remains a living place of worship: its ancient stones are saturated with prayers, hymns, and liturgies. Its passageways are occupied throughout the day with fervent cycles of processions sanctified with chant and incense.

Early Christians venerated the site, but the emperor Hadrian covered it with a pagan temple. When Constantine built Christianity's most beautiful basilica, he tore down the pagan temple and had Christ's tomb cut away from the original hillside. His mother, St. Helena, discovered the cross of Christ in a cistern not far from the hill of Calvary. Constantine's church consisted of separate constructions over the holy sites: a rotunda enclosing the holy tomb, a colonnaded atrium with the site of Calvary in one corner, and the great basilica for celebrating the Eucharist. The church was consecrated in 335, burned by Persians in 614, restored, destroyed by Muslims in 1009, and partially rebuilt. The Crusaders completed the reconstruction in 1149. The result is essentially the church that stands today.

Immediately upon entering the church from its courtyard, visitors see a steep and curving stairway that leads upward to the hill of Golgotha (in Aramaic) or Calvary (in Latin). At the top on the right is a window looking into the Crusader Chapel of the Franks, commemorating the stripping of Jesus's garments (the tenth station of the cross). Straight ahead is the Catholic Chapel of the Nailing to the Cross (the eleventh station). To the left is the more ornate Greek Orthodox Chapel of the Crucifixion where Jesus died on the cross (the twelfth station). A silver disc beneath the altar marks the place where the cross stood. Pilgrims may touch the

The Fourteenth Station at the rock-cut tomb of Jesus

Stairway leading to Calvary, the site of Jesus's crucifixion and death

The perfumed stone where the body of Jesus was anointed for burial

stone mound of Calvary through a round hole in the disc. The limestone rock upon which Jesus Christ was crucified lies beneath the altar, under glass. Between the two chapels, the Catholic Altar of the Stabat Mater (Our Lady of Sorrows) commemorates the place where Jesus was taken down from the cross and held in the arms of his mother (the thirteenth station).

Here on Calvary, Jesus was taunted and tormented; here soldiers gambled for his clothing and gave him vinegar to drink. Here Jesus cried out to God with a feeling of abandonment before he shouted out his final cry in torturous pain. At this abandoned rock quarry outside the north walls of ancient Jerusalem, Jesus suffered humanity's most memorable death. Rejected by those he ministered to, denied, betrayed, abandoned by his closest friends, and feeling totally forsaken, Jesus remained unconditionally loyal and demonstrated history's decisive victory of faithful love. There is no depth of human experience to which Jesus has not plunged. Yet, on the cross, he did more than tell us he shares our pain; he transformed it with his love, bringing light out of darkness and life out of death.

Another flight of steep stairs at the rear of the Chapel of the Crucifixion leads back to the ground floor. Here is a grand mosaic depicting, from right to left, Jesus being taken down from the cross, his body being prepared for burial, and his body being taken to the tomb. In front of the mosaic lies the Stone of Anointing, a slab of reddish stone flanked by candlesticks and overhung by a row of lamps. It commemorates the body of Jesus being anointed (an alternate location for the thirteenth station), and kneeling pilgrims kiss it with great reverence. A small circular slab with four pillars surmounted by a marble canopy is found in the corner. Here is the Armenian Station of the Holy Women, commemorating Jesus's mother and her companions who viewed the crucifixion from a distance.

Turning away from Calvary, visitors glimpse the rotunda of the church opening up on the right, surrounded by massive pillars and surmounted by a huge dome. Its outer walls date back to Constantine's original basilica. The dome is decorated with twelve rays of light representing the apostles. At the center stands the stone shrine enclosing the holy tomb (the fourteenth station), in which Jesus was buried and where he rose from the dead. Pilgrims enter two chambers: the outer Chapel of the Angel, in which stands a pedestal containing what is believed to be a piece of the rolling stone used to close the tomb, and the inner chamber, where a marble slab covers the stone on which the body of Jesus was laid to rest. Here pilgrims touch the stone, recite brief prayers, light candles, and recall the gospel of the resurrection.

Jesus was hastily taken down from the cross, wrapped in a linen cloth, and laid in the tomb on a Friday before sundown, when the Sabbath began. His disciples would rest on the Sabbath and return to the tomb at sunrise on Sunday, the third day, to complete the anointing of his body. The last station of the sorrowful Way of the Cross becomes the beginning of the glorious way of resurrection. The message of the angel, "Look, there is the place they laid him," continues to call pilgrims to see the empty tomb; but the other message, "He has been raised; he is not here," forever changed the lives of those disciples and his followers throughout the world. It assures us that the truest pilgrimage is going out to tell others the good news and living the new life given to us by our risen Lord.

The stone shrine (or edicule) enclosing the tomb was reinforced and restored in 2017 after many centuries of neglect. The reddish-cream marble of the edicule emerged cleaned of centuries of grime from candle smoke and freed from the exterior scaffolding of iron girders that braced it since the mid-twentieth century. During the restoration, a small window was cut into the southern wall of the inner chamber, allowing pilgrims to see and touch one of the limestone walls of the burial cave. Work continues to shore up the foundations of the edicule and rotunda.

Exiting the holy tomb, pilgrims find a Crusader arch that leads to the central worship space or catholicon, which was originally the main part of the Crusader church and is now the Greek Orthodox cathedral. Its dome contains the image of Christ the Pantocrator, ruler of the universe. Beneath the dome is a stone called the *omphalos* (navel), representing the spiritual center of the world according to a medieval tradition. The sanctuary is separated by the ornate iconostasis and on each side are thrones for the patriarch of Jerusalem and the patriarch of Antioch.

Returning to the Holy Sepulcher, on the side opposite the entrance, visitors find a tiny Coptic chapel. The chapel is attached to the edicule and reveals some of the natural rock of the tomb. Behind this chapel, in the walls of the rotunda from Constantine's church, stands the Orthodox Chapel of St. Joseph of Arimathea and St. Nicodemus. Within is the entrance to two complete Jewish tombs from the first century. Since Jews always buried their dead outside the city, this proves that the Holy

The empty tomb of Jesus, for he is risen indeed

Sepulcher site was outside the city walls at the time of the crucifixion. Joseph of Arimathea and Nicodemus, who took down and entombed the body of Jesus (John 19:38-42), are said to be buried here.

On the other side of the rotunda stands the Catholic altar dedicated to St. Mary Magdalene; then bronze doors lead to the Franciscan Chapel of the Apparition, commemorating the tradition that Jesus appeared to his mother after his resurrection. Inside the entrance of the chapel stands a section of a column, said to be the one to which Jesus was tied when he was scourged. Along the far wall, scenes of the Way of the Cross are depicted in wrought iron.

Returning past the altar of St. Mary Magdalene and turning left into the northern aisle, pilgrims encounter a series of columns from different periods, including richly decorated Corinthian columns from the original fourth-century church. Known as the Arches of the Virgin, they commemorate the belief that Mary made visits to her son's tomb. At the end of the aisle is a small square chamber called the Prison of Christ, based on a belief that Jesus and the two thieves were briefly confined here before the crucifixion. Further around the semi-circular aisle are two chapels on the left. The first is the Greek Chapel of St. Longinus, dedicated to the Roman soldier who pierced Jesus's side with his spear and then accepted him as the Son of God. Further along is the Armenian Chapel of the Division of the Raiment, recalling that the Roman soldiers divided Christ's clothes among them.

Next on the left is a stairwell, its walls inscribed with hundreds of crosses by pilgrims in past centuries. Steps descend to the underground Armenian Chapel of St. Helena. This was the crypt of Constantine's fourth-century basilica and is therefore the oldest complete part of the church. The Armenians have renamed the chapel to honor their national patron, St. Gregory the Illuminator. He is credited with converting Armenia from paganism to Christianity in 301, making it the first nation to adopt Christianity as its official religion. The chapel contains images of important events in the life of St. Gregory and the history of the Armenian nation. The altar to the left is dedicated to St. Dismas, "the good thief" crucified alongside Jesus, who repented and pleaded, "Jesus, remember me when you come into your kingdom" (Luke 23:39-43).

Another steep staircase leads to the Franciscan Chapel of the Finding of the Cross. This rough-walled area has been built within part of the ancient quarry, later converted into a cistern. Here St. Helena discovered the True Cross and other instruments of Christ's passion and crucifixion. A statue behind the altar shows her holding the cross. The remains of the cross and other relics of the crucifixion were relocated to Rome and are seen in the Basilica of the Holy Cross.

After ascending all the steps back to the ground floor, pilgrims see immediately on the left the Greek Chapel of the Derision. It commemorates the mocking of Jesus by the Roman soldiers. Under the altar is a fragment of a column said to be where Jesus sat when invested with royal robes and the crown of thorns. Further along, a glass screen protrudes slightly into the aisle and encloses the natural rock of Calvary. Around the corner is the Chapel of Adam, which is directly beneath the Chapel of Calvary upstairs. The fissure running through the stone was possibly caused by the earthquake at the time of Christ's death. Tradition suggests that Adam was buried here and that the blood of Jesus tricked down to his skull. More theological than historical, the tradition affirms that Christ's saving blood saved all of humanity from eternal exile and death.

The ownership of the Church of the Holy Sepulcher is shared between the Greek Orthodox, Catholics, and Armenian Orthodox. Three other communities—Coptic, Syriac, and Ethiopian Orthodox—have rights to use certain areas for worship. All the churches jealously guard their rights of possession. The rights of possession and use are spelled out by a decree, called the Status Quo, originally imposed by the Ottoman Turks in 1757, specifying that no changes may be made to the church unless all the parties holding rights agree. One notorious effect of the Status Quo can be seen above the main entrance on leaving the church. The immovable wooden ladder leaning against a window ledge has been there since the eighteenth century. Nobody really knows why it is there, but because it was in place when the Status Quo began, it must remain there.

Although we know that Jesus desired his church to be united, the church's contrasting architectural styles, its divergent ornamentation, and its differing liturgies attest to the rich variety of expression and devotion over the centuries within the church of Jesus Christ. But is this the place where Jesus died and was buried? History, archaeology, and tradition all point in the direction of a conclusive yes. If all these historical structures could be removed, we would stand with dirt and rocks under our feet, witnessing a former quarry with a mound of rock where Christ died and a new tomb where he was buried. The earliest Christians knew the place, and despite the Roman attempts to cause them to forget, they recovered the place so that countless pilgrims over two millennia could come to touch, remember, and pray.

Meditation

- What difference does it make to me that the tomb of Jesus is empty?

- How do I desire the good news of the Lord's resurrection to renew my life today?

Reading: Mark 16:1-8

Very early on the first day of the week, when the sun had risen, they went to the tomb. . . .

Response: "This is the day that the LORD has made; / let us rejoice and be glad."

O give thanks to the LORD, for he is good;
    his steadfast love endures forever!
Let Israel say,
    "His steadfast love endures forever" (Ps 118:1-2). R.

The right hand of the LORD is exalted;
    the right hand of the LORD does valiantly.
I shall not die, but I shall live,
    and recount the deeds of the LORD (Ps 118:16-17). R.

Open to me the gates of righteousness,
    that I may enter through them
    and give thanks to the LORD.
This is the gate of the LORD;
    the righteous shall enter through it.
I thank you that you have answered me
    and have become my salvation (Ps 118:19-21). R.

The stone that the builders rejected
    has become the chief cornerstone.
This is the LORD's doing;
    it is marvelous in our eyes.
This is the day that the LORD has made;
    let us rejoice and be glad in it (Ps 118:22-24). R.

Prayer: Risen Lord, you never abandon your disciples and your rising assures us that your word is trustworthy and true. By your cross and resurrection you have set us free; you are the Savior of the world. Help us to place our hope in you and entrust our future to you.

"He has been raised; he is not here. Look, there is the place they laid him."

Chapter XII

Outward on the Church's Mission

Often people wonder what it would have been like to live with Jesus and follow him throughout his earthly life. They imagine an intimate nearness with the Lord as they walk in his footsteps and enjoy an ongoing encounter with him. Yet, because Christ is risen, ascended, and has sent his Holy Spirit, we are truly able to live more closely to him now than we could have when he walked the earth. The first disciples lived "with" Jesus; but now we live "in" Jesus. Jesus became like us and lived in our world in order that we might become like him, that we might share in his own divine life.

The fifty days of the first Easter season, between the resurrection and Pentecost, marked a period of transition between the ministry of Jesus and the age of the church. In this age of the church, we should follow the instructions given to us in the first chapter of the Acts of the Apostles. We are challenged by the "two men in white robes" not to "stand looking up toward heaven" (Acts 1:10-11), but to use the gifts of the Holy Spirit to become missionary disciples. The parting words of the Lord to his disciples were these: "You will receive power when the Holy Spirit has come upon you; and you will be my witnesses in Jerusalem, in all Judea and Samaria, and to the ends of the earth" (Acts 1:8). Jesus will indeed return from heaven to earth, but in the meantime, the church has a mission, the outward-reaching evangelization of the world.

The nature of Christ's church as the community of missionary disciples challenges pilgrims to the Holy Land to discover the other side of pilgrimage. Conventional pilgrimage means going somewhere to find God in a new way; the other side of pilgrimage means going somewhere in order to bring God in a new way to that place. The call to be witnesses, not only in the Holy Land but "to the ends of the earth," convinces us that every place in the world can be a place of pilgrimage. We can discover God's presence in the least likely places, and we can bring the presence of God to places that wait in darkness for the dawning light of the risen Lord.

The remaining sites in this pilgrimage guide are all outward oriented: Emmaus and the coastal cities of Joppa and Caesarea. These places memorialize the early figures of the church as they seek to follow the Lord's mandate to proclaim the gospel and make disciples. They show us our own vocation to be missionary disciples, following in the way of Jesus.

1. Emmaus

Two pilgrims were returning home to Emmaus after celebrating Passover in Jerusalem. One of the pilgrims was named Cleopas, but the other was unnamed and represents each one of us. When the risen Jesus came up to them, he seemed to be just another pilgrim returning home. They expressed to him their sadness at the death of Jesus, their disappointment and shattered hopes, and their skepticism about the women's report that he was alive. Jesus then reproached them for not taking the Scriptures seriously regarding the suffering and glorification of the Messiah. Rather than referring to a particular Scripture passage, Jesus laid out for them the way in which "all the Scriptures" had led up to God's revelation of the cross and resurrection of Christ. He showed how the ancient texts, "beginning with Moses and all the prophets," prepared for the gospel and were fulfilled in him.

One of several churches claiming to be the site of Emmaus

The two disciples offered hospitality and convinced Jesus to stay with them. When at table with them, Jesus "took bread, blessed and broke it, and gave it to them." His liturgical gestures looked back to the action of the Last Supper and forward to the "breaking of the bread" in Acts. As the narrative reached its climax and Jesus vanished from their sight, the disciples realized they had been experiencing the presence of the risen Christ all along. They remembered that their hearts were catching fire with insight and love as Jesus was interpreting the Scriptures for them. Only after understanding the Scriptures were they prepared to recognize Jesus in the breaking of the bread.

Through the Emmaus account, the disciples and Luke's readers realize how the risen Lord will be present to his church. The encounter demonstrates the dynamic relationship between word and sacrament in the life of the church, and it reflects the twofold structure of Christian assembly. Both the interpretation of the Scriptures and the breaking of the bread are actions of the risen Christ in which his presence is made real for the church.

But the ancient narrative suggests the Christian Eucharist not only in word and sacrament, but also in the movement from table to witness. The disciples returned at once to Jerusalem to communicate their experience of how they came to know the risen Christ. The account begins with the disciples walking slowly and hopelessly from Jerusalem to Emmaus, and it ends with their movement hurriedly and expectantly from Emmaus to Jerusalem with the good news of the risen Lord.

The Emmaus narrative, like the resurrection itself, is both historical and transhistorical. Cleopas and his anonymous companion represent historical disciples and also you and me. Appropriately, we don't know for sure where Emmaus is, and today three different locations are identified as the biblical Emmaus. Luke said the village was seven miles (literally "sixty stadia") from Jerusalem, but he didn't specify in which direction. So, for those seeking a straightforward identification of the biblical site, Emmaus can seem puzzling and frustrating. Yet, it might help teach us that what happened on that Sunday is more important than where it happened and that encounters with the risen Christ are not confined to one time or place. So, if we want a peaceful place to reflect on the lessons of Emmaus, any of these three sites can offer a memorial to the Emmaus encounter.

Christians of the fourth century considered the site of Luke's Emmaus to be the city of Nicopolis, near today's Cistercian abbey of Latrun. In the first century this location was named Emmaus, and around 220, the town received the status of a city and changed its name to Nicopolis. St. Jerome wrote in a letter that the city had a church built at the house of Cleophas. This tradition may have resulted in scribes "correcting" some texts of Luke to read 160 stadia (about 18 miles) rather than 60 stadia. The town was wiped out by plague in 639 and its association with Emmaus was lost for many centuries, until its revival in the nineteenth century. Ruins of a large Byzantine church with mosaic floors, within which was built a smaller Crusader church, may be found there. The main factor against this location is its distance. It would have been exceedingly difficult for the disciples to walk here from Jerusalem and make the uphill return the same evening before the city gates were shut.

The site of El-Qubeibeh, just over 60 stadia northwest of Jerusalem, was suggested as the location of Emmaus during the time of the Crusaders, when a Roman fortress was found there which became known as Castellum Emmaus. The site was adopted in 1335 as the site of Emmaus by the Franciscans, who began an annual pilgrimage there. The present church was built in 1902, while excavations found evidence of occupation in Roman times and a section of Roman road, but no Jewish remains have been found there. Inside the church are the remains of what is suggested to be the foundation of the house of Cleophas.

The third site that could be the biblical Emmaus is Abu Ghosh, just over 60 stadia west of Jerusalem on the main road to Joppa. The town was previously known as Kiryat Yearim, the resting place of the ark of the covenant between being retrieved from the Philistines and being taken to Jerusalem by King David around 1000 BC. The Crusaders built a church there in 1140 and called the place Emmaus. The church is now restored as the Church of the Resurrection and remains one of the finest examples of Crusader architecture. The crypt contains a spring used by the Roman Tenth Legion when it camped here after capturing Jerusalem in AD 70. Its tranquil setting today adjoins a Benedictine monastery.

Meditation

- When does my heart catch flame within me as the Lord opens the Scriptures to me?

- What does the Emmaus account show me about the ways Jesus reveals his presence to me today?

Reading: Luke 24:13-35

Now on that same day two of them were going to a village called Emmaus, about seven miles from Jerusalem. . . .

Response: May our hearts burn within us in the presence of the risen Lord.

The Lord Jesus continues today to walk alongside his disciples, just as he did two thousand years ago. May we, who walk in his way, recognize his presence in every pilgrim on the road. R.

All the Scriptures, from Moses through all the prophets, speak of the Messiah in his suffering and glory. May we listen to God's word in a way that makes our hearts catch flame. R.

All disciples are tempted by discouragement and sadness, as were the first disciples. May followers of the risen Lord find courage and hope through hearing the word and sacramental communion with the risen Lord. R.

Many people seek the Lord and struggle to believe. May they be attentive to the fulfillment of Scripture and welcome into their hearts the incarnate and risen Lord Jesus Christ. R.

The church was born from the paschal announcement of the resurrection of our Lord. May the worldwide community of disciples be a continual witness and herald of the living Christ to all people of our time. R.

Prayer: Risen Lord, continue to open the Scriptures to us so that our hearts may catch flame with your understanding and love. Continue to open our eyes to recognize you in the breaking of the bread. As we continue our life of pilgrimage, may we be continually nourished with your holy word and the bread of life.

2. Abu Ghosh, Our Lady of the Ark of the Covenant Church

The ark of the covenant resided in the village of Kiryat Yearim, today's Abu Ghosh, before being brought up to Jerusalem by King David in about 1000 BC. Today the Church of Notre Dame de l'Arche de l'Alliance (Our Lady of the Ark of the Covenant) stands at the highest point of the village. According to Christian tradition, the church stands on the site of the house of Abinadab, where his son Eleazar was consecrated as the

Our Lady of the Ark of the Covenant Church at ancient Kiryat Yearim

ark's custodian (1 Sam 7:1). A Byzantine church was built here in the fifth century, and the present church from 1924 preserves pieces of floor mosaics from the ancient site. A statue of Mary holding the child Jesus in her arms towers above the church and can be seen across the village. The base of the statue is the ark of the covenant with cherubs' wings extended, and Jesus above the ark offers the Eucharist to God's people.

The ark of the covenant, a chest made of acacia wood and overlaid with gold, was created according to instructions given to Moses by God at Mount Sinai. Within it were stored the two tablets of the Ten Commandments, the rod of Aaron, and an urn filled with manna. Above the ark were the cherubim of glory overshadowing the mercy seat, the footstool for God's presence (Heb 9:4). The ark was housed in the tabernacle, which was filled with the glory of the Lord. The Levites carried the ark through the wilderness, across the Jordan, and into the Promised Land. When carried, the ark was concealed beneath a veil made of skins and blue cloth. Within the Holy Land, the ark resided in Shilo for more than two hundred years. When the Philistines captured the ark in battle, they subsequently sent it back because of the misfortunes that befell them. The ark remained at Kiryat Yearim for about twenty years. King David then brought it to Jerusalem, and King Solomon enshrined the ark in the holy of holies of the temple.

Early Christian theologians described the Virgin Mary as the new ark of the covenant. In the old covenant, the ark was the dwelling place of God; in the new covenant, Mary is the new place of God's dwelling. If God wanted his words inscribed on stone housed in a splendid container covered with pure gold within and without, how much more would he want his eternal Word to dwell in a noble sanctuary. The Virgin Mary is the living shrine of the word of God, the ark of the new and eternal covenant. As the cloud covered the ark of the covenant and filled the sanctuary as a sign of the divine mystery present in the midst of Israel (Exod 40:35), so the shadow of the Most High envelopes and penetrates the tabernacle of the new covenant that is the womb of Mary (Luke 1:35).

A comparison of David's bringing the ark of the covenant to Jerusalem (2 Sam 6) and the gospel account of Mary's visitation (Luke 1) indicates more ways in which the former foreshadows the latter. The ark remained in the house of Obed-edom for three months; Mary remained in the house of Elizabeth for three months, both locations in the hill country west of Jerusalem. David asked, "How can the ark of the Lord come to me?" Elizabeth asked, "How can the mother of my Lord come to me?" Dressed as a priest, David danced and leapt in front of the ark; John the Baptist, of priestly lineage, leapt in his mother's womb at the approach of Mary. In time, the ark came to Jerusalem, where God's presence is revealed; Mary eventually came to Jerusalem, where she presented God incarnate in the temple.

Luke understood the prefiguring in the account of the ark to reveal the place of Mary in salvation history. In the ark of the old covenant, God came to his people with a spiritual presence, but in Mary, the ark of the new covenant, God comes to dwell with his people bodily in the womb of a specially prepared Jewish girl. In the ark was

The Virgin Mary as the new ark of the covenant

the law of God inscribed in stone; in Mary's womb was the word of God in flesh. In the ark was the urn of manna, the bread from heaven that kept God's people alive in the wilderness; in Mary's womb is the bread of life come down from heaven that brings eternal life. In the ark was the rod of Aaron, the proof of true priesthood; in Mary's womb is the true priest who will offer his life for all. In the third century, St. Gregory the Wonderworker said that Mary is truly an ark: "Gold within and gold without, and she has received in her womb all the treasures of the sanctuary."

In the book of Revelation, John sees the temple in heaven opened, displaying the ark of the covenant (Rev 11:19). What had previously been hidden in the holy of holies is now revealed to all. In the next verse of the same vision (the text was divided by chapters centuries later), John sees "a woman clothed with the sun, with the moon under her feet, and on her head a crown of twelve stars" (Rev 12:1). While she cries out in birth pangs, a red dragon waits to devour her child when it is born. On one level of meaning, the woman is Mary, the personification of ancient Israel, giving birth to its Messiah. The dragon's eagerness to devour the child expresses the violent opposition Jesus met during his earthly life. The woman is also Mary, the personification of Christ's church, continually bringing Christ to birth in the world, while the forces of evil seek to destroy Christ and his church. While Christ was taken up to the throne of God, his church continues to experience the threat of suffering and persecution.

The vision offers us a two-level view of reality. On earth the church experiences continual opposition and the outcome seems uncertain. Yet, when we look to heaven, we see a cosmic battle, the outcome of which is clear: the dragon is beaten; the powers of Satan are vanquished. The defeat of the dragon represents the victory won by "the blood of the Lamb," the atoning death of Christ, and the witness of his followers.

Meditation

- In what ways do I experience my own life as a spiritual battle?
- What assures me that the victory has been won? How can I deepen my trust?

Reading: Exodus 25:10-22
They shall make an ark of acacia wood. . . .

Response: Mary, Ark of the Covenant, pray for us.

Then God's temple in heaven was opened, and the ark of his covenant was seen within his temple; and there were flashes of lightning, rumblings, peals of thunder, an earthquake, and heavy hail (Rev 11:19). R.

A great portent appeared in heaven: a woman clothed with the sun, with the moon under her feet, and on her head a crown of twelve stars. She was pregnant and was crying out in birth pangs, in the agony of giving birth (Rev 12:1-2). R.

Then another portent appeared in heaven: a great red dragon, with seven heads and ten horns, and seven diadems on his heads. His tail swept down a third of the stars of heaven and threw them to the earth. Then the dragon stood before the woman who was about to bear a child, so that he might devour her child as soon as it was born (Rev 12:3-4). R.

And she gave birth to a son, a male child, who is to rule all the nations with a rod of iron. But her child was snatched away and taken to God and to his throne; and the woman fled into the wilderness, where she has a place prepared by God (Rev 12:5-6). R.

Prayer: Lord God, you remained with your people Israel through the ark of the covenant, covered with gold inside and out, and you were born in the flesh through the womb of the Virgin Mary. As we continue our pilgrim way, may we experience the sufferings of our life in light of the suffering of Christ and of your people through the ages, and may we trust in the victory of Christ the Lamb over all the forces that oppose your people.

3. Joppa

Because of its natural harbor and defendable hill above, the seaport city of Joppa became an important stronghold with valuable access to the Mediterranean Sea. One of the oldest port cities on earth, Joppa was the Holy Land's link to the nations to the west before air travel. For centuries, pilgrims visiting the Holy Land arrived and departed from its natural harbor. The cedars of Lebanon used in the building of the temple, both at the time of Solomon (2 Chron 2:16) and of Zerubbabel (Ezra 3:7), were brought to shore here. The story of Jonah says that the prophet set sail

The seaside Church of St. Peter in Joppa

Fresco of Peter's vision on the rooftop in Joppa

from Joppa to flee the Lord's call and was then thrown up again on its shore by the great fish. Visitors today may survey its coastline, which has changed little in thousands of years, imagining merchants and pilgrims coming and going through the centuries.

While Peter was making pastoral visits to the communities of Jewish believers, he came to Joppa, where a beloved woman named Tabitha became sick and died, causing much grief within the church there. When Peter arrived at the upstairs room where her body lay, the widows were weeping and showing him the clothing she had made for them (Acts 9:36-43). Then, beseeching God in prayer, Peter directed Tabitha to get up, and Peter offered her his hand and helped her up. The account echoes the raising of Jairus's daughter in Luke's gospel. Peter's words of command in Aramaic would have been *"Tabitha, cumi,"* which is only slightly different from the words of Jesus to the young girl, *"Talitha, cumi."* Peter's ministry demonstrates that Jesus is still powerfully at work in his church.

While in Joppa, Peter stayed at the seaside house of Simon the Tanner, a site that may be seen at Simon the Tanner Street, number 8. The house is an inconspicuous private residence behind Jaffa's lighthouse. Here Peter went up on the roof to pray, fell into a trance, and was given a vision. The heavens opened and a sheet was lowered, filled with all sorts of animals, which he was told to eat. When he protested that some of the animals were unclean, a voice told him, "What God has made clean, you must not call profane" (Acts 10:15).

The same prohibitions that separated animals into clean and unclean also divided people from one another. Peter came to realize that his vision was not only about food laws but also about fellowship and acceptance. It expressed God's will to remove the barriers that divided Jews and Gentiles. If God is making unclean food clean, the Jewish Christians may share table fellowship with Gentiles and cross the barriers that prevented the gospel from being brought to all people. God was preparing him to travel up the coast to Caesarea where he would instruct Cornelius as the first Gentile convert to Christianity.

Peter's visit to Joppa is commemorated at St. Peter's Church, overlooking the waterfront. A towering belfry makes the church, just off Kedumim Square to the north, the town's most distinctive landmark. Beginning in 1650, the Franciscans had a guesthouse here to welcome the increasing number of pilgrims arriving through the port. The church was opened in 1894 on the site where the fortress of St. Louis IX, King of France, had stood at the time of the Sixth Crusade. Stained-glass windows by the artist

Franz Xaver Zettler depict events in the lives of Peter and other saints. An unusual wooden pulpit is carved in the form of a fruiting tree. The painting above the high altar represents St. Peter's vision.

Meditation

- Could God's vision of who is part of his people today be broader than mine? How might my narrow vision restrict the work of God?

- What are some barriers that divide people from one another? In what ways does the gospel break down these barriers?

Reading: Acts 10:1-23

Send men to Joppa for a certain Simon who is called Peter; he is lodging with Simon, a tanner, whose house is by the seaside. . . .

Response: Make us, Lord, your missionary disciples.

Lord Jesus, you chose Simon Peter your apostle to bring the grace of salvation to Cornelius and all the Gentiles. May all those who are searching find joy in your gospel. R.

Here in Joppa, the apostle Peter was the guest of a tanner who lived near the sea. May all visitors and pilgrims be welcomed and given hospitality through your church. R.

Lord Jesus, you founded your church on the faith of the fisherman from Galilee. May we who have received the grace of baptism see the church, the bishop of Rome, and all our bishops and pastors as charismatic guides as we follow them along the way of your gospel. R.

Here in Joppa, you prepared Peter to open the church to all people, both Jews and Gentiles. May everyone who approaches your church find its doors open for an encounter with your love. R.

Lord Jesus, you chose Peter to be the first among the apostles and the shepherd of your church. Make our hearts free of prejudgment and fear, and make us quick to be your witnesses to our neighbors. R.

Here in Joppa, Peter raised Tabitha from death by the power of his prayer. May our beloved dead rest in the peace of Christ and rise in glory. R.

Prayer: Risen Lord, through the ministry of your church your power is at work. The sick are restored to health, the dead are raised, the gospel is proclaimed, and people's hearts are turned to receive your redeeming grace. Give us missionary hearts to be witnesses of your gospel and to bring others to a saving encounter with you.

4. Caesarea Maritima

Not to be confused with Caesarea Philippi in Galilee, Caesarea Maritima ("by the sea") was founded by Herod the Great on the site of an ancient fortified town. In 22 BC, with no expense spared, Herod began building a new city and harbor. The forty-acre harbor was built using materials that would allow the concrete to harden underwater. Massive breakwaters gave safe anchorage to three hundred ships. Herod built his palace on a promontory jutting out into the sea. The pool in the center was nearly Olympic in size and was filled with fresh water. Paul may have been imprisoned on the grounds of this palace (Acts 23:35).

Herod built markets, baths, temples, public buildings, and wide roads. A vast hippodrome seated more than twenty thousand people at chariot races. Later an amphitheater was built to accommodate four thousand for gladiatorial combats, animal performances, and theatrical events. According to the historian Josephus, this is where the death of Herod Agrippa occurred (Acts 12:21-23). The theater is still in use today for dramas and concerts. To the north of Caesarea, visitors can view the Roman aqueduct that brought water into the city from the foothills of Mount Carmel. To ensure that the water would flow by the pull of gravity, the aqueduct was built on arches and the gradient was carefully measured.

Caesarea became the provincial capital of Roman Judea and the headquarters of the Roman procurators and their army. They resided here and came up to Jerusalem only during the Jewish feasts to quell nationalistic fervor and rebellion. Pontius Pilate was procurator from AD 26 to 36, during the time of Jesus's adult ministry. Near the amphitheater, a stone tablet was found with an inscription "Pontius Pilatus, Prefect of Judea." This tablet announces that Pilate consecrated a temple dedicated to Tiberius Caesar who nominated him as procurator. A replica of the stone may be seen at the site.

Pontius Pilate inscription discovered in Caesarea Maritima

Seated in the theater and looking toward the Mediterranean Sea, pilgrims may contemplate God's call to take the message of salvation to the world. Caesarea became the exit port for spreading the faith to the heart of the Roman empire in the western world. The way to Greece and Rome was across the sea. From Caesarea, Peter and Paul, and many other early evangelists, brought the gospel to the nations.

Cornelius was a Gentile centurion, a commander of the Roman army stationed in Caesarea. Since Peter concluded after his vision in Joppa, "God has shown me that I should not call anyone profane or unclean" (Acts 10:28), Peter took the chance of visiting the Gentile city of Caesarea and entering Cornelius's home. Although neither Peter nor Cornelius fully understood what God was moving each of them to do, God's guidance brought them together. Peter found in Cornelius not an enemy but a man

searching for God. Through them, God began to realize the divine plan for the Gentiles. Cornelius and his household heard the gospel from Peter, they opened their hearts as the Holy Spirit descended upon them, and Cornelius and his family were baptized. They became the first converts from paganism to be received into the church.

Peter's baptism of Cornelius, opening salvation equally to Jews and Gentiles, prepared the way for the ministry of Paul. Following the years of Paul's missionary journeys, he was arrested in Jerusalem and brought to Caesarea, where he was confined in Herod's palace. After two years had elapsed, and despairing of receiving a fair sentence, Paul exercised his right as a Roman citizen and appealed his case to Caesar (Acts 25:11-12). In about AD 60, the Roman procurator Festus heard Paul's case along with Herod Agrippa II and his wife, Bernice. Acts 26 recounts Paul's final defense before being sent for trial in Rome. Here Paul narrates his conversion from persecutor to missionary. At the end of Paul's defense, Agrippa hinted that if he were to listen any longer to Paul's persuasion, he might become a Christian. From Caesarea, Paul made his harrowing voyage to Rome, where he was imprisoned and put to death under the emperor Nero.

After the destruction of Jerusalem, Caesarea became the center of Christianity in Palestine. By the end of the second century, the city had a bishop, Theophilus of Caesarea, whose territory included Jerusalem. Church fathers who were active in Caesarea included Origen and Pamphilius. The library they built up was second only to that of Alexandria. By the seventh century, it held thirty thousand works. Eusebius, who became bishop in 314, was both the first church historian and the first biblical geographer. Without his book of place names, the *Onomasticon*, many biblical sites would never have been identified.

The city was destroyed during the Muslim conquest of the seventh century, then strengthened by the Crusaders into an important port. The remains of a Crusader walled city include a cathedral that was never completed because the vaults below, from an earlier period, were unable to bear the weight. After the Crusader retreat, the city was left in ruins, and its stones were reused in buildings throughout the region.

Caesarea is a geographical reminder of the essential Christian call to evangelize the world. An ancient legend says that after Jesus said to his apostles, "Go out and make disciples of all nations," they got out a map of the world and chose which countries each would evangelize. Although the sea may seem like a barrier to some, the Holy Spirit urges disciples to cross boundaries and to bring the gospel to all.

Meditation

- In what way is the encounter between Peter and Cornelius a critical moment for each of them?

- In what ways do the narratives of Peter and Paul in Acts inspire me to work for the gospel?

Reading: Acts 10:24-48

The following day they came to Caesarea. Cornelius was expecting them and had called together his relatives and close friends. . . .

Amphitheater in Caesarea looking westward to the Mediterranean Sea

Response: May we go out and make disciples of all nations.

Lord of all nations, as you enabled Peter to overcome the barriers that separated him from people longing for the gospel, open our minds to your universal rule and make us instruments of evangelization in your church. R.

Lord of all, through his encounter with Cornelius you taught Peter about your love for every person, and through his encounter with Peter, you gave Cornelius the light of the gospel. Show us how our meeting with each person is an opportunity to encounter your transforming grace. R.

Transforming Lord, as you gave your Holy Spirit to Cornelius and the other Gentiles with him, open the hearts of all people who do not know your gospel and pour out your Spirit on all who seek you sincerely. R.

Lord of all, you taught your church to transcend nations, races, genders, and all divisions. Convert our minds and hearts so that we may see other people as you see them and to offer them the love that you have for them. R.

Lord Jesus, may the grace of this pilgrimage grow in our hearts, making us messengers and witnesses of your word. May we feel the urgency of your missionary call and become evangelizing disciples. R.

Prayer: O Christ, the True Light of the world, through the inspiration and intercession of your holy apostles Peter and Paul, commission us to go forth and witness. Stir up the grace of our baptism and our pilgrimage, and make us your missionary disciples. May we be your instruments in preparing the hearts of the men and women of our time for the gift of everlasting life.

Chapter XIII

Returning Home

Most pilgrims are drawn to the Holy Land through a desire to see and touch the places we read about in Scripture, and indeed, after experiencing the sites where the history of our salvation unfolded, we are able to imagine the scenes of Scripture much more vividly. In this way, a pilgrimage to the Holy Land leads us to want to know the Bible more richly, to read and reflect on it each day. Through experiencing the holy ground of these sacred places, we hunger to experience the panorama of the whole Bible and to savor its sacred pages.[1]

When we read the books of the Bible, we notice that many of them seem incomplete, leaving us with the conviction that there is more to come. The Old Testament history convinces us that God's definitive work remains undone, and reading the New Testament helps us understand that the coming of Jesus completes the Torah and the prophets. But when we read the four gospels and the Acts of the Apostles, each book ends in a way that makes its story seem unfinished. In this way, these writings urge us to enter the text ourselves and continue the story they have begun. The life of Jesus continues in his church, a community of disciples that continues to be led by the glorified Christ. The Acts of the Apostles must continue into the lives of disciples in every age as they continue the work of Jesus—teaching, healing, evangelizing, doing the work of justice, and making disciples to the ends of the earth.

Similarly, all pilgrimages are incomplete. Christians usually end pilgrimages wanting more—more encounters with Christ, more experiences

---

1. To begin studying the Bible, see Stephen J. Binz, *Introduction to the Bible: A Catholic Guide to Studying Scripture* (Collegeville, MN: Liturgical Press, 2007); *Panorama of the Bible: Old Testament* (Collegeville, MN: Liturgical Press, 2016); and *Panorama of the Bible: New Testament* (Collegeville, MN: Liturgical Press, 2016).

of Scripture, more liturgical prayer, more communal involvement with other believers. Pilgrimage helps us grow in our discipleship, a growth that is never complete until we reign with the Lord in glory. Following Jesus is an ongoing journey, and pilgrimage teaches us how to direct and savor the ongoing events of life. Every person, place, and experience can be viewed as a sacred encounter, as part of life's pilgrimage, when we live with the heart of a pilgrim.

Continuing to reflect on Scripture and on our experiences of pilgrimage, we realize that the shrines of the Holy Land are representations of the holy temple that is our lives in Christ. He makes of those who believe in him a temple built of living stones, the pilgrim church: "Come to him, a living stone, though rejected by mortals yet chosen and precious in God's sight, and like living stones, let yourselves be built into a spiritual house, to be a holy priesthood, to offer spiritual sacrifices acceptable to God through Jesus Christ" (1 Pet 2:4-5). With him we construct the spiritual shrine of the new covenant, presenting our lives as living sacrifices to God. The witness of our lives is pleasing to God precisely because it is offered in Christ, through him and with him, the covenant in person.

Pilgrimage draws us in two directions: inwardly to holiness and outwardly to mission. The final material in this guide encourages us to grow in both holiness and mission as we return home and continue the pilgrimage of life. Reviewing our Holy Land pilgrimage in our imagination can help us rekindle the experience in our heart and continue to grow in discipleship. For this reason, these final pages include a series of "armchair pilgrimages" that may be easily made at home. Although a physical pilgrimage cannot be traveled in any kind of chronological order or thematic sequence, an armchair pilgrimage can be made in any order we wish. So depending on the season or our spiritual goal, we can make selected stops at the places described in this book, letting the biblical and historical description of each place lead us into meditation and prayer.

1. The Double Call to Holiness and Mission

The first appeal of Jesus to his disciples was "Come and see"; his final appeal was "Go and witness." They first learned the way of Jesus: they heard his call, listened to his sermons, shared his compassion, witnessed his resurrection, and felt his Spirit. Then they were impelled to go out and share what they had experienced with the world. This double calling—the call to holiness and the call to mission—is given to every disciple and is the calling given by the church today to all its members. The call to holiness is not just for those who dedicate their lives to prayer in monasteries; it is the vocation of us all. The call to mission is not just for those who leave their homes for foreign lands; it is the vocation of us all. The pursuit of this double call is necessary to be effective followers of Jesus Christ.

The early Christians experienced this double calling in their celebration of the Eucharist. They gathered to encounter the risen Lord, to hear the Scriptures, and to share his real presence in the breaking of the bread. Then, after receiving the Lord in word and sacrament, they went forth on their mission as his witnesses. This encounter that we see throughout the New Testament is what we experience in every celebration of the Eucharist today. We are called to come, to gather, to be formed as disciples, to hear God's word and to share intimately in the body and blood of Christ. Then, we are sent out, commissioned, sent on mission to the world. The final words of the Mass are critically important: *Ite Missa est*, "Go, You are sent forth," "Go and announce the gospel of the Lord," "Go in peace, glorifying the Lord by your life."

In order to be disciples of Jesus today, we must encounter him in ways that move us inward to deeper holiness and that move us outward to effective mission. We must experience this double dimension of the Christian life in all we do: reading Scripture, celebrating the Eucharist, and going on pilgrimage. These encounters result in a deeper oneness with God and a desire to join in the mission of God, a deeper faith in Christ and the mission to evangelize.

Pilgrimage without a connection to holiness and mission becomes spiritual tourism. Mark Nepo expressed it succinctly:

To journey without being changed is to be a nomad.

To change without journeying is to be a chameleon.

To journey and be transformed by the journey is to be a pilgrim.[2]

It is difficult in our culture today to truly be followers of Jesus. We live in an age of cynicism. Our materialistic culture has blurred our vision and

2. Mark Nepo, *The Exquisite Risk* (New York: Random House, 2006), 34.

muffled our hearing. Our attention is diverted from what really matters. Surrounded by consumerism, we can no longer discern what we truly desire. But there is nothing that cuts through this superficial culture more effectively than disciples who have truly cultivated a relationship with Jesus Christ. We know them when we encounter them, don't we? They have personally met the Lord, they are filled with his love, they have a deep sense of joy despite the struggles of life, and they have a compassionate concern for others.

When I seek models for discipleship, I turn to Peter and Mary Magdalene. They must have been amazing witnesses in the early church. They were credible missionaries because they were able to speak to others from their experience of knowing Jesus. Their faith in the Lord urged them to proclaim and share the good news with those they met. And, as history demonstrates, their witness bore tremendous fruit in the hearts of those who came to believe because of them. Today's witnesses must cultivate a personal relationship with Jesus Christ that will inform everything we do. Parents, catechists, all lay and clerical ministers in the church, and each one of us must be people who are passionately in love with Jesus Christ and have a deep desire to share his life with others.

In the two-volume work of Luke, his gospel and the Acts of the Apostles, he narrates this double call of discipleship. In his gospel, he leads us toward Jerusalem, toward an increasingly deep and more personal encounter with Jesus. Then, in Acts, he leads us away from Jerusalem, the outward-reaching evangelization of the world. The final words of Jesus before his ascension were these: "You will be my witnesses in Jerusalem, in all Judea and Samaria, and to the ends of the earth" (Acts 1:8). The first sphere of Christian witness is Jerusalem, the place where the disciples lived. For us this call to witness corresponds to our home, the domestic space within our families. The second area of mission is Judea, which corresponds to our neighbors, our parishes, and our local communities. The next sphere is Samaria, which the Jews of Jerusalem avoided. This relates to our mission to those who are shunned and rejected. And ultimately, the mission of the whole church together is to the ends of the earth, the missionary mandate of Christ to bring the gospel to the whole world.

When we return home from a pilgrimage to the Holy Land, we must continue the spirit of pilgrimage if we are to be transformed by our journey. Ongoing pilgrimage is the lifelong pursuit of holiness and mission, until we reach our goal. For when all is said and done, as the French novelist Léon Bloy wrote, "The only real sadness, the only real failure, the only great tragedy in life, is not to become a saint."[3]

One of the great challenges for the church today is the rapid rates of people becoming unchurched and giving up a belief in God. This is a tragedy for which we are all, in some way, responsible. Thomas Merton warned, "Do not be too quick to condemn the one who no longer believes in God: for it is perhaps your own coldness and avarice and mediocrity and materialism and selfishness that have chilled his faith." Jesus and the great tradition he founded holds the answers to the questions the world is asking, the best answers to the questions that well up from every human heart. Let us all continue to cultivate the spirit of pilgrimage within ourselves, investing time in Scripture reading, meditation, and prayer to come to know Jesus Christ more personally, so that we can become more effective witnesses for the sake of God's people.

2. Armchair Pilgrimages

Armchair pilgrimages allow us to remember various aspects of pilgrimage in the Holy Land after returning home. From the reflective environment of a comfortable armchair, we can review the sites of pilgrimage, focusing on particular aspects of the gospel accounts, seasonal Scriptures, or biblical themes. This kind of imaginative remembering can rekindle the experience within us and encourage further reflection on our experiences. For each armchair pilgrimage, read the biblical and historical description about each site, allowing it to lead you into deeper meditation and prayer.

Armchair Pilgrimage for Holy Week

This day-by-day timeline represents the major events of the days of Holy Week. Go on an imaginative pilgrimage in the steps of Jesus from Palm Sunday through Resurrection Sunday.

Palm Sunday: Jesus Triumphantly Enters Jerusalem (VIII.1—Bethphage, Sanctuary of the Palms)

---

3. Léon Bloy, *The Woman Who Was Poor*, quoted by Pope Francis, *Gaudete et Exsultate* 34.

Monday of Holy Week: Jesus Clears the Temple of Corruption (IX.1—The Temple Mount)

Tuesday of Holy Week: Jesus Gives His Olivet Discourse Concerning the Destruction of Jerusalem and the End of the Age (VIII.3—Eleona)

Wednesday of Holy Week: Jesus Stays with His Friends in Bethany (V.7—Church of Martha, Mary, and Lazarus)

Holy Thursday: Jesus Celebrates the Last Supper with His Disciples (X.2—The Cenacle, Upper Room)

Later on Holy Thursday: Jesus Prays in Agony (VIII.5—Basilica of the Agony)

Overnight on Holy Thursday: Jesus Is Imprisoned in the House of Caiaphas and Denied by Peter (X.1—Church of St. Peter in Gallicantu)

Good Friday: Jesus Walks the Way of the Cross and Is Crucified on Calvary (XI.5—Way of the Cross)

Holy Saturday: The Body of Jesus Lies in Its Tomb (XI.6—Church of the Holy Sepulcher)

Easter Sunday: Jesus Is Risen and Appears to His Disciples (XII.1—Emmaus)

Armchair Pilgrimage to the Signs of John's Gospel
      The signs of John's gospel are the seven miracles of Jesus that help readers believe that Jesus is the Messiah, the Son of God, so that they may have life in his name (John 20:30-31). These seven signs in the Book of Signs (John 1–12) are followed by the Book of Glory (John 13–21) and its great sign of Christ's resurrection.

First Sign: Changing Water into Wine at Cana in John 2:1-11 (II.6—Cana, Church of the Wedding Feast)

Second Sign: Healing the Royal Official's Son in Capernaum in John 4:46-54 (III.7—Capernaum, Synagogue)

Third Sign: Healing the Paralytic at Bethesda in John 5:1-15 (XI.3—Bethesda Pools)

Fourth Sign: Feeding the Five Thousand in John 6:5-14 (III.4—Tabgha, Church of the Multiplication of the Loaves and Fishes)

Fifth Sign: Jesus Walking on Water in John 6:16-24 (III.1—In a Boat on the Sea)

Sixth Sign: Healing the Man Blind from Birth in John 9:1-7 (IX. 4—Pool of Siloam)

Seventh Sign: The Raising of Lazarus in John 11:1-45 (V.8—Bethany, Tomb of Lazarus)

The Great Sign: The Resurrection and Appearances of Jesus (III.6—Tabgha, Church of the Primacy of St. Peter)

Armchair Pilgrimage of the Twenty Mysteries of the Rosary[4]
Gain a richer biblical and geographical understanding of each mystery of the rosary by exploring these sacred sites. Meditate and pray while taking an imaginative journey to the place of each mystery.

First Joyful Mystery: The Annunciation, Mary learns that she has been chosen to be the mother of Jesus (II.1—Nazareth, Basilica of the Annunciation)

Second Joyful Mystery: The Visitation, Mary visits Elizabeth who is pregnant with John the Baptist (V.1—Ein Karem, Church of the Visitation)

Third Joyful Mystery: The Nativity, Jesus is born in Bethlehem (V.3—Bethlehem, Church of the Nativity)

Fourth Joyful Mystery: The Presentation, Mary and Joseph bring the infant Jesus to be presented to God in the temple (XI.2—Church of St. Anne)

Fifth Joyful Mystery: The Finding of Jesus in the Temple, Jesus is discovered discussing with the teachers (IX.1—The Temple Mount)

First Luminous Mystery: The Baptism of Jesus, God proclaims that Jesus is his beloved Son (VI.2—Baptism Site on the Jordan River)

---

4. Stephen J. Binz, *Mysteries of the Rosary* (New London, CT: Twenty-Third Publications, 2005).

Second Luminous Mystery: The Wedding Feast at Cana, At Mary's request, Jesus performs his first miracle (II.6—Church of the Wedding Feast)

Third Luminous Mystery: The Proclamation of the Kingdom of God, Jesus calls all to conversion and service to the Kingdom (III.3—Mount of Beatitudes)

Fourth Luminous Mystery: The Transfiguration of Jesus, Jesus is revealed in glory to Peter, James, and John (II.9—Mount Tabor, Basilica of the Transfiguration)

Fifth Luminous Mystery: The Institution of the Eucharist, Jesus offers his Body and Blood (X.2—The Cenacle, Upper Room)

First Sorrowful Mystery: The Agony in the Garden, Jesus prays in the Garden of Gethsemane on the night before he dies (VIII.5—Basilica of the Agony)

Second Sorrowful Mystery: The Scourging at the Pillar, Jesus is lashed with whips (XI.4—Chapel of the Flagellation)

Third Sorrowful Mystery: The Crowning with Thorns, Jesus is mocked and crowned with thorns (XI.4—Chapel of the Condemnation)

Fourth Sorrowful Mystery: The Carrying of the Cross, Jesus carries the cross that will be used to crucify him (XI.5—Way of the Cross)

Fifth Sorrowful Mystery: The Crucifixion, Jesus is nailed to the cross and dies (XI.6—Church of the Holy Sepulcher)

First Glorious Mystery: The Resurrection, Jesus is raised from death to life (XI.6—Church of the Holy Sepulcher)

Second Glorious Mystery: The Ascension, Jesus returns to his Father in heaven (VIII.2—Chapel of the Ascension)

Third Glorious Mystery: The Feast of Pentecost, The Holy Spirit comes in flame to inaugurate the church (X.2—The Cenacle, Upper Room)

Fourth Glorious Mystery: The Assumption of Mary, At the end of her life on earth, Mary dies and is taken body and soul into heaven (X.3—Abbey of the Dormition)

Fifth Glorious Mystery: The Coronation of Mary, Mary is crowned as Queen of Heaven and Earth (VIII.6—Tomb of the Virgin Mary)

Armchair Pilgrimage in the Way of Mary the Theotokos

As an integral part of God's saving plan for the world, Mary is the beloved daughter of the Father, the tender mother of the Son, and the intimate spouse of the Holy Spirit. Let the journey of her life lead you to a closer relationship with Jesus.

Mary's Birth and Childhood in the Shadow of Jerusalem's temple (XI.2—Church of St. Anne)

Gabriel Announces to Mary that She Is to Be the Mother of Israel's Messiah (II.1—Nazareth, Basilica of the Annunciation)

Mary Travels to Be with Her Cousin Elizabeth (V.1—Ein Karem, Church of the Visitation)

Mary Gives Birth to Jesus in the Cave of Bethlehem (V.3—Bethlehem, Church of the Nativity)

The Angels Announce the Birth of Jesus to the Shepherds (V.5—Beit Sahour, Shepherds' Fields)

Mary Nursed the Infant Jesus with Her Milk as the Holy Family Sought Refuge from Herod's Massacre (V.4—Bethlehem, Milk Grotto)

Mary and Joseph Enter the Temple Gates for the Presentation of the Infant Jesus (IX.3—Jerusalem Archaeological Park)

Mary and Joseph Discover Their Lost Son in the Temple at Age Twelve (IX.1—The Temple Mount)

At Mary's Request, Jesus Performs the First Sign of His Adult Ministry (II.6—Cana, Church of the Wedding Feast)

Mary Fears for the Life of Her Son after His Rejection at Nazareth (II.5—Nazareth, Mount Precipice)

Mary Encounters Her Suffering Son along the Way of the Cross (XI.5—Way of the Cross)

Jesus Entrust Mary to His Beloved Disciple as He Dies on the Cross (XI.6—Church of the Holy Sepulcher)

Mary Devotes Herself to Prayer and Waits in the Upper Room for the Descent of the Holy Spirit (X.2—The Cenacle, Upper Room)

Mary Dies in the Company of the Disciples (X.3—Abbey of the Dormition)

Mary Is Buried and Assumed into Heaven (VIII.6—Tomb of the Virgin Mary)

Mary Is the New Ark of the Covenant (XII.2—Abu Ghosh, Our Lady of the Ark of the Covenant Church)

Mary Is Honored as the Guiding Star for All Travelers (II.7—Mount Carmel, Stella Maris)

Mary Is Honored by Jews, Christians, and Muslims throughout the World (II.3—Nazareth, Mary of Nazareth International Center)

Armchair Pilgrimage in the Footsteps of Peter the Apostle[5]
   A journey through Peter's life takes us from the place where he dropped his net to follow Jesus to the place where he gave his life out of love for his Lord—from Galilee, to Jerusalem, and to Rome. Learning from Peter, we can embrace the reality that God works through broken human beings to accomplish truly beautiful things.

Peter the Fisherman Called to Discipleship by Jesus (III.1—In a Boat on the Sea)

The House of Peter Becomes Home to Jesus's Ministry in Galilee (III.8—Capernaum, House of Peter)

Peter Affirms that Jesus Has the Words of Eternal Life (III.7—Capernaum, Synagogue)

Peter the Rock Given the Keys to God's Kingdom (II.8—Caesarea Philippi)

Peter Encounters the Transfigured Lord on the Mountain (II.9—Mount Tabor, Basilica of the Transfiguration)

Peter Fails to Stay Awake and Pray with Jesus in Gethsemane (VIII.5—Basilica of the Agony)

Peter Denies Knowing Jesus at His Arrest and Trial (X.1—Church of St. Peter in Gallicantu)

Peter Commissioned by the Risen Lord to Shepherd His Church (III.6—Tabgha, Church of the Primacy of St. Peter)

---

5. Stephen J. Binz, *Saint Peter: Flawed, Forgiven, and Faithful* (Chicago: Loyola Press, 2015).

Peter Receives the Holy Spirit at Pentecost and Preaches the Church's First Sermon (X.2—The Cenacle, Upper Room)

Peter's Vision Prepares for the Church's Universal Mission (XII.3—Joppa)

Peter Opens the Way for the Mission to the Gentiles by Baptizing Cornelius (XII.4—Caesarea Maritima)

Index of Places

Note: References in **bold** are to major entries.